THIS GREEN AND GROWING LAND

THE AMERICAN WAYS SERIES

GENERAL EDITOR: John David Smith

Charles H. Stone Distinguished Professor of American History,
University of North Carolina at Charlotte

This series provides concise, accessible treatments of central topics in the American experience. Titles first appear in hardcover and eBook editions for a general audience and subsequently appear in reasonably priced paper editions for classroom use.

CURRENT TITLES IN THE SERIES

How America Eats: A Social History of U.S. Food and Culture,
by Jennifer Jensen Wallach

Popular Justice: A History of Lynching in America, by Manfred Berg

Bounds of their Habitation: Race and Religion in American History,
by Paul Harvey

National Pastime: U.S. History through Baseball, by Martin C. Babicz
and Thomas W. Zeiler

A harmonious relation to land is more intricate, and of more consequence to civilization, than the historians of its progress seem to realize. Civilization is not, as they often assume, the enslavement of a stable and constant earth. It is a state of mutual and interdependent cooperation between human animals, other animals, plants, and soils which may be disrupted at any moment by the failure of any of them.

—ALDO LEOPOLD, "The Conservation Ethic," 1933

THIS GREEN AND GROWING LAND

Environmental Activism in American History

Kevin C. Armitage

ROWMAN & LITTLEFIELD
Lanham • Boulder • New York • London

Published by Rowman & Littlefield
A wholly owned subsidiary of The Rowman & Littlefield Publishing Group, Inc.
4501 Forbes Boulevard, Suite 200, Lanham, Maryland 20706
www.rowman.com

Unit A, Whitacre Mews, 26-34 Stannary Street, London SE11 4AB

British Library Cataloguing in Publication Information Available

Library of Congress Cataloging-in-Publication Data
ISBN 978-1-4422-3707-0 (cloth : alk. paper)
ISBN 978-1-4422-3708-7 (electronic)

∞™ The paper used in this publication meets the minimum requirements of
American National Standard for Information Sciences—Permanence of Paper
for Printed Library Materials, ANSI/NISO Z39.48-1992.

Printed in the United States of America

CONTENTS

ACKNOWLEDGMENTS

WRITING A book is a solitary affair made possible by rich social networks of colleagues, friends and family members. I'm fortunate to be part of a vibrant community of environmental thinkers at the Institute for the Environment and Sustainability. I have the pleasure of working on environmental issues with many excellent scholars, especially Jonathan Levy, Dave Prytherch, Susie Zazycki, Dave Gorchov, Tom Crist, and Peggy Shaffer.

I have the great fortune to engage with superb colleagues in the Western Program. Nik Money is a mycologist and Milton scholar, a friend, mentor and leader. Hays Cummins is a great friend, lover of tropical nature, bon vivant and co-teacher from whom I have learned a great deal. Donna McCollum is an ecologist, deep environmental thinker, and amazing finder of natural treasures. Nik, Donna and especially Hays have expertly explained a lot of science to me over the years.

Environmental history is a rich and growing field. Scholars who have engaged with my thoughts on environmentalism include Brian Drake, the indefatigable and always helpful Mark Hersey, Michael Egan, Lisa Brady, Andy Kirk, Kip Curtis, Brian Black and Adam Rome.

Mark Harvey took the time to write greatly helpful comments on my wilderness chapter when I was particularly vexed in my approach to the subject. Any mistakes in fact or interpretation are, of course, my own.

Like all scholars, I depend on the good works of librarians. In particular, I wish the thank the staff of both King Library and the BEST library at Miami University of Ohio; the Old Rock Community Library in Crested Butte, Colorado, and the staff at the Denver Public Library, especially those working in their outstanding Conservation Collection.

At Rowman & Littlefield, Jon Sisk and Kate Powers worked diligently to see the manuscript to completion; John David Smith provided expert reading, commentary, and editing of this book.

The title of this book comes from the folk singer Phil Ochs's song "Power and the Glory." I chose it because the song's lyrics connect the love of land with patriotism and social conscience—prominent themes in this book.

My parents, Ken and Katie Armitage, lovingly support everything I do. My father read and commented on drafts of two chapters. My brother Keith Armitage is a physician and alpinist who always wanders off trail and rarely reaches his stated destination—the best kind of hiking. My sister Karole is an amazing and renowned choreographer who has tackled the climate issue through ballet with her Fables of Global Warming. It was on the porch of her house in Crested Butte, Colorado, just eight miles from our childhood summer home, that I wrote the bulk of this book. More than anyone else I must thank my wife Helen Sheumaker and daughter Rita Armitage for their love, support and good cheer. I love you both. Finally, Tipper dog is always happy and unendingly enthusiastic for a long walk.

CHAPTER 1

THE HORNS IN DOCK CREEK

When the well's dry, we know the worth of water.
–BENJAMIN FRANKLIN (1706–1790),
Poor Richard's Almanac

IN THE eighteenth-century, noxious wastes plagued Philadelphia's Dock, a commercially thriving neighborhood of printers and barrel makers. Part of the fastest growing city in America, the Dock was bounded to its east by the Delaware River; a tidal tributary, Dock Creek, ran through the neighborhood. But Dock Creek was little more than an open sewer. Slaughterhouses and tanneries used it as their dump. Neighbors described the creek as "a Receptacle for the Carcases of . . . Carrion, and Filth of various kinds." Exposed to the elements, the carcasses would "putrify" and become "extremely offensive and injurious to the Health of the Inhabitants." Residents of the Dock thus faced a question central to the history of environmentalism: did private interests have the right to befoul the shared environment?

For Benjamin Franklin (1706–1790), the answer was a resounding "no." He strongly condemned the contamination of Dock Creek, decrying how refuse from tanneries "choaked the Dock . . . with . . . Tan, Horns, etc." Animal rendering, continued Franklin, gave off "many offensive and unwholesome smells." The wastes and odors diminished the "Value of . . . Lots and Tenements" in the neighborhood. Repulsed by the pollution, in 1739 Franklin and his neighbors petitioned the Common Council that governed the city to remove the tanneries so as to keep the "great number of tradesmen from being poisoned by a few, and restore to them the liberty of breathing freely in their own homes." The tanneries asserted their rights as businessmen to pollute. But for Franklin, justice demanded that public rights and health take precedence over the tanneries' and slaughterhouses' ability to pollute the local waters.

Franklin's work for the Dock was not his only campaign for environmental quality. His decades-long concern with Philadelphia's water supply was so great that he helped found its municipal water system. He spent much of the 1760s leading a commission that attempted to regulate city waste collection and water pollution. Crucially, Franklin worked to ensure that the commission abated industrial and municipal waste as well as household refuse. This work eventually gave rise to the Philadelphia Water Commission. In 1747, he even helped propose a plan to restore Dock Creek. His commitment to clean water extended all the way to his will, which bequeathed monies to purchase forest lands in the Schuylkill watershed to protect Philadelphia's water supplies.

Urban sewage and pollution were hardly the only environmental problems that engaged Benjamin Franklin. Conservationist by nature, Franklin was particularly interested in energy efficiency. Noticing that chimney smoke was unhealthy, Franklin lobbied his fellow citizens to improve Philadelphia's air quality by using their chimneys less. He designed the Franklin stove to produce more heat using less fuel. His justification for the new stove noted that overharvesting had made trees scarce, so a benefit of his design was that it "us'd much less wood . . . a considerable Advantage where Wood is dear." He also invented a four-sided street lamp that resisted the buildup of soot that plagued the common globe-shaped street lamp. The soot required laborious daily cleaning and let off excess smoke—thus the new design was more efficient in its use of natural and human resources. He proposed maximizing daylight waking hours (initially in jest) to exploit the use of sunlight and more generally engage in efficient resource use.

Although Franklin was primarily an urban man, his expansive interests included another subject fundamental to the history of North American environmental reform: agriculture. Most prominently, Franklin championed agricultural research. His plan for the American Philosophical Society included investigations into domestic and imported "plants, herbs, trees, roots . . . and methods for propagating them" as well as "improvements in planting, gardening, and clearing land." When the society formed, it included a section devoted to "husbandry and American improvements." In this way Franklin anticipated the agricultural experiment station and even the charge of the land grant university.

Nor was Franklin's interest in agriculture merely theoretical. His inventive nature extended to agronomy, and he continually urged North American farmers to experiment with new foodstuffs. Franklin introduced American farmers to Scottish kale and rhubarb, Chinese soybeans and kohlrabi, and Swiss barley. Most famously Franklin worked to establish a North American silk industry, advocating for the planting of mulberry trees—from which silkworms spin their silk—in hedgerows and for household shade, thus doubling their usefulness. Franklin's reputation for agricultural innovation was global. While serving as ambassador to France, Franklin was sought out for his knowledge on how to protect fruit trees from frost and how to control insect pests by ensuring healthy bird populations. An integrator of social and natural thinking, Franklin was also the first to propose crop insurance to protect farmers against the damages wrought by natural disasters.

Franklin's contributions to Enlightenment science made him a forefather of ecological thinking. This vital mode of thought can be seen in the way Franklin responded to Joseph Priestley's experiments with oxygen, which tested the conditions in which plants and animals could thrive in terrariums. Franklin championed Priestley's work and maintained an extensive correspondence with him. Priestly was working out the role of plants in producing salutary environments, specifically demonstrating that the air we breathe is not an unalienable physical phenomenon like gravity but rather a product made by plants. Franklin, remarkably, understood Priestley's work in global terms, grasping the interconnected nature of animals, plants, and atmospheric gases. Nature, it seemed, created the environments conducive to its own flourishing. In making such conclusions, Franklin and Priestley were helping pioneer ecosystem thinking.

Franklin grasped that such a new worldview had profound implications for human behavior. Given the new understanding that trees produce oxygen, Franklin wrote that "I hope this will give some check to the rage of destroying trees that grow near homes," a common practice because many people considered forest air unhealthy. From his own "long observation" Franklin felt sure "that there is nothing unhealthy in the air of woods"; now he could draw upon science to support his intuition that trees supported rather than retarded human health. Most fundamentally Franklin embodied the notion that scientific innovation and ecosystem thinking demanded new social thinking and the consequent alteration of human behavior in accordance with new understandings about how the world works.

Franklin's writings on population further evinced the beginnings of ecosystem thinking. In his "Observations Concerning the Increase of Mankind, Peopling of Countries, & etc." he worried that if one country controlled a fishery that employed "great numbers" and "makes the food and subsistence of the people cheaper," competition from another nation could "make it more difficult to subsist a family." Though Franklin was clearly most concerned with the political control of resources, such an analysis also assumed that natural resources such as fisheries are defined and limited. Furthermore, while Franklin also posited a wildly fecund earth—"there is," he wrote, "no bound to the prolific nature of plants and animals"—he also understood that competition could interfere "with each other's means of subsistence." This observation was quoted by Thomas Malthus, and via Malthus this line of thought profoundly impacted Charles Darwin. Nature, these thinkers were discovering, was simultaneously abundant and limited, fecund yet constrained. Franklin, then, helped found the lines of inquiry that developed into evolutionary theory and hence is part of the Enlightenment modes of thought that eventually gave rise to ecological science.

Franklin's concerns—water quality, pollution, agriculture, new sources of energy, efficient use of resources, ecological thinking, population, crop insurance, and governmental regulation of waste and pollution—are remarkably contemporary and profoundly environmental. Most broadly, Franklin was an environmentalist who championed quality of life through quality environments, both urban and rural. Time and again he supported the environmental public good against the privileges of private polluters. His solutions to environmental problems were often technical—he was, after all, one of the master inventors of his time—but also social. The rights of the majority in the Dock to enjoy a clean environment trumped the ability of tanneries to dump wastes into Dock Creek.

As such Franklin anticipated modern environmentalism in yet another way: environmental issues have never simply been a dry application of science to the problems of resource allocation and distribution. They are always social problems, problems of values and of governance; Franklin seemed to understand the truth that when we manage nature we create society. Every social action or governmental policy affects the environment in some way. This was true in the past and will remain true in the future. As policy historian Richard Andrews observes, "Today and for the foreseeable future, in a world in which human population growth, technological capabilities, and material and energy consumption now impact the earth's natural processes on a global scale, managing the environment requires managing ourselves as well." The key to environmental thinking—and the possibility for sound management—is that it integrates nature and society rather than bifurcating the human from the rest of the natural world.

Franklin may have been an environmentalist, but he would not have recognized the term. Activists, drawing on the science of ecology, popularized the term "environment" two centuries after Franklin's time, in the 1960s and 1970s. Which brings up an important question: what is an environmentalist anyway? As with any historically complex and interesting word, its meaning is contested, which is to simply say that its meaning has been debated—fiercely, passionately, searchingly—and has changed over time. This book investigates those changes, highlighting the ways that environmentalism is the integration of natural and social systems thinking. Most broadly, environmentalism may be thought of as a philosophy and social movement that seeks protection for the natural world. That protection in turn promotes a healthy human society that benefits from the clean air, water, and other natural properties that allow for human flourishing.

An example from the burgeoning environmental movement of the early 1960s demonstrates the intertwined nature of social and natural goods. First Lady Claudia "Lady Bird" Johnson was known for her work on highway beautification and wildflower protection. But rather than mere aesthetic improvements enjoyed mostly by the middle classes, she understood that even such anodyne projects as planting wildflowers and regulating unsightly billboards involved profound social questions. Elaborating on her beautification campaign she observed that, "though the word 'beautification' makes the concept sound merely cosmetic, it involves much more: clean water, clean air, clean roadsides, safe waste disposal and preservation of valued old landmarks as well as great parks and wilderness areas. To me . . . beautification means our total concern for the physical and human quality we pass on to our children and the future." Johnson's grasp of the socially integrated nature of environmental quality highlights the best and most salient qualities of environmental thought and policy.

Environmentalism, then, might be thought of as the natural world corollary that must be present in all social thinking. Readers will likely have heard some version of the proverb that if you "give a person a fish, they eat for a day; but teach them to fish and they eat for a lifetime." Everyone can recognize the profound vision for social betterment, independence, and self-reliance contained in this pronouncement. But environmentalists must also see it as deeply, even fatally, limited. For, even if taught to fish, one will not be able to eat fish for a lifetime if the fishery has been "fished out"; that is, overfished so that fish stocks cannot replenish. Nor will anyone be able to eat for a lifetime if, as with the tanneries abusing Dock Creek, hazardous wastes have been dumped into the fishery. Those wastes can either kill the fish or make them poisonous for human consumption via biomagnification. (Biomagnification describes the concentration of poisons increasing up the food chain as larger animals ingest plants or animals in which poisons are more widely dispersed.) No one eats from lifeless waters.

Many environmentalists would also contend that species other than humans have some rights to live too—is planet Earth really only for people? The environmentalist Rachel Carson described this dilemma as "the problem of sharing our earth with other creatures." And what happens to those humans deprived of the ability to fish by the toxins that foul the fishery? This issue has plagued the world recently as Somali fisherman, unable to make a living because overfishing crashed coastal fish stocks, have turned to piracy in a desperate bid for financial support.

More broadly, if global fish stocks continue to decline, one in ten people worldwide will suffer from malnutrition. Social problems, it seems, are always already environmental problems.

Like most Americans, environmentalists have not always successfully integrated social and natural thinking. Indeed, they often failed to do so. This, too, is a legacy of the Enlightenment of which Franklin and the American founding was such a prominent part. Indeed, the fact that historians usually separate Franklin's interests in agriculture and science from his democratic impulses and anti-slavery views is an example of how our culture habitually separates scientific and social thought. Franklin did not understand his work for Dock Creek and Philadelphia's water quality as essentially different from his joining and eventual presidency of the Society for Promoting the Abolition of Slavery and the Relief of Negroes Unlawfully Held in Bondage. Franklin understood both environmental quality and the abolition of slavery as the same thing: that is, as advancements of the public good. But many other Enlightenment thinkers did separate the social from the natural, mostly due to the belief that social action involved questions of morality while interacting with nature did not.

Enlightenment thought bequeathed wide varieties of both nature hating and nature loving to the modern West. And if one hates nature, or views it merely as a machine—a dominant metaphor of the Enlightenment—then it will rarely figure into an understanding of human welfare as anything more than an exploitable resource. The mechanized and sterile view of nature can be readily seen in the philosophy of Francis Bacon (1561–1626), the British author, scientist, statesman, jurist, and proponent of British colonization of the New World. Bacon championed the careful, empirical, and inductive study of nature through procedures that minimized the ability of investigators to mislead themselves. The modern, organized scientific method grew in large part from Bacon's divorce of human cognition from metaphysical abstractions and his insistence on methodological controls to combat self-deception. With this method in place, Bacon passionately proposed that society would continually improve due to constant advancements in the physical sciences and mechanical arts. The betterment of human life came from the better understanding of nature, which allowed for the better control of it.

Indeed, for Bacon progress came from humans aggressively dominating nonhuman nature. Control over the green world allowed for the "enlargement of the bounds of Human Empire, to the effecting of all things possible." Ignorance was the only check on human behavior; morally humans should dominate nature for "the world is made for man, not man for the world." Given that nature was a mere repository of parts to be forged in new ways by human ingenuity, it followed for Bacon that mastery over nature equaled improvement of it. "We make [orchards and gardens] by art greater much than their nature" contended Bacon. Humans made "their fruit greater and sweeter and of differing taste, smell, color, and figure, from their nature." Animals, too, were experimental fodder: "We have also parks and enclosures of all sorts of beasts and birds, which we use not only for view or rareness but likewise for dissections and trials. . . . We also try all poisons and other medicines upon them as well."

Bacon's arguments for the human domination of nature derived from not just his science but from his theology. As Bacon's scathing critique of philosophic method, *The New Organon*, makes clear, his objective was to recover the dominion that humans held over nature before the Fall and subsequent expulsion of people from Eden. "For man by the fall fell at the same time from his state of innocency and from his dominion over creation" argued Bacon. "Both of these loses however can even in this life be in some part repaired; the former by religion and faith, the latter by arts and sciences." The manipulation of the natural order thus did not violate God's plan; indeed, dominion over nature was part of the original state of innocence to which humans should aspire. By coupling innocence with domination, Bacon averted theological or moral constraints upon human interaction with the natural world. Nature was merely a resource, a blank, unfeeling thing subject to human manipulation. Considering how that manipulation might affect society—how the wastes of tanneries poisoned the entire Dock neighborhood—lay beyond Bacon's understanding.

One way this lineage of Enlightenment thought affected the relationship of colonial Americans to their environment was that they tended to see nature as compartmentalized, a collection of isolated and extractable units. The English colonial historian Edward Johnson wrote in 1653 that "In a very little space everything in the country proved a staple commodity . . . nor could it be imagined that this Wilderness should turn a mart for Merchants in so short a space." In his classic work of environmental history *Changes in the Land*, William Cronon demonstrates that

Johnson's attitude was typical of how Europeans viewed the New World environment with "an eye to its mercantile possibilities." This attitude is revealed in their descriptions of the land that "often degenerated into little more than lists."

Thus colonists such as James Rossiter described the coastal vegetation of Maine as "the profits and fruits which are naturally on these Ilands." And many of those profits and fruits seemed not just abundant but inexhaustible and of stupefying quality. In 1584 Sir Walter Raleigh reflected upon the nature of the New World by asserting that "This island had many goodly woodes and [is] full of deere, conies, hares and fowle even in the middest of summer, in incredible aboundance." Other colonists quickly understood such "aboundance" in terms of wealth and nobility. The Reverend Francis Higginson declared that "A poor servant here that is to possesse but [fifty] Acres of land may afford to give more wood for timber and fire as good as the world yeelds than many Noble men in *England* can afford to do."

Colonists were eager to describe the abundance of the New World, particularly its fish, birds, and forests. The great quantities of New World fish, wrote Francis Higginson in 1630, "are almost beyond believing." Colonialist William Wood found alewives (anadromous herring) "in such multitudes as is almost incredible, pressing up shallow waters as will scarce permit them to swim." Legends began to circulate that a person could walk across a creek without getting wet feet by stepping on the backs of the fish that overstuffed the waters. Cod were so numerous and so large that many colonists boasted of landing fish that were as large as people. In 1497 a report on John Cabot's return to England from the New World stated, "The Sea there was swarming with fish which can be taken . . . in baskets let down with a stone." Cape Cod was named after its plentiful resource, enticing new settlers to the land of plenty.

Fish were hardly the only foodstuffs available in staggering numbers. Birds, too, could fill the bellies, and through sale, the pocketbooks of colonial Americans. William Wood described how some hunters of waterfowl "killed a hundred geese in a week, fifty ducks at a shot, forty teals at another." Such success "may be counted impossible though nothing is more certain." Turkeys were fat, delicious, and plentiful. Franklin was a fan of turkeys—he wrote to his daughter that they are "respectable . . . and a true original Native of America . . . and a Bird of Courage"; he did not however, as is often asserted, want the turkey to be the National

Bird. As with other resources, birds were assumed to exist for the benefit of human consumption. In 1622, Captain Richard Whitbourne said sailors harvested the flightless Great Auk "by hundreds at a time as if God had made the innocency of so poor a creature to become such an admirable instrument for the sustenation of Man." Overhunting pushed the North American Great Auk into extinction by the early 1800s.

More than any other bird, flocks of passenger pigeons astonished European settlers. John Josselyn estimated the numbers in one flock to be in the "millions of millions"; one diarist, Thomas Dudley, wrote of "many flocks of doves, each flock containing many thousands and some so many that they obscured the light." In the early 1800s the ornithologist Alexander Wilson described a flock so numerous that "I took [it] for a tornado"; he estimated that it was 240 miles long and contained over two billion birds. As with fish the abundance was so stupefying that settlers felt the need to defend the veracity of their accounts. John J. Audubon found "The multitudes of Wild Pigeons in our woods . . . astonishing. . . . Indeed, after having viewed them so often, and under so many circumstances, I even now feel inclined to pause, and assure myself that what I am going to relate is fact. Yet I have seen it all, and that too in the company of persons who, like myself, were struck with amazement." Another colonist simply averred that "Those who did not see them might think it was not true, but it is very true."

The rich, beautiful, and plentiful forests of the New World—at the time of colonization forests covered about 45 percent of the land that became the coterminous United States, most of that east of the Great Plains—stunned the colonists who encountered them. The abundant oaks, hickories, chestnuts, and pines of southern New England prompted Francis Higginson to note that despite cold winters, "here we have plenty of Fire to warm us." A visitor to Plymouth described it as "good ground in abundance, with excellent good timber." British colonial policy attempted to reserve the tallest, strongest trees, those suitable for use as ship's masts, by having agents mark them with a protecting "broad arrow." In 1711, the White Pine Act of Parliament extended Broad Arrow protections to all trees suitable for masts.

The British were especially keen to preserve the most useful trees due to their own famine in timber. About two thousand years ago Julius Caesar described Britain as "one horrible forest." But an increasing population committed to clearing fields for agriculture rapidly axed the beeches, oaks, poplars, maples, and ash trees that covered the British countryside. A royal proclamation of 1615 lamented the lost former wealth of "Wood and Timber," especially the kind of wood that is "not only great and large in height and bulk, but hath also that toughness and heart, as it is not subject to rive [violent splitting] or cleave, and thereby of excellent use for shipping." The lack of wood—the single most important heating and building material—made it increasingly costly in the years leading up to the English Civil War (1642–1651). In response the people of England more and more turned to coal to power their country's economy, with social and environmental consequences that greatly affect the world to this day.

While colonial Americans reveled in the natural abundance of the New World, nature also scared them, especially the forest. Forests were the edge of civilization, the place where the wild and untamed lurked—and tempted or endangered otherwise moral and safe citizens. The people colonialists considered uncivilized—either outliers from their own society, or, more commonly, the indigenous inhabitants of the Americas—also threatened members of civil society. Thus colonists enacted Bacon's philosophy: by turning the forest into commodities they overcame the "savages" who lived there and profitably safeguarded their own moral and economic standing.

The French American writer J. Hector St. John Crèvecoeur, in his celebrated essay "What is an American?" (a chapter from his widely read *Letters from an American Farmer*), made the comparison explicit. The American, argued Crèvecoeur, "must greatly rejoice that he lived at a time to see this fair country discovered and settled. . . . Here he beholds fair cities, substantial villages, extensive fields . . . where a hundred years ago all was wild, woody and uncultivated!" Lest anyone fail to understand the connection between the taming of wild nature and moral improvement, Crèvecoeur goes on to argue that those who want to truly appreciate the American should visit the frontier where "men appear to be no better than carnivorous animals" and are "not sanctified by the efficacy of a few moral rules." Happily, "the first labours of the mode of clearing the earth . . . will change in a few years that hitherto barbarous country into a fine fertile, well-regulated district." Subduing nature was a moral and economic necessity. Edward Johnson, writing in 1653, attributed to "God's providence that 'a rocky, barren bushy, wild-woody wilderness' was transformed in a generation into 'a second England for fertileness.'"

Europeans may have assumed that the nature they encountered was a barren bushy, wild woody wilderness extant in pristine, undisturbed form, but it was in fact a land extensively managed by its native inhabitants. Some New England native peoples would settle in a forested area for a generation and greatly abuse the land, clearing it of timber and overhunting its game. After overharvesting made the area unfit for continued habitation, they would move and the land, its disturbances localized, would quickly recover so that in time it appeared untouched.

Native peoples used timber harvesting and controlled fires to maintain a mosaic of forest and meadowlands. Indians throughout North America used fire to increase the production of berries, seeds, nuts, and other gathered foods. Creating this patchwork of meadow and forest enhanced the "edge effect"—the boundaries of two or more different habitats that are the preferred environments of game animals such bison, turkey, and deer—of the areas that were frequently hunted by native peoples. Thus patchwork forest clearing could increase the amount of available game. Some animals such as the heath hen, a subspecies of the greater prairie chicken, greatly benefited from the edge effect management of native peoples. Loss of native habitat management and overhunting from Europeans led to their drastic decline and eventual extinction when the last few passed away from a fire on Martha's Vineyard in 1916.

In general, native peoples in New England and elsewhere employed a strategy of seasonal subsistence, altering their diets and food-gathering techniques to conform to the changing time of year. Many native peoples in the South spent springtime harvesting from the enormous runs of anadromous shad, alewives, herring, and mullet that swelled southern rivers. Indians in Florida and elsewhere along the Atlantic coastal plain fished with nets and spears, or with hooks and lines. In autumn and winter—especially in the piedmont and uplands—the natives turned for sustenance away from fish and more to deer, bear, and other game animals. Because they required such animals in quantity, Indians used fire to drive deer and other game into areas where the animals might be more easily harvested.

The South benefited from a long growing season and generally plentiful rainfall. Southern Indians took advantage, developing a complex system of agriculture primarily based on the "three sisters" of corn, beans, and squash. Native peoples cleared farmland using fire and stone axes to remove small brush and timber. They then girdled trees by stripping the bark all the way around the trunk of larger trees so that those trees sprouted no leaves and eventually died. Native farmers, most often women, subsequently planted corn, beans, and squash together in hills beneath the dead and dying trees. The three crops usually grew well under such conditions. Beans "fixed" nitrogen (i.e., converted inert N2 into biologically useful NH3) and thus helped replace the nitrogen leached from the soil by corn. Cornstalks provided structures for the beans to climb, and broad-leaved squash plants helped minimize weed growth and erosion. This farming system likely allowed native populations to increase in the millennium before European contact. Some of the larger native cultures numbered in the tens of thousands.

The introduction of European economic systems interacted with native economies and the natural world in devastating ways. A good example is the deerskin trade. Native peoples of the South—mostly Catawba, Cherokee, Creek, Chickasaw, and Choctaw—participated in this new economy with relish. The deerskin trade began in earnest in sixteenth-century Spanish Florida. Europeans turned deerskins into breeches, gloves, harnesses, saddles, and bindings for books. In exchange for providing deerskins, Indians received manufactured goods, particularly guns and ammunition, but also kettles, iron hoes, axes, and knives, as well as dry goods like duffel, flannel, and cotton. The deerskin trade reached fabulous proportions in the 1690s and 1700s; as many as eighty-five thousand skins were exported each year from Charleston and Virginia combined. In the 1750s it reached as high as 178,000 skins. By the middle of the eighteenth century, the deerskin trade grew to hundreds of thousands of skins. But due to overhunting the deerskin trade collapsed and was as good as dead by 1800. Deer teetered on regional extinction. Native peoples had no experience with a massive, extractive economy or with being dependent upon trade. Being swept up on European economic systems disrupted native cultures and led directly to the devastation of whitetail deer populations in the southeast. The Choctaw and other Indian tribes agreed that their futures were as farmers, as there were no deer left.

The bountiful nature that Europeans encountered, then, was due in part to native peoples' administration of it. Blind to native management, one reason Americans such as Crèvecoeur could rejoice at the clearing of the earth was that they assumed, deerskins notwithstanding, that its resources were inexhaustible. The cultural historian Jackson Lears labeled this view a "fable of abundance." The fable of abundance is the complex desire for material plenty initially assumed to derive from a fecund Earth, and later, as the industrial revolution progressed, from the efficient factory churning out seemingly endless streams of consumable goods.

While the desire for material plenty is likely in some ways universal, the bedrock belief in Earth's abundance was particularly acute in the United States, a country that mythologizes itself as one with limitless horizons and eternal frontiers. Environmentalists, aware of nature's limits, came to decry this myth. Secretary of the Interior Stewart Udall's 1964 book *The Quiet Crisis*, for example, criticized "the myth of superabundance." Udall defined the myth of superabundance as the belief that "There was so much of everything—so much land, so much water, so much timber, so many birds and beasts that man simply did not envision a time where the planet would not replenish what had been sowed." As we shall see, this analysis is central to much of environmentalism.

Franklin's activism on behalf of the Dock, a creek whose waters were not abundant enough to absorb the wastes being tossed into it, is not the only example of colonial environmentalism. One important illustration comes from Benjamin Rush, the colonial physician (who served as surgeon general to the Continental army), social reformer, patriot, and founder of Dickinson College. Rush was troubled by the overharvesting of sugar maple trees (*Acer sacharinum*), and his concerns combined environmental and social reasoning. In a 1791 letter to Thomas Jefferson, Rush noted the many uses of sugar maple sap: it made "a most agreeable molasses, and an excellent vinegar" and could even "compose the basis of a pleasant summer beer." Thus "to transmit to future generations, all the advantages which have been enumerated from the maple tree, it will be necessary to protect it by law." Moreover, making the sugar maple the primary source of sugar would render "the commerce and slavery of our African brethren, in the sugar Islands as unnecessary, as it has always been inhuman and unjust." For Rush, environmental protection could help enact worthy social outcomes.

Thomas Jefferson was similarly concerned with long-term resource viability. Writing to James Madison on September 6, 1789, Jefferson outlined an environmental philosophy based on intergenerational equity. Jefferson asked whether future generations must "consider the preceding generation as having had a right to eat up the whole soil of their country, in the course of a life?" In other words, did those who managed the soils of their day have a duty to leave them to future generations unharmed—or at least in healthy enough shape to support the next generation's agriculture? The answer, for Jefferson, was a self-evident truth: "Every one will say no; that the soil is the gift of God to the living, as much as it had been to the deceased generation." Soils—and by extension the environment as a whole—are the rights of all, and not to be abused by one generation at the expense of the future.

Worry over the ongoing viability of soils or economic importance of the sugar maple was typical of colonial environmentalism, which was mostly concerned with long-term viability of valuable species. Wildlife protection laws, often prompted by overhunting and overfishing, were common colonial statutes. In 1647 Massachusetts declared free public right of access to fisheries but also established, as wildlife protection measures, closed seasons for fishing in 1652 and deer hunting in 1691. Massachusetts also prohibited unauthorized dams that blocked navigation and fish migration in 1709. In 1726, South Carolina prohibited pollution that was harmful to fish, especially targeting the use of fish poisoning as a harvesting method. Connecticut created an annual season for deer in 1739; in 1772 New York established closed seasons on quail and partridge.

Most of these and similar statutes were attempts to abate conflict over common resources. What became abundantly clear is that the weak central authority of the Articles of Confederation (written in 1777, ratified in 1781) hindered effective policy. What was needed was a new common law that would allow for uniform standards across the states that could make the laws governing shared resource use (and everything else not confined to a single state) practical and enforceable. No longer a loose confederation of states, but an integrating national power, the new nation required a new supreme law.

The men who gathered at the constitutional convention in Philadelphia in 1787—eighty-one-year-old Ben Franklin among them—did not consider the problem of nature's limits. They were most absorbed with the difficulties of political representation and the question of how to distribute power in a government that substantially increased centralized authority. For the most part, the framers of the Constitution viewed nature as a mere storehouse of natural resources available for human manipulation. They had strikingly little, if any, appreciation for the idea that human life occurs within the context of natural limits. The Constitution contains no formal consideration of the natural world or any human responsibilities toward it.

And yet the Constitution is an environmental document for both its assumptions about private property—the Fifth Amendment mandates that the government justly compensate any property it takes for public use—and its framework for how social conflict would be adjudicated. Beyond constitutional fragmentation of power among various branches, it encourages private property, requires government agencies to provide scientific or economic rationales for their actions, and allows citizens to challenge the government through an independent judiciary—a framework that set much of environmental activism on its course. The supreme law of the land supports the "general welfare" and contains several specific passages of particular importance for the history of environmental politics. We will briefly investigate three of them: the commerce clause, the property clause, and federal supremacy.

The Commerce Clause refers to Article 1, Section 8, Clause 3, of the U.S. Constitution, which grants Congress the power "to regulate commerce with foreign nations, and among the several states, and with the Indian tribes." Among the most reliably controversial of federal powers, the commerce clause became the constitutional basis for a great deal of environmental policy. Because waterways were central to commerce—rivers were sometimes referred to as "highways of commerce"—courts allowed the federal government to regulate them. Thus the federal government could aide navigation by dredging rivers or constructing lighthouses. Later extensions of this policy allowed the federal government to promote commerce by funding water resource development projects by agencies such as the Army Corps of Engineers and the Bureau of Reclamation. Moreover, that authority is the basis of most environmental law enacted by Congress that protected public health and the environment, including such foundational environmental statutes as the 1970 Clean Air Act, the Clean Water Act of 1972, and the Endangered Species Act of 1973.

The commerce clause is also the basis of many other vitally important federal statutes as well, including civil rights laws, laws that regulate employer wage and hour abuses, laws that condemn trade in unsafe food products, as well as laws prohibiting unfair labor practices such as targeting unions. It may strike readers as odd that the commerce clause is so important to questions of environmental and social justice. Yet the Supreme Court has repeatedly made clear that Congress is free under the commerce clause to legislate against public health problems as well as moral and social problems as long as those problems also burden interstate commerce.

Article 4, Section 3, Clause 2, of the Constitution, colloquially known as the property clause, grants congress the power "to dispose of and make all needful Rules and Regulations respecting the Territory or other Property belonging to the United States." The clause is crucial because the federal government owns property in every state and about 30 percent of the landmass of the United States overall; the property clause allows it to regulate and govern those lands. Because of the property clause, the government can establish such environmental goods as national parks or forest reservations and wildlife refuges. Moreover, the property clause is also significant to water resource policy. The "prior appropriation" doctrine of water rights states that water rights are determined by priority of beneficial use. This means that the first person to use water or divert water for a beneficial use or purpose can acquire individual rights to the water. By virtue of being the first formal owner of public lands, the federal government can own and manage water resources as it sees fit. When it creates a water resource such as the Tennessee Valley Authority, it owns that resource and can manage it accordingly.

The manner in which the constitution adjudicated power between the states and the federal government also substantially impacted the future development of environmental law. Federal supremacy, as defined by Article 6 of the Constitution, is simply the recognition that federal law prevails over state laws if the two conflict. Closely related to federal supremacy is the doctrine of federal preemption: federal law preempts state law should the laws disagree. Hence a federal court can require a state to stop actions it believes interfere with, or are in conflict with, federal law. Questions arise when federal law overlaps with those powers reserved to the states. The federal power to regulate pollution, for example, overlaps the police power of the states to regulate health and good order. In such a case, should federal or state law take precedence? There is no broad finding or general principle that resolves the issue. Though supremacy remains intact, the assertion (or not) of federal supremacy usually happens on a case by case basis.

Supremacy has been a double-edged sword in the history of environmental policy. One example of supremacy helpful to the cause of conservation is the Migratory Bird Treaty Act of 1918. The act established federal authority over migratory birds that were harmed by either lax or conflicting regulations in different states along their flyways. The stronger federal protections prevailed over the weaker efforts of some states. By 1920 the federal government established a series of seventy federal wildlife refuges in part to ensure healthy bird populations. Federal supremacy can prevent a race to the bottom in such matters; for example, federal law can supersede the states who try to compete for industry by offering weak regulations meant to entice businesses from another state that imposes stricter regulatory standards.

But federal supremacy can work both ways, preempting strong state laws in favor of weak federal statutes. Minnesota, for example, sought to impose strict regulations on nuclear power plants, policies much more stringent than those enforced by the federal Atomic Energy Commission. But the courts forbade Minnesota's regulations on the grounds that federal regulations preempted such an action, thereby forcing a regulatory regime on Minnesota against its wishes. Whether one favors the doctrine of preemption generally depends on the outcome of a particular conflict. If federal supremacy supports the policy goals of environmentalists they generally applaud it; if it favors, say, manufacturers, they often decry the infringement on local control and vice versa. The general trend over time is that the federal government has gained more power over policy and has extended its reach into areas previously understood to be reserved to the states.

Questions of federal power greatly impacted the relationship of nineteenth-century Americans to the environment, but the lessons of Franklin's Dock Creek did not. The myth of the superabundant eternal frontier prevailed. Even when local resources proved to be limited, Americans looked toward the untrammeled nature that lay further west. There was little pollution and plenty of resources further out on the frontier. Americans engorged those resources throughout the century, a profligacy that begat the beginnings of the environmental movement.

CHAPTER 2

THE SCIENCE AND NATURE OF EMPATHY

What is the use of a house if you haven't got a
tolerable planet to put it on?—If you cannot
tolerate the planet that it is on?

–HENRY DAVID THOREAU,
Familiar Letters (1865)

WHEN IN 1782 Hector St. John Crèvecoeur
asked "What is an American?" his question
tapped into cultural anxieties that vexed the
early republic: What was original about the United States
and not derivative from Europe? To many it seemed that
Europe had history and culture, America only the wilderness. One way to combat this problem was to make a
virtue of necessity and define the land itself as what was
unique about America. Because America lacked the glorious historical icons of Europe, editorialized the *North
American Review*, the forest "must be the monument of
our country." American identity became tied to the land.

In the nineteenth century as Americans were simplifying and commodifying landscapes at stunning rates, they were also embracing an environmental nationalism that eventually led historian Perry Miller to dub the United States "Nature's Nation."

The story of nineteenth-century environmentalism is how the people of Nature's Nation turned from understanding nature as raw material to be turned into commodities to an understanding that began to value and sympathize with nature itself. That change came from many directions. Naturalists began to understand how biological systems supported human well-being. Others began to use nature as a way to critique society—to posit the natural world as a counterpoint to the crass materialism of a culture obsessed with commodity acquisition. Still others connected access to the natural world with republican ideals, to the ability of people to craft meaningful and fulfilled lives. All such motivations depended on varieties of empathy with nature, on the ability to understand how nature functioned and how those functions intersected with human lives.

That empathy first manifested itself when early naturalists tied American identity to not only forests but the many wonderful and varied environments of the New World. Naturalists were not yet conservationists, but in celebrating American nature they helped establish some of the key values embedded in environmental thought: the balance of nature, the divinity of the natural world, and the sublimity of the unaltered landscape. Moreover, what began as teleological assumptions about the purpose of natural forms grew into an appreciation of the interconnectedness of nature—that is, into early ecological thought. The Harvard naturalist Benjamin Waterhouse, for example, argued in 1811 that the woodman sees the tree as something "to bear nuts; [or] to be cut into boards to burn to keep him warm or cook his victuals." But the naturalist "will tell you that [trees] are an important, nay indispensable link in the chain of human existence." As naturalists began to comprehend both the usefulness and the interconnectedness of nature, they developed empathy for it. Nature was no longer understood as an inexhaustible catalogue of raw materials, but as an interconnected system upon which people depended.

The lack of European institutional structures also gave early naturalists some advantages. For one, the scarcity of institutional credentialing allowed those without formal education entry to the world of natural science. It gave American natural history a democratic cast absent in

Europe where natural history maintained a genteel if not aristocratic bent. The openness to amateurism and the more republican style of natural history in America also fed into values that became prominent in environmental thought: a suspicion of wealth and its corrupting effects, duty to the common good, and the beauty of simplicity. These values promoted an interest in the natural world. By 1837 the *North American Review* could editorialize that by turning inward Americans found that, "the vast natural riches of our land are no longer trodden under foot with the slightest investigation, nor its majestic and beautiful scenery passed by with a heedless glance."

This Romantic inclination—which is to say an inclination based on emotion and subjective values as well as science—enabled an appreciation of nature. It also led to calls for nature's preservation. In 1793 Pennsylvania's Benjamin Smith Barton noted that the Susquehanna once supported many elk and, given their disappearance, recommended laws to "prevent many of our animals from being almost entirely extirpated in a few years through the whole . . . of the United States." His stupefied appreciation of the green world led Barton to rethink the relationship between people and the rest of nature. After describing beaver lodges in vivid architectural terms, Barton confessed that "I have sometimes been so extravagant as to wish that the laws of my country were extended, in their influence, to the protection of this sagacious quadruped."

Other early writers who urged conservation combined Romantic, nationalistic, and pragmatic reasons for doing so. In his 1793 "An Essay on those Inquires in Natural Philosophy, which at Present Are Most Beneficial to the United States of North America," Nicholas Collin, rector of the Swedish Churches in Pennsylvania, described America's forests as a "national treasure deserving the solicitous care of the patriotic philosopher and politician." Furthermore, Collin argued that citizens should preserve all natural forms with the pragmatic justification that we do not yet understand their role in fostering human economy and security:

> The great herds of buffaloes in the Western country, are a valuable national possession; a wanton destruction of them should be checked. . . . The greater number of birds in the old settlements have been described; but many equivocally: and our knowledge of their habits is in general very small. We should not indiscreetly destroy those deemed of no value; who knows what part is assigned

to them in the oeconomy of nature? perhaps our numerous tribes of woodpeckers save many trees from destructive worms? As to the useful and ornamental birds, they demand our protection against licentious and greedy tyranny: the beautiful and melodious birds diminish fast; and the Turkeys once so abundant, have long ago been drove into the remote woods.

Even John James Audubon, the frontiersman, field naturalist, and artist who killed thousands of birds (he once complained that he failed to collect enough birds to examine "when I shoot less than one hundred per day") came to decry the devastation of seabird colonies by "eggers" who looted their nests and was dismayed at seeing bison killed for sport.

By midcentury naturalists drew upon many different kinds of arguments for forest preservation. Forests were important for economic reasons. They also provided cool for people and crops, conserved moisture, and provided a sanctuary for many other species. But specific scientific rationales provided arguments for forest protection with a convincing, authoritative tone. In 1831, *The Naturalist* summarized the emerging opinion about the usefulness of forests among American natural scientists:

> Independent of ornamenting the earth and of furnishing us with timber and fuel, forests arrest the progress of impetuous and dangerous winds; maintain the temperature of the air; diminish extreme cold, and regulate intense heat; oppose the formation of ice and shelter the earth from the scorching rays of the sun; produce an abundance of water in the streams and impose a barrier to washing away or undermining their banks; preserve and enrich soil on hills and mountains; discharge the electricity of the atmosphere, and serve as laboratories for purifying the air we breathe.

Given this empathetic understanding of forest ecology, it only made sense to conserve them. Thus a dismayed George Emerson, in his 1846 *Report on the Trees and Shrubs Growing Naturally in the Forests of Massachusetts*, found it "difficult to account for the thoughtless destruction of rich resources of this kind, in a land where so universal and laudable an economy prevails in the use of all things that are worth money."

By the mid-nineteenth century many naturalists were becoming concerned with the destruction of nature, but no naturalist paid more close attention to the forested world or wrote more affectingly of its many great values than Henry David Thoreau (1817–1862). Thoreau and his mentor Ralph Waldo Emerson remain the two most prominent Transcendentalist philosophers, a major school of American Romantic philosophy in the nineteenth century. Emerson, especially, was a Neoplatonic philosopher, instructing his readers to value nature, but chiefly as an inspired (if degraded) reflection of the One or "Oversoul." Humans were to transcend imperfect nature to find a more perfect order. Transcendentalism is thus plagued by a dualism that divides this world from an assumed world that exists beyond this one. Part of Thoreau's continuing relevance, however, may derive from his more thorough and concrete reconciliation of obdurate nature with his notion of the divine.

To reconcile the two, Thoreau got his feet wet. Or muddy. Or up in a tree—nature was a tonic for Thoreau and a subject of his friendly but intense and precise scrutiny. Writing about the connections between people and nature in his classic meditation upon simple living and self-reliance, *Walden; or, Life in the Woods* (first published in 1854), he contended that, "Our village life would stagnate if it were not for the unexplored forests and meadows which surround it." It would stagnate because when the world is too much with us and getting and spending dominate so much of our lives, humans "need the tonic of wildness,—to wade sometimes in marshes where the bittern and the meadow-hen lurk, and hear the booming of the snipe; to smell the whispering sedge where only some wilder and more solitary fowl builds her nest."

Thoreau also embraced spiritual meanings given to the natural world: "My profession is always to be on the alert to find God in Nature," he wrote. "Heaven is under our feet as well as over our heads." Given the importance of the wild to human vitality, it followed that "Each town should have a park, or rather a primitive forest, of [five hundred] or a thousand acres, where a stick should never be cut for fuel, a common possession forever, for instruction and recreation." Yet very few of these primitive forests were being saved from the axe. As he claimed in his classic essay "Walking," "Nowadays almost all man's improvements, so called, as the building of homes and the cutting down of forests and of all large trees, simply deform the landscape." Rather than such waste, we need to promote a "culture in sympathy with surrounding nature," for "In Wildness is the preservation of the World."

This has been the environmentalists' Thoreau. Though largely ignored in his own time, since the late nineteenth century he has been revered as one of our most passionate advocates for a close relationship with the natural world. The problem with this Thoreau is that, like Benjamin Franklin before him, we often remember only a part of his legacy, stripping one measure of Thoreau's life—the love of nature—out of its larger context of social thought and action. For Thoreau was a master naturalist, but also a compelling social critic, an educator, and a passionate abolitionist. This matters, for Thoreau's environmental thought was embedded in his social outlook. As Rebecca Solnit writes, a stripped-down Thoreau "permits no conversation, let alone unity, between Thoreau the rebel, intransigent muse to Gandhi and Martin Luther King, and that other Thoreau who wrote about autumnal tints, ice, light, color, grasses [and] woodchucks."

When Thoreau decamped for his famous stay at Walden Pond, a mere mile and a half from the Concord village green, he did not do so to abandon the city—indeed, he was a frequent visitor to town so he could eat, visit his mother (who did his laundry for him), talk with friends, and perform the odd jobs that helped support him. He went to Walden Pond so he could, as he explained, live "deliberately" to "front only the essential facts of life. . . . I wanted to live deep and suck all the marrow out of life." Commodity culture distracted people from the essentials of life, and thus affronted his sensibilities. "Our inventions are wont to be pretty toys, which distract our attention from serious things," he wrote. "They are but improved means to an unimproved end." He sought the individual agency and self-improvement that an overcivilized existence focused on crass materialism precluded. He began *Walden* with a chapter on "Economy" that stressed the wrongness of materialism both for its spiritual emptiness and its undermining of republican ideals. It was not a celebration of "wilderness" that opposes society, but rather a thoroughgoing criticism of an avaricious culture. Nature was Thoreau's retreat to be sure, but it was not the antithesis of human culture or of urban life.

Most importantly, his deeply felt hatred of slavery was bound up in his environmental critique. Some of his visitors at Walden Pond were escaped slaves whom he helped along their way. Thoreau famously spent a night in jail in protest of government sanctioning of slavery and the Mexican War, which Thoreau and other abolitionists regarded as a

Figure 2.1 For Thoreau, living the good life meant combining his intense interest in the natural world with his social conscience. Portrait by Benjamin D. Maxham.

means to expand slavery into the western territories. Less well known is that he wrote about slavery as an ecological as well as a social ill. "Slavery and servility have produced no sweet-scented flower annually, to charm the senses of men, for they have no real life: they are merely a decaying and a death, offensive to all healthy nostrils," he wrote in his important essay, "Slavery in Massachusetts." Burying slavery, Thoreau argued, would allow for a more just society to sprout. In other writings Thoreau christened slavery a "pollution" that degraded people and the land. Conversely, ecological and social justice fused together. In *Wild Fruits* Thoreau argued for the superiority of huckleberries that grow "wild all over the country—wholesome, bountiful and free" compared to the "culture of tobacco" that required "inventing slavery and a thousand other curses for that purpose, with infinite pains and inhumanity."

Thoreau's ecological critique of slavery was similar to that of black abolitionists who also denounced slavery as a social and ecological evil. Former slave Charles Ball, in his compelling narrative *Slavery in the United States*, consistently tied the use of slave labor to the degradation of once productive farmlands. Ball described farms in Pennsylvania as

> originally . . . highly fertile and productive . . . but the gentle-men [farmers] . . . supplied themselves with slaves from Africa, cleared large plantations of many thousands of acres—culti-vated tobacco—and became suddenly wealthy . . . but . . . they . . . exhausted the kindly soil by unremitting crops of tobacco, declined in their circumstances, and finally grew poor. . . . Finally, pinched by necessity, at last sold their slaves.

He repeatedly noted how the slave economy, predicated on violently exploited forced labor, transformed once productive landscapes into exhausted and sterile fields.

Frederick Douglass made similar ecological criticisms of slave society in his second autobiography, *My Bondage and My Freedom*. In it Douglass despaired for the farm of his birthplace and the "worn-out, sandy, desert-like appearance of its soil." This desolation was further expressed by "the indigent and spiritless character of its inhabitants." But he found other natures. As a young man he was thrilled to encounter a landscape

> of almost Eden-like beauty . . . rabbits, deer, and other wild game, might be seen, peering and playing about, with none to molest them or make them afraid. The tops of the stately poplars were often covered with the red-winged black-birds, making all nature vocal with the joyous life and beauty of their wild, warbling notes. These all belonged to me.

The palpable intensity of Douglass's affection for this landscape informed his reaction as a free man to New Bedford, Massachusetts, which he found "surrounded by more comfort and refinement . . . than a majority of the slaveholders on the Eastern Shore of Maryland." Slavery was not required to produce wealth. Beyond such practical evaluations, Douglass's moral admonitions to end slavery are also ecological: In allowing slavery "we are made a reproach and a by-word to a mocking earth, and we must continue to be so made, so long as slavery continues to pollute our soil." Slavery was not just a moral evil, but an ecological one too.

Like Douglass, Thoreau understood that slavery was in Massachusetts because the cotton grown with slave labor was spun into garments there. (Massachusetts, once a center of the colonial slave trade, abolished slavery via a series of court decisions culminating in an abolitionist state Supreme Court ruling in 1783.) He criticized both this extension of slavery and the dehumanizing effects of industrial production more generally. "I cannot believe," he wrote in *Walden*, "that our factory system is the best mode by which men may get clothing. The condition of the operatives is becoming every day more like that of the English; and it cannot be wondered at, since . . . the principle object is not that mankind may be well and honestly clad, but unquestionably, that the corporations may be enriched." The Romantic, ecological critique of capitalism, then, extended from distress over rampant materialism to the use of forced labor that exhausted once-productive farmlands. It also entered the factory where not just Thoreau but the workers in industrializing cities such as Lowell, Massachusetts—just fifteen miles north of Concord—expressed a nascent understanding of how factory pollution could harm their health and a full bore Romantic juxtaposition between the satanic mills that were their workplace and the ministering balm of the green world.

The factory girls of Lowell—mostly young women from rural New England—experienced the factory system first hand and quickly understood its ill effects on their well-being. One wrote that we must aid the young women "who are shut up within the 'Prison walls of a Factory' where we are continually inhaling cotton-dust, lamp smoke, and away from wholesome pure air." Wholesome and pure air—what one factory laborer described as an escape to the "purest of society, with brook and bird, and flower and tree"—powerfully juxtaposed "the haunts of selfish men." One Exeter, New Hampshire, worker complained that "you don't realize how unpleasant it is for females to be confined in a factory month after month with no time to enjoy the sunshine and flowers—the blue sky and the green grass." Escaping from "being pent up in a cotton mill and factory house" for a short trip to the country, wrote another young millworker, allowed factory workers to "appreciate the pleasures of a journey through the country, when the earth is dressed in her richest roves of green, bedecked with flowers, and all smiling with sunlight." The trip affirmed her belief that "man had made the town, but God made the country." The trip could also be mental; one worker, E.D., lasted through the workday by indulging her "waking dream" that nostalgically returned her to "the green hills of my childhood."

These reactions arose because the nineteenth century was, especially in America, the golden age of capitalist economic growth and consequent commodification of nature. Originating in Great Britain and Europe, the industrial revolution came full bore to the United States between 1820 and 1870. The building of transportation infrastructure—first roads and canals, soon the railroad—opened the whole continent to the world market. By 1840 the United States had the most railroads in the world, with three thousand miles of track; by 1860 the country had added twenty-one thousand more miles of track. Train tracks seemed to be everywhere; they even bordered Walden Pond.

For the homesteaders moving west—encouraged by government policies such as the Homestead Act of 1862 (which granted settlers 160 acres of land for a mere twenty-six dollars as long as they resided upon it and "improved" it)—the railroad offered transportation of their goods to eastern markets, and in turn, the ability of consumer goods to be shipped to them. Railroad development and the Homestead Act often worked together, for the government subsidized the railroads with land grants under the assumption that settlers would follow and put down roots along the right of way. They did, and the flow of Americans westward counts as one of the great migrations of human history. By the end of the century, more than eighty million acres had been granted to over 480,000 successful homesteaders. In total, about 10 percent of the United States was settled because of the Homestead Act, in what Theodore Roosevelt later described as "the great leap Westward."

The railroad was thus a stunning engine of economic growth; by the 1850s it accounted for about 15 percent of all investment in the United States. It also amounted to a mind bogglingly massive handover of publicly owned natural resources to private interests. Regional railroad grants included rights of way and ten alternating 640-acre sections of land on either side of the tract per mile. Railroad companies took all the timber and stone they needed from these grants free of charge. The government subsidized transcontinental railroads even more, as they received not ten but twenty sections of land per mile. Furthermore, they could select "lieu lands," not just lands adjacent to the railroad, anywhere they wished from the public domain. The Northern Pacific railroad alone received in transfer about forty million acres of public lands, an area nearly the size of New England. Between 1862 and 1872, the government transferred over ninety-four million acres of public land directly to the railroad industry, an area as big as the fourth largest state, Montana. This aggressive economy and policy worked; by 1890 scholars declared the frontier closed.

The environmental costs of westward expansion were monumental. Forests were cut and cleared, dams built, prairies turned to monoculture, mines excavated, and pollutants were dumped in waters, soils, and cities. Michigan, for example, was nearly completely deforested. Scarcely inhabited by Euro-Americans in 1820, by 1897 they had logged and shipped 160 *billion* board feet of white pine timber from the state, leaving only 6 billion still standing, a loss of 96 percent. The great economist Thorstein Veblen, writing in the early 1920s, understood westward expansion as a massive squandering of public wealth. Granting natural resources to corporations as "free income" encouraged waste, wrote Veblen. Lumbering waste alone was so great "that this enterprise of the lumber-men during the period since the middle of the nineteenth century has destroyed very appreciably more timber than it has utilized."

Beyond barren, cut-over forests, denuded land baked under the broiling sun and branches stripped from shipped trees—"slash"—provided ample fuel for fires. Many ignited, including the most destructive fire in U.S. history, the Peshtigo, Wisconsin, fire of 1871. Drought and unusually hot temperatures combined with the effects of logging that October to spark a fire that burned nearly 1.28 million acres of northeastern Wisconsin and upper Michigan. The fire claimed some fifteen hundred lives. Survivors reported that the firestorm generated a fire whirl (described as a tornado) that tossed rail cars and houses into the air. Neither entirely natural or social, the fire is an example of environmental and social factors combining to produce a devastating result.

By the mid-nineteenth century many Americans began to see deforestation as a national problem. William Cullen Bryant, the poet and great liberal reformer—he was an abolitionist and agitator for women's suffrage, organized labor, and immigrants—also became an environmentalist. Writing in the June 1865 *Evening Post* on "The Utility of Trees," Bryant argued that in its "disposition of the public domain" Congress should not simply give land to the railroads, but preserve forests. "It will be an act of provident wisdom to reserve considerable tracts of forest in different parts of the country, as the public domain, with a view of preventing the destruction of trees," reasoned Bryant. To effect this policy, Bryant recommended "a body of foresters . . . must be retained in the pay of the Government." Despite his poetic sensibilities, Bryant largely defended his ideas in utilitarian terms: "forests protect a county against drought, and keep its streams constantly flowing, and its wells constantly full." Other poets lamented the loss of forest with a full-bore sentimentality. Lydia Huntly Sigourney, among the most popular poets of her day, began her poem "Fallen Forests" by asserting "man's warfare on the trees is terrible" and ended it by asking the Father to grant Americans the grace to "mourn the rashness time can ne'er restore." Despite such pleas most Americans ignored the problem of resources, sure that plenty more awaited them in the West.

Westward expansion was justified by a new colonial terminology: Manifest Destiny. John O'Sullivan of the New York *Democratic Review*, arguing in favor of the annexation of Texas, first coined the term "Manifest Destiny" in 1845, giving name to an ideology already well established. By the 1830s advocates of westward expansion added the secular justification of scientific and civilizational progress to the initial rationale of subduing nature as God's work. The jurist James Kent, for example, seeking in 1832 a legal basis for seizing land from Native Americans, argued that the continent was "fitted and intended by Providence to be subdued and cultivated, and to become the residence of civilized nations." If God's providence drove colonists to subdue the eastern forests, Manifest Destiny drove them to the Pacific. The celebrated French observer of American society, Alexis de Tocqueville, described the attitude toward nature of westward-flowing Americans in this way: "In Europe, people talk a great deal of the wilds of America, but the Americans themselves never think about them; they are insensible to the wonders of inanimate nature and may be said not to perceive the mighty forests that surround them till they fall beneath the hatchet."

Environmental myths helped justify the movement west. The first was a way to ignore the indigenous inhabitants of western lands by assuming that the land itself was in untouched or "virgin" condition. John O'Sullivan assured his readers that western lands were unoccupied and simply awaiting the kindly hand of the American settler: "We are entering on . . . untrodden space," he wrote in 1839, "with the truths of God in our minds." Other myths proffered an ostensibly scientific rationale to promote western settlement. Land speculator Charles Dana Wilber, writing in 1881, sold the idea that human improvements altered the climate of the more arid part of the West. "God speed the plow. . . .

By this wonderful provision, which is only man's mastery over nature, the clouds are dispensing copious rains," claimed Wilber. The plow "is the instrument which separates civilization from savagery; and converts a desert into a farm or garden. . . . To be more concise, *Rain follows the plow*." For Wilber and other proponents of westward expansion, civilization created the nature it needed to prosper.

Two important early environmental thinkers attempted to work on behalf of nature and the native inhabitants of the West. The first was a Philadelphia portrait artist George Catlin (1796–1892), who in the 1820s encountered a delegation of "some ten or fifteen noble and dignified-looking Indians." The experience profoundly affected him; in the 1830s he left Philadelphia for six years to preserve through painting the disappearing peoples and landscapes of the American West. His art attempted a kind of rescue anthropology, and during those years, he painted three hundred portraits and nearly 175 landscapes and ritual scenes. The West was full of meaningful contradictions for Catlin. He was appalled by "the profligate waste of the lives of . . . noble and useful" buffalos. He also was deeply empathetic to the native peoples of America, challenging repugnant stereotypes by writing "The Indian's misfortune has consisted chiefly in our ignorance of their true character and disposition" and painting them in a humanizing, even reverential manner. In 1841 Catlin published the two-volume *Letters and Notes on the Manners, Customs, and Condition of the North American Indians* which featured approximately three hundred engravings. Three years later he published *Catlin's North American Indian Portfolio*, a collection of twenty-five plates.

Most important to the history of environmentalism, in 1832 Catlin proposed one solution to the problem of vanishing landscapes and peoples: the national park. Catlin imagined nature and native peoples

> As they *might* in future be seen (by some great protecting policy of government) preserved in their pristine beauty and wildness, in a *magnificent park*, where the world could see for ages to come, the native Indian in his classic attire . . . amid the fleeting herds of elks and buffaloes. . . . A *nation's Park*, containing man and beast, in all the wild and freshness of their nature's beauty! [Emphasis in original]

Though his proposal had little effect, Catlin deserves much praise for suggesting the great innovation that became the national park and for including both people and nature in his vision for the future. But many troubling assumptions also infest Catlin's proposal. He presumed native peoples were somehow outside of history, unchanging—and thus saw a place for them in a preserved area, not as part of a developing society. He also assumed and wrote that Indians were destined to be a "vanishing people," thereby powerfully if inadvertently supporting President Andrew Jackson's policy of Indian removal. His writings on economy contained similar contradictions. Catlin was both a shrewd exhibitionist concerned with turning paintings into profit and a proponent of ethical commerce: "I travel not to trade," wrote Catlin, but to "herald the Indian." In the end Catlin's typical assumptions about progress and civilization limited the efficacy of his work on behalf of nature and native peoples—problems that haunt American civilization to this day.

Catlin did not confine his interests in native peoples to those in the United States. He traveled to other parts of the world to investigate native peoples, notably to South America to find the peoples encountered by the great German naturalist-explorer Alexander von Humboldt (1769–1859). Humboldt is currently undergoing a revival in American intellectual circles, and it is long overdue. In his time, Humboldt was fervently celebrated; Emerson called him "one of the wonders of the world." And he was. One of the inventors and great practitioners of ecosystem sciences, Humboldt was also a deeply humanitarian radical who denounced slavery (a "disgrace") and decried the oppression of Native Americans as a "stain" on the nation. As historian Aaron Sachs contends in *The Humboldt Current*, Humboldt remains one of the few thinkers who understood that colonialism, with its raw extraction of resources and callousness toward indigenous populations, inevitably led to ecological devastation. Humboldt bequeaths to environmentalism what Sachs terms its "social edge," what I have previously called the integration of social and natural thinking. Humboldt thus foreshadowed social ecology, the analysis of how social power shapes the ways that a society interacts with the environment.

Born into a wealthy Prussian aristocratic family, Humboldt became known for his five-year long voyage to Latin America. He not only studied the ecology of the New World, but defended the sophistication and cultural integrity of the indigenous peoples he met there. He visited the United States in May of 1804, spending a week in Washington where he regaled President Thomas Jefferson with information about Mexico and South America. "We have little knowledge" of the Spanish colonies, a grateful Jefferson told Humboldt, "but through you." Humboldt loved the United Sates enough that for the rest of his life he called himself "half an American."

Humboldt's most astonishing and consequential idea was the now-familiar concept of the "web of life." Prefiguring the Gaia hypothesis, Humboldt considered the world a single unified organism. "Everything," he wrote, "is interaction and reciprocal." Rather than just studying the structure of organisms, he attempted to understand the structures of nature and how individual organisms fit into them. Building on the work of Joseph Priestley, Humboldt was the first scientist to theorize how climate emerged from the "perpetual interrelationship" between land, ocean, wind, elevation, and organic life—what he called a science of "mutual dependence and connection." Departing from Linnaeus, he championed the idea of classifying plants by climatic zones—taking into account the altitude, temperature, latitude, and other factors of location—instead of relying upon taxonomy alone. Noting the puzzle-piece geography of Africa and South America led him to postulate an "ancient" connection between the continents, an inference confirmed in recent decades by the contemporary science of plate tectonics. He had a profound effect on Charles Darwin and such environmental luminaries as John Wesley Powell, John Muir ("How intensely I desire to be a Humboldt," confessed the young Muir), and Aldo Leopold.

Humboldt pushed his observations to logical conclusions—and into the need for conservation. The decline of one species, for example, could have cascading effects on others; "In this great chain of causes and effects," reasoned Humboldt, "no single fact can be considered in isolation." Thus deforestation doubly harmed the land because denuded fields were subject to unfettered rains that washed topsoil away. Forests needed protection because of soils and their effects on regional climates—Humboldt explained how forests cooled the climate by releasing oxygen, storing water, and providing shade. He wrote how overfishing could deplete "future generations" of life, and he denounced the "insatiable avarice" of humans, the future consequences of which were "incalculable." Humboldt provided the nineteenth century's most advanced intellectual architecture that housed both humans and nature, and the need to conserve both.

Humboldt died just before the beginnings of the Civil War, but George Catlin lived until late December 1872, just long enough to see a great protecting policy of government, the creation of Yellowstone National Park. The area that became Yellowstone had long attracted the attention of Euro-Americans. In 1806, the Lewis and Clark expedition, having reached the Pacific Ocean a year and half after they set out from St. Louis, Missouri, was returning east through what is now Montana. They allowed a member of their party, John Colter, to venture out on his own; a year later he rejoined the group with wild tales of mountain canyons, boiling lakes, and rivers that flowed upward. Many dismissed his accounts as crazy, and the area that became Yellowstone was derisively dismissed as "Colter's Hell." But subsequent expeditions, most importantly a surveying group led by Henry Washburn, collaborated Colter's early descriptions.

But it was another expedition in 1871 led by geologist Ferdinand Hayden that included painter Thomas Moran and photographer William Henry Jackson that proved most important for the creation of the park: visual representations of the area captured congressional and public attention. Hayden suggested that the unique and beautiful area be set aside as a park, lest tacky commercial development despoil it as had happened to the glorious Niagara Falls. On March 7, 1872, President Ulysses S. Grant signed *The Act of Dedication* creating Yellowstone National Park. The act declared that Yellowstone was "dedicated and set apart as a public park or pleasuring-ground for the benefit and enjoyment of the people." Park supporters were successful in large part because they argued that it would cost nothing to create the park. Congress took the financial argument to heart. When Yellowstone National Park became the first national park in the history of the world, it had no budget or administrative structure. The position of park director was entirely volunteer and initially held by a man who visited the park only twice during his seven years as director.

In making his suggestion, Hayden drew upon at least one precedent for the federal government setting aside lands for public use. California underwent exponential growth following the discovery of gold in 1849; the striking cliffs, domes, and waterfalls in Yosemite Valley experienced large-scale tourism and ecological damage. In 1864, to ward off further commercial exploitation, conservationists convinced President Abraham Lincoln to declare Yosemite Valley and the Mariposa Grove of giant sequoias (some of the largest and oldest organisms on earth) a public trust of California. The Yosemite Grant, as it was called, bequeathed the land to California as a park for "public use, resort and recreation." As would happen with the debate over Yellowstone, a key point for conservationists was that protecting the lands would cost nothing. This marked the first time the U.S. government protected land for public use and enjoyment.

Though Catlin lived to see his idea of a park created, he did not get to see parks used as living space for native peoples. Native American tribes were expelled from Yellowstone in the 1870s and 1880s. Before park status, about a half-dozen tribes made seasonal use of Yellowstone; a group of Eastern Shoshone known as the "Sheepeaters" inhabited the land year-round. The Sheepeaters left Yellowstone in 1868, after ceding the lands, but not their rights to hunt, to the U.S. government. But the United States never ratified the treaty and refused to recognize the usufruct claims of the Sheepeaters. Though the larger nineteenth-century policy goal of "subduing" and confining native peoples to reservation lands clearly directed Indian policy for Yellowstone, the park had the further burden of providing "uninhabited" nature and abundant wildlife for its visitors. It thus lacked the means to accommodate native peoples and their economies.

And yet the early history of the national parks, which are probably the most thoroughly democratic institutions in American society, also significantly involved nonwhite peoples. Because parks were not accorded a budget, the task of administering them fell to the army. And the parks needed administration; lax oversight meant that logging, hunting, and other unmanaged resource use continued unabated. The U.S. Calvary took control of Yellowstone in 1886 and managed the park for the next thirty-two years. The managers and rangers of the early parks—the California parks Yosemite, Sequoia, and General Grant (later named Kings Canyon) were added in 1890—were largely Buffalo Soldiers, the regiments of black forces renowned for their exploits in the Indian wars of the late nineteenth century. They served as both rangers and as administers. Captain Charles Young, the third black man to graduate from West Point, served for a year as superintendent of Sequoia and General Grant National Parks. Approximately five hundred of his fellow Buffalo Soldiers worked in Yosemite National Park and nearby Sequoia National Park, evicting poachers and timber thieves as well as extinguishing forest fires. Buffalo soldiers were the first guardians and many of the first rangers of the national parks.

The national parks are just one lasting legacy of nineteenth-century conservation; the centuries' environmental innovations and reforms were also urban as well as rural. Some strains of nineteenth-century thought exulted in urban hybrid landscapes rather than bifurcations between the wilderness and the city. Indeed, wilderness could be thought of as the wild within such civic landscapes as Mount Auburn cemetery, located just outside Boston, Massachusetts. Mount Auburn was founded as a cemetery and a rural garden; it has also served as an arboretum. Joseph Story, an associate Supreme Court justice mourning the loss of his ten-year-old daughter to scarlet fever, delivered in 1831 a powerful commemoration at the opening of Mount Auburn. He took solace from nature's gifts. Story extolled nature's "varied features" of "beauty and grandeur" such as "the sheltered valley; the deep glen; the grassy glade; and the silent grove." Visitors to Mount Auburn, in Story's estimation, "breathe a solemn calm, as if we were in the bosom of a wilderness." As would happen with national parks, such lands were open to all citizens of the United States, a striking break from European traditions that most often reserved access to garden and park spaces to the moneyed elite.

Thinking creatively about nature in city and small town spaces characterized some of the great urban planners of the nineteenth century. The Hudson valley landscape architect Andrew Jackson Downing, for example, was not merely an elite and influential Gothic Revival "taste-maker" who moralized about the benign influence of the well-kept country home. Rather, Downing advocated for exhaustive civic planning—not unrestrained capitalist sprawl—and more importantly argued for the democratic purpose of common lands. Like Thoreau's, Downing's ideal town contained one "indispensable" feature: "a large open space, common or park, situated in the middle of the village—not less than twenty acres; and better if fifty or more in extent . . . held as joint property, and for the common use of the whole village." Downing held culturally exclusive ideas about what constituted proper behaviors in such spaces, but nevertheless advocated for "country villages" that offered Americans "a neighborhood where, without losing society, they can see the horizon, breathe fresh air, and walk upon elastic greensward." Downing held that for the United States to be truly "republican" its citizens needed "public parks, public gardens, public galleries, and tasteful villages."

Children, too, were thought of as crucial citizens for such spaces. Playing outdoors was fun, and the ennobling effects of contact with nature would help ensure republican citizenship. Thus the landscape architect H.W.S. Cleveland, author of the important *Landscape Architecture as*

Applied to the Wants of the West; with an Essay on Forest Planting on the Great Plains, emphasized the importance of developing cities so that children—and especially "the children of the poorer classes"—would have access to open spaces and clean air. All children should enjoy "the presence of trees and shrubs, and flowers and grass" and experience the "wonder and delight" that derives from "love of nature." More broadly, Cleveland advocated for civic planning opposed to giving free reign to "the selfish greed of real estate developers" who were "callous to the sufferings they inflict upon future inhabitants." Rather than real estate developers, Cleveland explained in a letter to Frederick Law Olmsted, planners should create cities with planted trees at the town center and have "the elements of beauty . . . everywhere present, pervading all portions of the city." For Cleveland, wise use of nature in urban planning could improve the beauty of the city and provide recreational and social spaces for its inhabitants.

The idea of using hybrid spaces such as parks to promote republican virtue was widespread among the planners and designers of the mid-nineteenth century. This includes the man best remembered for his efforts, Frederick Law Olmsted, designer (along with his partner Calvert Vaux) of New York's Central Park, the Boston Fens, and the Capitol grounds in Washington, District of Columbia. Central Park was not Olmsted's idea. It had been championed for years by figures such as William Cullen Bryant (who in 1844 pleaded to "give our vast population an extensive pleasure grounds for shade and recreation") and Andrew Jackson Downing, who, like Olmsted, wanted the park to be an inclusive institution of democratic society. As Olmsted put it, Central Park should "supply to the hundreds of thousands of tired workers, who have no opportunity to spend their summers in the country, a specimen of God's handiwork." This was especially innovative, because as one European observer noted about cities in the United States, they had a near "total absence of public gardens or pleasure-grounds" for the working classes. But for Olmsted, it was a moral responsibility of society to provide democratic natural spaces.

Nor was the park a mere occasional relief from the built environment. Olmsted advocated for citywide park systems that ensured the broadest access to green spaces instead of individually designed parks. The belief in planning for the entire society extended to Olmsted's view of national parks. He argued that without government protection places like Yosemite would devolve into "rich men's parks." He served a one-year appointment on the Board of Commissioners of the Yosemite state reserve, and his 1865 report to Congress, based on the board's recommendations, urged congress to protect Yosemite's "value to posterity." Indeed, Olmsted claimed that "It is a scientific fact that the occasional contemplation of natural scenes of an impressive character, particularly if this contemplation occurs in connection with relief from ordinary cares, change of air and change of habits, is favorable to the health and vigor of men . . . beyond any other conditions that can be offered them." Like Andrew Jackson Downing, Olmsted held middle-class Protestant norms of proper behavior for the users of parks. But that legacy must be understood in the context of radical civic design meant to help the poor and working classes in an age when government, at best, ignored them.

National parks and hybrid civic grounds were not the only landscapes that attracted the attentions of nineteenth-century environmentalists. So did agricultural lands. Early critics of colonial agriculture, noting that farmers regularly exhausted their fields, decried the absence of an enduring society based on an enduring agriculture—what today we would call sustainability. Much of the problem had to do with methods of cultivation. Soils are more susceptible to erosion when tilled—the rooted plants that hold the earth together are ripped out by the plow. Loosened earth then easily drifts away, especially when wind or rain brush the plowed field.

Observers of colonial agriculture noted these problems. Pehr Kalm, a student of Linnaeus who was commissioned by the Royal Swedish Academy of Sciences to collect North American agricultural specimens, became deeply critical of the colonial agriculture he encountered. North American "agriculture was in a very bad state" reported Kalm in his 1753 volume, *Travels into North America*. Initial crops were "excellent," but the "same land, after being cultivated for several years in succession, without being manured, finally loses its fertility of course." Beyond abusing soils into infertility Kalm found that, "the grain fields, the meadows, the forests, the cattle, etc. are treated with equal carelessness; and the characteristics of the English nation, so well skilled in these branches of husbandry, is scarcely recognizable here." Kalm blamed colonial farmers who had "their eyes fixed on the present gain" with such an unwavering gaze that it left them "blind to the future."

Another critic of the blind future of American agriculture was James Madison, who after his time in elective office became the president of the agricultural society in Albemarle County, Virginia. In an 1818 speech before the society he elucidated the "errors of husbandry." Madison fiercely decried "The evil of pressing too hard on the land," which has "also been much increased by the bad mode of ploughing it. Shallow ploughing, and ploughing up and down hilly land have, by exposing the loosened soil to be carried off by rains, hastened more than any thing else, the waste of its fertility." Among solutions Madison proposed "cultivation in horizontal drills, with a plough adapted to it," what today we would call contour plowing, a proven method for reducing soil erosion.

Madison also recognized that the belief in endless new frontiers prevented farmers from adopting enduring improvements. The neglect of manures, for example, "may be traced to the same cause with our excessive cropping. In the early stages of our agriculture, it was more convenient and more profitable to bring new land into cultivation, than to improve exhausted land." Fortunately, new farming methods could correct the old errors. "Fertility may be preserved or restored," continued Madison, "by giving to the earth animal or vegetable manure equivalent to the matter taken from it." Madison was not the only one making this case. As *The Farmer's Manual* put it one year after Madison's address, "The face of the country is changed; the quality of the soil has changed; and if we will live as well, and become as rich and respectable as our fathers, we must cultivate their virtues; but abandon their system of farming."

One reformer who tried to help his fellows abandon their father's system of farming was Jesse Buel (1778–1839), proprietor of a profitable printing business that he left to pursue agricultural reform. He later combined his two passions by becoming editor of the *Cultivator*. Agricultural reform was Buel's calling; he explained his motivations by noting that, "Agriculture is truly our nursing mother, which gives food, and growth, and wealth, and moral health and character to our country. It may be considered the great wheel which moves all the machinery of society." But that great wheel was broken because farmers refused to cultivate their fields to fertility. "It is your province and your duty to husband and apply the vegetable and most essential element of fertility— MANURES." Happily, it was only poor methods of farming that led to soil exhaustion. If farmlands were "judiciously managed" they would not "wear out or become exhausted of their fertility." For Buell, fertile soil was a "gift of a beneficent Creator" entrusted to the judicious farmer who is "bound to transmit [it] UNIMPAIRED, to posterity."

Like other reformers, Buell thought about the ecology of agriculture systematically, which he called "the farmer's magic chain." For Buell, "Cattle and sheep make manure,—manure makes grain, grass and roots—these, in return, feed the family, and make meat, milk and wool." And meat, milk, and wool make money, "the great object of the farmer's ambition." All is well unless the chain "is broken or suffered to corrode by neglect." For Buell, also a Whig politician, the productivity of the farm was directly related to the character of the farmer. That character could be improved through education. Buell noted that New York boasted schools for science, engineering, law, medicine, and war, but lacked them for agricultural instruction.

Madison also wished for agricultural education: "But, whilst all are sensible that agriculture is the basis of population and prosperity, it cannot be denied that the study and practice of its true principles have hitherto been too generally neglected in the United States." Those true principles were largely ignored in the Unites States until 1862 with the passage of the Land-Grant College Act (popularly known as the Morrill Act). The Morrill Act provided land to states to finance the establishment of colleges specializing in "agriculture and the mechanic arts," and was meant in part to help ensure the success of the agricultural settlers enticed west by the Homestead Act.

Agricultural reformers such as Buell and Madison connected the sustainable farm to republican virtue. The Virginian Edmund Ruffin (1794–1865) sought to use his striking innovations in agrochemistry to entrench slave agriculture. Best remembered as a "Fire Eater" advocate of state's rights who advocated secession and argued for the moral superiority of chattel slavery against northern wage labor, Ruffin had previously made his reputation as an agricultural reformer. After he inherited his family plantation at age sixteen, Ruffin crushed fossil shells into its fields as a means to add marl (sedimentary rock consisting of clay and lime) to worn-out soil. The results were dramatic: he improved corn yields by a half and nearly doubled his wheat crop. Ruffin reasoned that the addition of calcium carbonate neutralized soil acidity and thus returned soils to fertility. He presented his methods to the public in 1832 as "An Essay on Calcareous Manures," and subsequently published an important journal of agricultural reform, *Farmer's Register*. Beyond marl, Ruffin championed organic manures and diversified crops as well as careful cultivation that avoided topsoil erosion.

Despite Ruffin's efforts to use reform to stabilize and entrench slaver society, poor agricultural practices figured into the causes of the civil war. Southern agriculture exhausted soils, which diminished the availability of farmable lands. This had the effect of increasing the monetary value of both productive land and slaves, which in turn concentrated the ownership of each into fewer and fewer hands. The majority of white farmers were forced onto marginal lands. Exhausted soils also contributed to the defense of slavery. Because worn-out lands had little commercial value, slaves became an ever more important source of wealth. Proslavery advocates such as J.D.B. De Bow (1820–1867), editor of the influential and widely circulated *De Bow's Review*, noted in 1852 that "The best [southern] lands have become exhausted . . . [and] the only increase to be found in the elements or means to procure wealth, consists of the increase of slaves." In this manner environmental degradation helped further entrench the slave system.

The Civil War itself was a great ecological disaster—as are all wars. General William T. Sherman's famous "hard hand of war" was seen in the devastated ecologies he left in the wake of his march to the sea during November and December 1864. "We devoured the land," he explained in a letter to his wife. In fact, every theatre devoured the land. Soldiers noticed. Captain (and future military historian) Theodore Dodge of New York wrote from Virginia, "it is wonderful how the whole country round here is literally stripped of its timber. Woods which, when we came here, were so thick that we could not get through them any way are now entirely cleared." Historian Megan Kate Nelson estimates that two million trees were killed during the war. Each year the Union and Confederate armies consumed four hundred thousand acres of forest for firewood alone. In a letter to his wife, Private William Paynton of the Twenty-First New Jersey Regiment described the use of trees for fire: "You can imagine the size of them when I tell you that we use as much woods as you could put on a cart in one fire . . . our Regt, will burn perhaps fifty loads every day." Multiply the destruction of trees by horses, fields, rivers, crops, animals both domestic and wild, disease organisms, human bodies, and the spread of poisons both chemical and from munitions, and one begins to imagine the ecological devastation of the first modern war.

Civil War soldiers employed Romantic tropes to understand the devastation of war on human and nonhuman nature alike. The word "stumps" acquired dramatic and horrifying new meanings; tree stumps and amputated limbs mirrored each other. Some soldiers made this connection explicit. The Union officer Morris Schaff described corpses in the Battle of the Wilderness as "human legs and arms, resembling piles of stove wood." Destroyed trees were "dead, or half-dead, dangling limbs." Even against such terrible destruction, however, Schaff understood that trees could offer "sweet shade to the dying soldier." Herman Melville's poem "The Armies of the Wilderness" witnessed the "stumps of forests for dreary leagues/Like a massacre show." Conversely, the beauties of nature highlighted the ugliness of war. Confederate General Robert E. Lee wrote his wife in 1861 from what is now West Virginia, that "I enjoyed the mountains, as I rode along. The views are magnificent—the valleys so beautiful, the scenery so peaceful. What a glorious world Almighty God has given us. How thankless and ungrateful we are, and how we labour to mar his gifts."

Not only did the war itself mar his gifts, but so did the transformation of the country that happened in its aftermath. The end of the war wholly opened the West to settlement. The transcontinental railroad and industrial-scale resource extraction followed in the war's wake. Even more fundamentally, it cemented the economy of the future as an industrial and chemical one. Both North and South experimented with chemical weapons during the war. On June 4, 1861, *The Richmond Daily Dispatch* argued that, "It is well known that there are some chemicals so poisonous that an atmosphere impregnated with them, makes it impossible to remain where they are by filling larges shells of extraordinary capacity with poisonous gases and throwing them very rapidly" into an enemy-held position. In May 1862, President Lincoln, who remained very keen to explore new methods of warfare, received a letter from a New York schoolteacher, John W. Doughty, urging that he fill heavy shells with a choking gas of liquid chlorine, to poison the enemy in their trenches.

The Civil War also cemented industrial production based upon fossil fuels. Coal in particular was crucial to mobilization of the North and South, and its use permanently altered the American economy. It is no accident that the first detailed scientific attempt to calculate the amount of carbon being released into the atmosphere, by Irish scientist John Tyndall, began on the eve of the war in 1859. Pollution from coal was not the only Civil War outcome that was severely detrimental to wildlife. The arms industry produced weapons in staggering numbers, and innovated new designs and technologies such as the repeating rifle that remade reloading—and offered postwar hunters unprecedented new abilities to kill game in massive quantities. Over time, the conservationist response to the industrial transformation of landscapes, poisons, fossil fuels, and the ability to kill game in tremendous numbers defined much of the following century and a half of environmentalism.

The most important of the immediate conservationist responses to the Civil War arose from Lincoln's State Department—his minister to Italy, George Perkins Marsh (1801–1882). Marsh devoted his Civil War years to writing his 1864 masterpiece *Man and Nature*. It made Marsh perhaps the most important of the early, prophetic voices of conservation. Born in 1801 to a Vermont farmer, Marsh was a stunning polymath: he spoke and read twenty languages, was a lawyer (even if, in his own words, "an indifferent practitioner" of law), newspaper editor, sheep farmer, mill owner, lecturer, Whig politician who served as a congressman from Vermont (where he championed women's education and helped to found and guide the Smithsonian Institution), U.S. ambassador to Turkey, and, for his final twenty-one years, ambassador to Italy.

Like many conservationists, the young Marsh delighted in nature; I was "Forest-born," he reminisced, "the bubbling brook, the trees, the flowers, the wild animals were to me persons, not things." As a boy he had "sympathized with those beings, as I have never done since with the general society of men, too many of whom would find it hard to make out as good a claim to personality as a respectable oak." Marsh attended Dartmouth College at age fifteen, where he read the cutting-edge conservationist writings coming from Europe. His world travels were also crucial to his intellectual development. Marsh witnessed the denuded hillsides of the Mediterranean firsthand; he also studied land and land use in Asia. His extensive travels and wide reading in science and history all combined in 1864 when Marsh published the book that Progressive-era forester Gifford Pinchot described as "epoch-making": *Man and Nature; or, Physical Geography as Modified by Human Action.*

Pinchot's reaction was likely due to the fact that Marsh's book helped pioneer a now-familiar genre: scientifically informed environmental writing. *Man and Nature* ranged widely across the globe; Marsh attributed the decline of the Roman empire in part to severe soil erosion begat by deforestation that led to the desiccation of the soil. The parts of the earth that suffered under such poor management evince "a desolation almost as complete as that of the moon." Even more broadly, Marsh noted that, "man everywhere is a disturbing agent. Wherever he plants his foot, the harmonies of nature are turned to discord . . . of all organic beings, man alone is to be regarded as essentially a destructive power." His examples from the rest of the world contained great lessons for Americans: "But we are, even now, breaking up the floor and wainscoting and doors and window frames of our dwelling." In words that should singe the mind of contemporary climate change denialists, he even warned that "climatic excess" might lead to the "extinction of the [human] species."

Though Marsh at times attributed environmental destruction to an ahistorical agent he termed "man," he was at other times more precise in his appraisals. For one, he sternly rebuked the greed-driven development of the country unleased by corporate capitalism. "The unscrupulousness of the private associations that now control the monetary affairs and regulate the transit of persons and property," argued Marsh, must be counteracted by a civic-minded populace working for the common good. Informed people must make sound decisions because "joint-stock companies have no souls; their managers . . . no consciences." He even called for a new kind of frontiersman, or settler of wild lands, one who was a "coworker with nature in the reconstruction of the damaged fabric which the negligence or the wantonness of former lodgers has rendered untenable." Marsh combined clear-eyed understandings of environmental destruction with pragmatic belief in the ability of people to reform and change their destructive relationship to the natural world.

Marsh's book was also informed by ecological thinking and full of examples of how short-sighted destruction of the natural world ended up harming people. "All Nature is linked together by invisible bonds and every organic creature, however low, however feeble, however dependent, is necessary to the well-being of some other among the myriad forms of life," instructed Marsh. Thus insect pests will proliferate if people thoughtlessly kill the birds that predate upon them. "Hence, in his wanton destruction of the robin and other insectivorous birds, the *bipes implumis*, the featherless biped, man, is not only exchanging the vocal orchestra which greets the rising sun for the drowsy beetle's evening drone, and depriving his groves and his fields of their fairest ornament, but he is waging a treacherous warfare on his natural allies."

By detailing the effects of human action on the landscape, Marsh also demonstrated that nature was not just, or no longer, separate from human influence; people had made many of the landscapes they inhabit. Thus while Marsh did not value untrammeled wilderness, he did evoke

Figure 2.2 George Perkins Marsh originated much of conservationist thought—its practical, problem solving orientation, its global reach and its apocalyptic worry about the human maltreatment of nature.
Library of Congress Photo Archive

great hope that smart management could improve the human relationship with nature. By the late nineteenth century, America began to follow some of Marsh's suggestions. At the state level, Marsh's neighbors in New York began to heed his specific worry that continued cutting of the Adirondack forest would deplete the amount of water available for downstate cities' consumption. He recommended that the Adirondack forest should become "the inalienable property of the commonwealth." In 1885, based on the endorsement of a state forest commission, New York created its Forest Preserve in which state-owned forests would remain in the public domain and therefore be "forever kept as wild forest lands." In 1894 New Yorkers added the "wild forever" language to the state constitution, which barred logging on state land in Forest Preserve counties.

Nationally, the federal government began its first, tentative steps into forest conservation. Marsh's warnings led the American Association for the Advancement of Science in 1873 to petition Congress for a national forestry commission. From this emerged the beginnings of a forest reserve system with the 1873 Timber Cultures Act. This law allowed homesteaders an additional 160-acre land claim if they planted trees on forty (later reduced to ten) of the acquired acres. The act was revised in 1891 as the Forest Reserves Act. The legislation empowered the president to set aside forested headwaters to protect downstream water supplies and otherwise remove forest lands from settlement. President Benjamin Harrison quickly protected thirteen million acres in fifteen forest reserves. He also added the Yellowstone Forest Reserve, effectively expanding the park by 1.2 million acres. Grover Cleveland followed in Harrison's footsteps, using the Forest Reserves Act to set aside twenty-one million acres of forest lands in thirteen reserves. The law marked a profound shift in federal policy: no longer would public lands be mere temporary holdings on their way to privatization, but genuine reserves owned in common by the American people.

The federal government also began to institutionalize scientific forestry. Franklin Benjamin Hough, a naturalist and former Civil War physician, was among the growing chorus of Marsh-inspired forest reformers in the United States. He formalized his concerns in a paper entitled "On the Duty of Governments in the Preservation of Forests," delivered at the August 1873 meeting of the American Association for the Advancement of Science. The paper asserted that, "This growing tendency to floods and droughts, can be directly ascribed to the clearing up of woodlands, by which the rains quickly find their way into the streams, often swelling them into destructive floods, instead of sinking into the earth to reappear as springs." Three years later, Congress hired him to report on forestry and lumbering. He promptly produced a highly critical four-volume series of *Reports on Forestry*. In 1881 Hough was appointed the first chief of the new Division of Forestry created within the Department of Agriculture. Though his conservationist proposals were ignored, the federal government institutionalized the possibility that forestry might be conducted with forethought rather than sheer rapaciousness.

Like Hough, Marsh favored intervention in nature. But he wished for humans to do so as stewards, not as conquerors. Being stewards entailed sacrifices: Unless "the sacred right of every man to do what he will with his own" were rescinded, wrote Marsh, a wise use of the earth could not prevail because "Man has too long forgotten that the earth was given to him for usufruct alone, not for consumption, still less for profligate waste." Moreover, Marsh was conservative in his approach to stewardship; he noted that humans are essentially "incapable of weighing their immediate, still more their ultimate consequences." We are bound to interfere in the natural world in ways we cannot anticipate. Even a small change may seem "insignificant because its measure is unknown, or even because no physical effect can now be traced to it" but might prove significant in the future. And overdetermined science provides no ultimate guide for stewardship: "The world cannot afford to wait," asserted Marsh, "till the slow and sure progress of exact science has taught it a better economy." We must conserve now, not knowing what the future will hold.

Aside from Civil War destruction and Marsh's grave warnings, the emotional punch that turned many Americans into conservationists was species extinctions and near extinctions. Increasing the force of the blow was the fact that the species lost were among the most populous on the continent: passenger pigeons, the American bison, and, to a lesser extent, the Eskimo curlew. All of these species congregated together in large groups. The massive numbers—passenger pigeons likely numbered in the billions, bison in the tens of millions, and Eskimo curlews in the hundreds of millions—are examples of an anti-predator adaptation known as predator satiation. High population density can both intimidate predators and make it less likely that any one individual will be preyed upon. It was a brilliant evolved strategy, but proved especially vulnerable to the combination of habitat loss, disease, and overhunting that Americans inflicted on these animals.

The sheer, nearly unimaginable size of passenger pigeon flocks astonished those who encountered them. Aldo Leopold dubbed them a "biological storm" and a "tempest" that "roared up, down and across the continent." George B. Thompson of Henderson County, Texas, recalled the "many times when I was on my way to school at about [eight] o'clock in the morning a humming sound would begin in the northwest without warning, and in almost no time the horizon would be covered by such a dense cloud of birds that it completely covered the sky east, north, west and south, with not a white spot of sky showing. So dense was the light that it made twilight of the morning." The revered nature writer John Burroughs, in his important book *Wake Robin*, recalled how "Wild pigeons, in immense numbers, used to breed regularly in the valley. . . . The treetops for miles were full of their nests, while the going and coming of the old birds kept up a constant din."

The fact that animals in such astonishing numbers could disappear and disappear so quickly—flocks were regularly encountered in the Civil War years, but the birds were likely extinct in the wild by 1900—stunned many Americans. Desperate rumors circulated insisting that the birds had simply moved to South America or Czechoslovakia; in reality the last pigeon, Martha, a captive in the Cincinnati Zoo, passed away in 1914.

Bison met a similar fate. Once numbering nearly thirty million in the southern herd, by the late 1880s a little over one hundred wild Bison remained. Overall, North America's nearly sixty million hoofed animals declined to a mere one to two million.

Similar to the passenger pigeon, the Eskimo curlew was once one of the most abundant shorebirds in North America. Though they bred in the remote Beaufort Sea, their spring migration traveled across the great plains. Overhunting (they were canned and marketed as "doughbirds"), the concurrent extinction of the Rocky Mountain grasshopper (an important food source), and habitat loss, mostly due to the extension of agriculture, combined to force the curlew into likely extinction by 1905. Yet another well-known bird, the beautiful yellow-headed Carolina parakeet, the only parrot species native to the eastern and plains states, was extinct in the wild by 1904, exhausted by overhunting and habitat loss.

These extinctions forcefully imprinted the idea of nature's vulnerabilities and limits on a generation of Americans. Many conservationists encountered pigeon flocks as children; by their middle-aged years the birds were gone. How could anyone assume limitless resources when even passenger pigeons could be used up? And how sad is it that future generations can never know the thrill of encountering their colossal flocks? Some Americans even wondered whether pigeons, too, might have a right to exist. Conservation thus became central to the stunning array of reforms and new institutions that we now call the Progressive Era. Beginning in the 1890s many Americans demanded a new social order, one that put nature and its conservation at the center of American democracy. For the first time, the social order would deeply consider the natural order that made it possible.

CHAPTER 3

A WILDERNESS SOCIETY

There is a love of wild nature in everybody an ancient mother-love ever showing itself whether recognized or no. . . . In God's wildness lies the hope of the world—the great fresh unblighted, unredeemed wilderness.

–JOHN MUIR, quoted by Donald Worster,
A Passion for Nature

IN 1902 John Muir exulted in a new trend coursing through American culture: popular gratitude for wild lands. His book celebrating and defending that trend, *Our National Parks*, began with an appreciation for those who toured wild nature:

The tendency nowadays to wander in wildernesses is delightful to see. Thousands of tired, nerve-shaken, over-civilized people are beginning to find out that going to the mountains is going home; that wildness is a necessity; and that mountain

parks and reservations are useful not only as fountains of timber
and irrigating rivers, but as fountains of life.

Drinking from the fountain of life made visitors more likely to work on
its behalf. Muir applauded the "growing interest in the care and preservation of forests and wild places in general, and in the half wild parks
and gardens of towns." Muir felt that even those tourists whose appreciation of nature was superficial, motivated by the "scenery habit" and
who trekked while adorned in garish, impractical attire ("arrayed more
gorgeously than scarlet tanagers"), did so in fulfillment of the deep and
universal human need for wild nature. "This is encouraging," declared
Muir, "and may well be regarded as a hopeful sign of the times." That
need was especially acute in industrial society. As with Thoreau and the
factory girls of Lowell, Muir contended that "Few in these hot, dim,
strenuous times are quite sane or free; choked with care like clocks full of
dust, laboriously doing so much good and making so much money,—or
so little,—they are no longer good for themselves."

Muir's wilderness writings combine the two great forces that have
created national parks and wilderness areas: the exalted reverence for
untamed nature and the pragmatic and political business of securing
legal protections for wild lands. This is what makes wilderness special
and secures its champions a unique place in the history of American
environmentalism. Wilderness is an ancient idea, but it is a modern practice. The idea of wilderness has changed substantially over time, and so
have the expedient political mechanics of securing its preservation. Muir
was remarkably adept in both worlds, praising sublime nature while
making pragmatic political alliances—Muir worked with grassroots and
corporate allies alike—to secure conservationist goals. Wilderness may
be transcendent but securing its preservation is entirely worldly.

John Muir's (1838–1914) impulse to share the wilderness was autobiographical and social. Born in Dunbar, Scotland, in 1838, Muir immi-
grated with his family to Wisconsin when he was eleven. His abusive
Calvinist father raised the young Muir through meager living, unrelent-
ing labor, and severe beatings for trivial lapses. Despite this upbringing,
Muir delighted in the natural world near the family farm and distinguished himself as an inventor. He briefly attended the University of
Wisconsin before finding employment in an Indiana factory that made
spokes for wagon wheels. Muir's diligence and inventiveness—he

performed shrewd time and motion studies for his employer—set him on the path for a successful industrial career. He was on the cusp of becoming the prototypical self-made man. But he found the work "terrible" and after nearly being blinded when the point of a file flew up and pierced his right eye, he decided to take a walk—from Indiana to Florida. He gloried in the nature he encountered along the way, and later chronicled his adventures in *A Thousand-Mile Walk to the Gulf.* Rather than returning to school or signing up for an industrial apprenticeship, Muir studied at what he later called the "University of the Wilderness."

Muir's life work was to try to enroll everyone in that university. Muir argued that all people benefited from wilderness and that everyone should "climb the mountains and get their good tidings," which would allow for "nature's peace [to] flow into [them] as sunshine flows into trees." He was loquacious, egalitarian, and democratic. Those who encountered him on the trail—Anglo farmers, former slaves, ministers, women of all ages, Sierra Club trekkers, scores of fascinated schoolchildren, the Tlingit Indians he met along the Alaska coast—found him charming, if sometimes a bit overwhelming, and unendingly enthusiastic in sharing his passions. Muir was nature's poet laureate, providing anyone who would listen (or read his wonderful essays) with a language of reverence for wild landscapes. As such Muir did not care for expedient values when he ventured into the woods. A Sierra Club member, Albert Palmer, recalled Muir's reply when asked about the word "hike." "I don't like either the word or the thing" thundered Muir:

> People ought to saunter in the mountains—not hike! Do you know the origin of that word 'saunter'? It's a beautiful word. Away back in the Middle Ages people used to go on pilgrimages to the Holy Land, and when people in the villages through which they passed asked where they were going, they would reply, 'A la sainte terre,' 'To the Holy Land.' And so they became known as sainte-terre-ers or saunterers. Now these mountains are our Holy Land, and we ought to saunter through them reverently, not 'hike' through them.

Though Muir abhorred expedience when sauntering, he kept an eye on the practical use of forests. When speaking about "The National Parks and Forest Reserves" to a meeting of the Sierra Club (at the time an organization of mountain enthusiasts) in 1895, Muir emphasized utilitarian uses of the forest: "The Sierra forests are growing just where they do the most good and where their removal would be followed by the greatest number of evils," contended Muir. "The welfare of the people in the valleys of California and the welfare of the trees on the mountains are so closely related that the farmers might say that oranges grow on pine-trees, and wheat, and grass." The preservation of sacred trees watered the farmer's fields. He ended his talk noting that "Forest management must be put on a rational, permanent scientific basis, as in every other civilized country." For Muir people benefited spiritually and economically from wild forest reserves.

Muir's spiritual, inclusive, and democratic sensibility is no accident. His commitment to parks and the public good were part of the larger, momentous struggles for reform that defined his age: human rights (particularly the abolition of slavery), equality for women, education for all. Some authors of the time connected the love of nature to democracy and its institutions. As shown in Donald Worster's brilliant biography of Muir, *A Passion for Nature*, Alexis de Tocqueville argued that democratic revolutions encouraged strong passions for nature. Those passions often supplanted traditional Christianity and its social hierarchies in favor of a pantheistic love of nature. The pantheistic critique extended to the extractive economy as well—if nature evinced God, should we not revere it rather than turn it into commodities? Thus for those like Muir who found God in nature, materialism, especially in its vulgar capitalist forms, was sacrilegious. The noble born and reverently Catholic Tocqueville abhorred these developments, but they were exactly what Muir hoped would come to define American culture. Of course not all citizens of democracy love wild nature or swell with pantheistic feeling, but the enduring popularity of Muir and the countless writers, activists, and everyday people he has inspired suggest that Tocqueville identified a prominent theme in American culture.

As with the other reform movements Muir supported, he adopted the view that a democratically controlled government can be a useful tool for securing the public good. *Our National Parks* explained that

> Any fool can destroy trees. They cannot run away; and if they could, they would still be destroyed—chased and hunted down as long as fun or a dollar could be got out of their bark hides,

Figure 5.1 The always garrulous John Muir loved nothing more than sharing his love of the outdoor world.
Courtesy of John Muir Papers, Holt-Atherton Special Collections, University of the Pacific Library

> branching horns, or magnificent bole backbones. . . . God has cared for these trees, saved them from drought, disease, avalanches, and a thousand straining, leveling tempests and floods; but he cannot save them from fools—only Uncle Sam can do that.

By saving trees Uncle Sam could extend the benefits of civilization to all citizens and even to the wild things of nature itself. The love of nature could be a common bond for people and forge a new ethics that included nature as a worthy recipient of value and humane consideration.

Muir had plenty of help spreading the wilderness gospel. One of his most important supporters was Robert Underwood Johnson

(1853–1937), editor of the widely read New York–based magazine *The Century*. Johnson was committed to preserving the West's spectacular natural heritage from the frenzied laissez-faire attack on western resources. His best means of achieving that end was Muir's pen: Johnson tirelessly pressed Muir for his detailed descriptions of the western landscape and for editorials advocating the need to protect spectacular landscapes from exploitation by moneyed interests. Thanks in no small part to his contributions to *The Century*—mostly in the 1890s—Muir became a leading national voice in the conservation movement.

Muir's Calvinist forefathers would hardly have recognized his feelings for wild nature. When Puritan settlers came to the New World they were infused with notions about wilderness derived from the Judeo-Christian tradition. Ancient Hebrews regarded wilderness as cursed land chiefly defined by a lack of water. Indeed, biblical authors often used "wilderness" and "desert" interchangeably. When the Lord wished to reward virtuous people he promised (in Isiah 35:5) that "in the wilderness shall waters break out, and streams in the desert." Moreover, wilderness was often juxtaposed with nature, which was depicted as a garden or a settled agrarian landscape. Thus after Adam and Eve are expelled from the original Garden, Joel 2:3 teaches its reader that "the land is as the garden of Eden before them, and behind them a desolate wilderness." While biblical texts also exhorted humans to be stewards of creation, they instilled fear of primal wilderness.

When Puritan settlers—who firmly believed they were God's new "chosen people"—reached New England, they interpreted the landscapes they encountered through this biblical lens. William Bradford, English separatist leader and governor of Plymouth Colony, would write in his *History of Plymouth Plantation* that the lands they settled were "a hideous and desolate wilderness, full of wild beasts and wild men." Similarly, the Puritan minister and poet Michael Wigglesworth's 1662 poem "God's Controversy with New-England" described the new world as "A waste and howling wilderness/ Where none inhabited/ But hellish fiends, and brutish men/ That Devils worshiped." An anonymous seventeenth-century writer found the wild to be a condition of the stomach: "Wilderness is a damp and dreary place where all manner of wild beasts dash about uncooked!"

Forests were not the only wilderness to fear. Puritans equated wetlands with sin—bogs were conceived as the Sloughs of Despond (swamps of despair) in John Bunyan's 1678 allegory, *The Pilgrim's Progress*. Swamps evoked not only despair but the Puritan foreboding of wild nature. Indian medicine men used the "dark and dismal swamps" to congregate "in a horrid and devilish manner," claimed William Bradford. Clearly the errand into the forest and wetland wilderness meant transforming wild landscapes into a sedate garden. As Isaiah 51:3 instructed, "the LORD shall comfort Zion: he will comfort all her waste places; and he will make her wilderness like Eden, and her desert like the garden of the LORD."

But to dismiss Puritan thought as solely fearful and hateful toward wilderness is to miss the origins of the idea that wilderness can be a spiritual and meditative refuge from the burdens of everyday life. For also in biblical literature is the idea that one ventures into the wilderness to meditate, to escape the confines of culture and society, and thus gain unmediated access to the deity. Sometimes this was done precisely because life in the wilderness is difficult—many Christians understood luxury and ease to inhibit introspection and communion. But it also was the beginnings of the idea that nature can be a place to escape the confines of society to enable understanding of greater personal or spiritual truths. The fiery preacher Jonathan Edwards (1703–1758)—most often remembered for his riveting sermon "Sinners in the Hands of an Angry God"—would ramble through the gentle woodlands of the Berkshire Mountains to appreciate God's creation and to find quiet places to commune with his deity. His 1739 "personal narrative" found God in "every thing; in the sun, moon, stars; in the clouds and blue sky; in the grass, flowers, trees; in the water, and all nature."

Other spiritual seekers did not view New England as a "desolate" wilderness so much as a landscape teeming with natural wealth. Thomas Morton, upon arriving at Plymouth in 1622, announced that the more he viewed the landscape, "the more I liked it . . . in my eye t'was nature's Masterpiece; her chiefest magazine of all where lives her store: if this land be not rich, then is the whole world poor." Not coincidentally, Morton also maintained better relationships with the native peoples of the New World, with whom he traded and even danced. Over time the idea that Bradford and Morton shared in common—that wilderness is spiritually significant—gave rise to the American tradition of spiritual reverence toward wilderness. Muir built upon the minority traditions of figures such as Edwards and Morton by simply (if radically) turning his forbear's spiritual fear of wilderness on its head.

Muir's new kind of spirituality was not the only heterodox wilderness idea he propagated. For while Muir (especially in his youth) often trekked alone, his instincts for sharing his experiences and for promoting parks and wild lands were profoundly social. That communalism, however, departed from an early nineteenth-century tradition of wilderness love that was intensely individual. This individualism can be seen in the paintings and writings of a group of landscape artists known as the Hudson River School. Led by Thomas Cole (1801–1848), Asher Durand (1796–1886), and Albert Bierstadt (1830–1902), these artists depicted wild, untamed nature in the form of deep forests, harsh crags, lush valleys, and majestic, if imposing, mountains.

These painters understood nature through their own unmediated experience with it. Over and over again, Hudson River School canvases depicted a middle or foreground of people dwarfed by the magnificence of wild nature. At times their paintings sought the reconciliation of a middle landscape that existed between civilization and wilderness, but not at the expense of wilderness values for wild nature was the source of the divine. Their canvases are widely credited with helping promulgate the notion that American wilderness helped create a uniquely American national identity.

The writings of Thomas Cole exemplify wildlands nationalism and a spirituality based on individual wilderness contemplation. In his 1835 "Essay on American Scenery," Cole claimed that "the most distinctive and perhaps the most impressive, characteristic of American scenery is its wildness." This wildness distinguished the American landscape from Europe where "the primitive features have long since been destroyed or modified." Cole valued wildness "for those scenes of solitude from which the hand of nature has never been lifted. . . . Amid them the consequent associations are of God the creator—they are his undefiled works, and the mind is cast into the contemplation of eternal things." Wilderness, then, was for individual communion with the creator.

As with others who valued wilderness, Cole recoiled at industrial intrusions upon sublime landscapes. In his 1841 poem "Lament of the Forest," Cole reported that "Our doom is near; behold from east to west/ The skies are darkened by ascending smoke;/ Each hill and every valley is become/ An altar unto Mammon." Cole's reverence for wild nature and fear of its passing led him to advocate for the "necessity of saving and perpetuating its features." So too with Cole's friend Asher Durand who forthrightly combined nationalism and individualism in his calls for a wilderness art. In his "Letters on Landscape Painting" published in *The Crayon*, a mid-nineteenth-century New York art periodical, Durand argued that the "true province of Landscape Art is the representation of the work of God in the visible creation." One finds God not in the trammeled landscapes of Europe, but in "the virgin charms of our native lands." Those lands would provide inspiration as long as they were "spared from the pollutions of civilization." As the country moved West, so did the Hudson River School. Albert Bierstadt's paintings of the mountains in the West, particularly his magnificent depictions of the Yosemite Valley, earned him the sobriquet of representing the "Rocky Mountain School" of Hudson River painters. Bierstadt produced massive canvases that depicted the sublimity of the most famous landscapes in the American West: Yellowstone, Yosemite, and the Grand Canyon.

This emphasis on individual experience with nature was buoyed by a contemporary of the Hudson River School painters, philosopher Ralph Waldo Emerson. The most renowned of the Transcendental philosophers, Emerson venerated nature as the physical manifestation of God. People were connected to nature through a divine spark found in the natural world—what Emerson called the "transparent eyeball." Inseparable from Emerson's views about nature was his radical individualism. In his great essay "Self Reliance," Emerson admonished his reader that "the great man is he who in the midst of the crowd keeps with perfect sweetness the independence of solitude." Emerson's true individual is the one who interacts with the green world to create uniqueness. "The power which resides" in an individual, wrote Emerson, "is new in nature." For Emerson, the integrity of the person demands a radical individualism.

The problem with this tradition of finding one's spiritual identity via ecstatic communion with divine wilderness is that it has been exclusionary. The idea of an individual connection to the deity forged though communion (as opposed to, say, works) is an intensely Protestant one, excluding other faith traditions. Moreover, the depiction of the lone man in the wilderness is just that—a solitary man. Communal and feminine traditions find few representations here. Last but not least, the lone worshiper in ecstatic communion with nature's God is inevitably depicted as white. This tradition has thus given wilderness and those who work for its protection an aura of being the exclusive provenance of white men. Muir's open and democratic invitation to the wild notwithstanding, many Americans have not found parks and wilderness areas, despite their fundamentally democratic nature, accepting, let alone inviting.

Notwithstanding these limitations, the national parks have been enormously popular and have hosted many hundreds of millions of Americans in all their identifying variety. None have ever denied entry to Americans based on race, class, religion, or gender. (The exception is Hot Springs National Park in Arkansas; the southern parks Shenandoah and the Great Smoky Mountains maintained segregated picnic and camping facilities from the 1930s through World War II.) Since 1904, when about 120,000 people visited parks, there have been more than 13.5 billion visitors to National Park Service sites. In 2015 alone, national parks hosted more than 307 million visitors. The parks themselves come in stunning varieties, from the 13.2 million acre Wrangell St. Elias park in Alaska—over twice as large as Maryland—to the Philadelphia house of Polish freedom fighter Thaddeus Kosciuszko, a mere 0.02 acres in size. National parks have their own dedicated federal agency—the National Park Service—which manages over 412 sites.

But even when excluding the historical sites, monuments, battlefields, scenic rivers and trails, shorelines, and the White House itself, all of which are managed by the Park Service, a powerful question arises: are the big parks wilderness? Are Yosemite, Yellowstone, the Grand Canyon, and the Great Smoky Mountains wilderness—or are they something else? The question has vexed parks and park management because parks have two, often-contradictory mandates: to protect nature and to provide recreational opportunities for the public. That conflict has driven much of the history of public lands. Indeed, conflict over the use of ostensibly protected park lands led to the creation of the National Park Service. And the problem of managing both nature and tourist infrastructure led to the creation of wilderness areas.

To understand the unique and consequential roles of development and preservation within the American public lands system, think of a lovely glacial valley in Yosemite National Park. Miwok Indians named the valley Hetch Hetchy after a species of edible grass that grew on the flat valley floor. Despite its beauty, the steep and narrow canyon had long interested water developers. In the 1850s, the Tuolumne Valley Water Company proposed to dam the valley; the City of San Francisco made several similar proposals in the late nineteenth and early twentieth centuries. The proposals were all rebuffed due to legal wrangling over the water rights, and, most importantly, due to the fact that Hetch Hetchy was part of the first public lands set aside from development in the United States. In short, the valley was protected. Until it wasn't.

The change came from the great San Francisco earthquake of 1906 which killed an estimated three thousand people, many from the fires that followed the earthquake, and left half the population—about two hundred thousand people—homeless. San Francisco needed to rebuild its municipal infrastructure, including its water lines, most of which the earthquake severed. The city once again proposed the Hetch Hetchy valley as a source for its future water supply. Because Hetch Hetchy was owned by the federal government, any such alteration to the valley required federal approval. By definition, the future of Hetch Hetchy was a national issue. After such a disaster as the earthquake, many Americans naturally felt that San Francisco should not in any way be inhibited in meeting its needs. Conversely, opponents of the dam worried not only about the valley itself, but for the precedent set if the project moved forward. If Congress allowed for industrial development within one national park, what kind of protection could any park expect in the future?

Muir was outraged by San Francisco's proposal. He considered the Hetch Hetchy valley second in sublimity only to the Yosemite Valley itself. (Muir, after writing about the ease of tourist travel to the valley, described Hetch Hetchy as "one of Nature's rarest and most precious mountain temples.") To that end he opposed the dam with some of his most intense rhetorical salvos:

> These temple destroyers, devotees of ravaging commercialism, seem to have a perfect contempt for Nature, and, instead of lifting their eyes to the God of the mountains, lift them to the Almighty Dollar. . . . Dam Hetch Hetchy! As well dam for water-tanks the people's cathedrals and churches, for no holier temple has ever been consecrated by the heart of man.

Moreover, the Yosemite protected area had already been reduced in size. In 1905, President Roosevelt approved legislation that removed 542 square miles from the park so that it could be logged and mined. Contemporary studies have demonstrated losses of biodiversity and ecosystem services due to this habitat fragmentation. For Muir, such destruction must not happen again; he marshaled the Sierra Club membership to oppose the dam and wrote hundreds of letters and editorials in favor of preserving the Hetch Hetchy valley. He pilloried dam proponents as "despoiling gain-seekers and mischief-makers of every degree from Satan to Senators." The park had been created through open, democratic processes to favor one very small bit of the natural world from the crazed rush of development. Does all nature need to be subject to commercial exploitation?

Opposition to Muir came from the City of San Francisco, particularly its former mayor (and future U.S. Senator) James Phelan, and one unexpected source: Muir's old friend and comrade in conservation, forester Gifford Pinchot. Pinchot and Muir were social friends and in 1896 both served on the National Forest Commission (a comprehensive survey of western forests). They took numerous camping trips together; Pinchot described their relationship as "like a pair of schoolboys." But Pinchot supported the dam. After years of political wrangling over the issue, in 1913 the House Committee on Public Lands sought to finally resolve the Hetch Hetchy question. It held hearings that featured Gifford Pinchot as the star witness in favor of the dam. During his testimony Pinchot reduced the Hetch Hetchy question to the formula of "whether the advantage of leaving this valley in a state of nature is greater than using it for the benefit of the city of San Francisco." Pinchot confirmed that he wished to protect wilderness, but in this case he felt that the needs of the City of San Francisco outweighed wilderness values. "The fundamental principle of the whole conservation policy is that of use," testified Pinchot. Conservation aimed to take nature "and put it to that use in which it will serve the most people." Pinchot simply differed from his "old and . . . very good friend" John Muir; for him the greater good was not the park but San Franciscans' need for reliable water.

Historians and environmentalists have often portrayed Hetch Hetchy as a battle between Muir's wilderness ideals and Pinchot's use-based pragmatism, even going so far as to find in their conflict two separate political movements: one for preservation, the other for conservation. But these interpretations are severely limited. For one, Muir, a former forester and sheepherder, was never the simple-minded devotee of "preservation" that such interpretations claim. "It is impossible in the nature of things to stop at preservation," wrote Muir. Forests are like "perennial fountains" that can be "made to yield a sure harvest of timber, while at the same time all their far-reaching uses may be maintained unimpaired."

Nor was Muir unmoved by San Francisco's plight; he supported using another part of the park, Lake Eleanor, as a water supply for San Francisco. (One compromise Muir supported was reached in 1908. It allowed San Francisco to dam Lake Eleanor with the understanding that it would only dam Hetch Hetchy if the waters of Eleanor proved inadequate to meet demand.) He also supported San Francisco developing other water sources outside park boundaries. Furthermore, Muir called for tourist development in Hetch Hetchy—a road, hotels, riding stables, and trails. This is hardly an unyielding preservationist stance that opposes all development.

For his part Pinchot expressed plenty of spiritual regard for the Yosemite. As a young man he camped in the valley and wrote that Half Dome was "marvelous"; seeing it he could grasp its "poetic appeal." Nevada Falls prompted him to muse that "nothing so fine, so graceful, so great and yet so delicate ever came in my way before." Lamenting his short visit, Pinchot wished that "I could spend a month in the valley." Pinchot's conservationism was much more than an unfeeling, development-oriented utilitarianism. Because both Muir and Pinchot supported some kinds of use for the Hetch Hetchy, the battle over the dam was not a dispute between "preservation" and "conservation" but of two different ways of using the valley. To muddy the river even further, some progressive reformers like Pinchot wished to dam Hetch Hetchy precisely because it was publicly owned. Public ownership of water could spare the citizens of San Francisco the price gouging commonly associated with the unscrupulous private corporations that controlled many western water utilities. The public good intersected with the Hetch Hetchy valley in complicated and competing ways.

In organizing support for Hetch Hetchy, Muir came to rely upon women, whom the conservation movement was attracting in large numbers. Prominent women such as Harriet Monroe, the poet and editor who founded *Poetry* magazine, became effective allies for Muir. Monroe even penned a lovely verse in praise of the valley, "Hetch Hetchy." But with greater female participation came the gender stereotypes that opponents used to discredit Hetch Hetchy supporters. Women, dam proponents charged, were mere bird lovers, motivated by sentimentality, unable to grasp the big picture. Dam supporters, on the other hand, were hard-headed realists, professional men unmoved by emotion, making the difficult but necessary decisions. One Sierra Club member who supported the dam, Marsden Manson, delivered a memorable bit of gender bias and homophobia when he quipped that opponents of the dam were "short-haired women and long-haired men." An editorial cartoon in the San Francisco *Call* even portrayed Muir as a stout old woman wearing a dress, apron, and bonnet, attempting to sweep back the surging waters of Hetch Hetchy.

The fiercely emotional battle over Hetch Hetchy spanned three presidential administrations, but in the end Muir lost. Congress approved the Raker Act (named after California congressman John Raker), the bill that allowed San Francisco to dam the pristine canyon under three hundred feet of water, on December 19, 1913. Typical of many western water development projects, the dam did not come online until 1934, and at double its original estimated cost.

But while Muir lost that battle, he nevertheless seemed to have won over many of the congressmen who voted for the dam. Just over two years later in 1916, Congress passed the National Park Service Organic Act, creating the National Park Service. Following the Hetch Hetchy debate, Congress created a federal body dedicated to managing the parks. The act also created the Park Service's confounding dual mandate "to provide for the enjoyment of the [parks] in such manner and by such means as will leave them unimpaired for the enjoyment of future generations." The dual mandate often resulted in a kind of selective preservation—an emphasis on preserving spectacular landscape features rather than ecosystem integrity. A citizen watchdog group, the National Parks Association (now the National Parks Conservation Association) arose in 1919.

Muir and his battles for park lands inspired other activists. Enos Mills (1870–1922), a guide and lodge owner from Estes Park, Colorado, met Muir on a Pacific beach when he spied a man "intensely explaining" a handful of plants to a group of rapt listeners. Mills joined the group and—like so many who encountered Muir—fell into deep conversation with the garrulous botanist. Muir encouraged Mills to not only wander in nature but to write and agitate for conservation. Mills soon styled himself after his new friend, hoping to accomplish for the Rocky Mountains what Muir had achieved for the Sierras. Mills dedicated to Muir his 1909 book, *Wild Life on the Rockies*; in it Mills conceived of experience in nature as a unifying force for humanity. "The forests of the earth are the flags of Nature," argued Mills. "Enter the forest and the boundaries of nations are forgotten. It may be that some time an immortal pine will be the flag of a united and peaceful world." Writing eight years later against the backdrop of World War I, Mills continued with the idea that "Nature is universal. She hoists no flags of hatred. Wood-notes wild contain no barbaric strains of war. The supreme triumph of parks is humanity."

Mills wanted to make the wild Rockies a "climate for everybody and scenery for all." Like Muir, Mills was an indefatigable champion of his chosen park; he lectured, wrote, and lobbied for its preservation. Also like Muir, he at times had powerful allies, including the Denver Chamber of Commerce and the Colorado Mountain Club. His efforts paid off. In 1915, just two years after damming Hetch Hetchy, President Woodrow Wilson signed the Rocky Mountain National Park Act into law. A grateful *Denver Post* dubbed Mills "The Father of Rocky Mountain National Park," though Mills himself would surely agree that if he was the father, Muir was the grandfather.

National parks (despite severe underfunding in recent decades) have continued to flourish; fifty-one parks have been created since the Hetch Hetchy controversy. They remain wildly popular. Today the Park Service employs twenty thousand people who safeguard fifty-nine national parks and another 352 national monuments, historical sites, and recreation areas. In 1983, writer and historian Wallace Stegner bluntly asserted that national parks are "the best idea we ever had. Absolutely American, absolutely democratic, they reflect us at our best rather than our worst." In 2016, an astonishing 95 percent of Americans told pollsters that protecting national parks was important to them. The American parks system has inspired similar efforts in at least one hundred other countries.

If not parks themselves, then, perhaps the greatest loss from the Hetch Hetchy debate comes from the way we remember the controversy. By portraying Muir as a narrow and unyielding preservationist, historians and anti-environmentalists have contributed to the perception that wilderness advocates were unconcerned with social issues. Muir's "temple destroyers" rhetoric is remembered at the expense of his compromises and his inclusive, democratic spirit. Understanding Hetch Hetchy in such a narrow way has added to the perception that wilderness is for elite men who are unencumbered by the concerns of the less well off.

Similar themes run through the history of establishing wilderness areas. All public lands face the same problem as parks: how to reconcile preserving what visitors want to see with providing visitors the means to see it. The problem was one that vexed Aldo Leopold, then a young forester. Writing in 1921 on "The Wilderness and Its Place in Forest Recreation Policy," Leopold explained that, "recreational plans are leaning toward the segregation of certain areas from certain developments, so that having been led into the wilderness, the people may have some wilderness left to enjoy." Setting aside wilderness was not merely a way to preserve natural resources such as timber and water, but a means to create level-headed policy concerning public lands recreation. In wilderness areas, Leopold found a way to preserve lands from recreational overuse, particularly road building. Preserving land from road building was key; it kept habitats intact and inhibited the other kinds of development that road building inevitably generates.

Wilderness areas were needed due to the explosion of outdoor recreation that followed World War I. This boom in tourist activity grew from the great increase in wealth, transportation infrastructure, and information about parks and other public lands. To maintain the authentic experience tourists wished to have, the forest service implemented Leopold's suggestion in 1924. After the Forest Service initially proposed an expanded road network in New Mexico's Gila Forest, Leopold, mostly motivated to save some primitive land for hunting, teamed with local activists to establish it as a wilderness area instead. They persuaded the Forest Service to set aside 755,000 acres as the Gila Wilderness, the world's first designated wilderness area.

Leopold and his ideas about wilderness on public lands reflected ongoing concerns from a number of different groups. As with Muir's supporters in the fight for Hetch Hetchy, many of those concerned were women. The General Federation of Women's Clubs (f. 1890; active through the 1950s) was disturbed by the commercialization of public lands, condemning billboards, for example, "as preventing the full enjoyment of outdoor beauty." Other women were rebelling against the compromises of land management agencies and the citizens' groups that were their ostensible watchdogs. Rosalie Edge and her organization, the Emergency Conservation Committee, objected to the frequent Forest Service practice of building roads for timber companies—what she termed "a madness of roads." Rather than public monies being used to subsidize private interests, Edge wanted them to protect wildlife. "Roads and more roads are dividing, shrinking and destroying the remnants of the wilderness," charged Edge. "Only trails belong to deep forests; a road into a wild region is the prelude to its destruction."

Robert Marshall (1901–1939) also criticized roads as a prelude to forest destruction. Marshall was a principle founder of the Wilderness Society. Born in New York City to one of the country's most prominent constitutional lawyers, Marshall combined the love of wild nature he developed while summering in the Adirondacks with commitments to the social good and liberal-socialist politics. Armed with a broad grin, the lanky, witty, gregarious, and intelligent Marshall completed a doctorate in plant physiology from Johns Hopkins and became a professional forester. He directed the Forest Service's Division of Recreation and Lands, and spent his free time mountaineering or skiing. He eventually summited all forty-six Adirondack peaks over four thousand feet.

Like Leopold and Edge, Marshall viewed roads as the primary destroyer of wilderness. Marshall feared for the "days to come, when all the once wild places in the country are dissected with highways and the honk of the auto horn on one road can be distinctly heard on the next." He formalized such thoughts against the "automobile majority" in a 1930 essay he published in *Scientific Monthly*, "The Problem of Wilderness." In it he concluded that, "There is just one hope of repulsing the tyrannical ambition of civilization to conquer every niche on the whole earth. That hope is the organization of spirited people who will fight for the freedom of the wilderness."

In 1935, Leopold, Marshall, and six others founded an organization of spirited fighters for wilderness freedom, the Wilderness Society. (Rosalie Edge, alas, was not among the founders. Marshall later wrote to her—the two warily admired each other—that in his "unsystematic" way he "did not happen to think" of Edge when organizing the group.) Marshall bequeathed the organization one thousand dollars to begin operations. Although they did not reach out to Rosalie Edge as one of their founders, they did adopt part of the Emergency Conservation Committee's mission statement: "The Wilderness Society is born of an emergency in conservation which admits of no delay." The urgency came from automobiles and their roads. The new organization was needed, wrote Marshall, "to counteract the propaganda spread by the Automobile Association of America . . . and the innumerable Chambers of

Commerce, which seem to find no peace as long as any primitive tract in America remains unopened to mechanization."

Being anti-car did not mean depriving everyday people the ability to access wild landscapes. Marshall proposed subsidized travel for low-income families so they could experience the beauty of remote lands. Marshall also connected the protection of wilderness to the cultural survival of native peoples. Marshall had lived for fifteen months with the Koyukuk people in Alaska. He donated half the proceeds from the 1933 book he published about his experiences, *Artic Village*, to the Koyukuk people he wrote about. He thought hard about what kind of government policies could help native peoples retain control over their destinies.

After Marshall was named the director of the Indian Forest Service in 1933, he was able to suggest specific policies regarding wild lands and Indian peoples. For one, he argued that the size of the native land base should be substantially increased. Secondly, he proposed setting aside wilderness areas on native lands; he eventually persuaded his superior, John Collier, commissioner for the Bureau of Indian Affairs, to protect sixteen Indian wilderness areas. He intended the policy to bolster Indian cultural autonomy against outside threats such as road building. Writing about the Navajo Nation he argued that, "highways bringing the interior of the reservation into intimate contact with the outside world should be eliminated." Without such roads, reasoned Marshall, Indians could retain the autonomy that would allow them to freely determine their own way of life. He also supported Indian usufruct rights on wilderness lands.

Marshall thus built on George Catlin's idea of using preserved public lands as living space for native peoples. But also like Catlin, Marshall's good intentions floundered on the larger cultural assumptions embedded within them. Most importantly and despite his personal connections with native peoples, Marshall did not consult with any of them when formulating his policy suggestions. Such paternalism assumed that Indian peoples did not want the trappings of industrial civilization; of course many did. Marshall further proposed that native peoples could act as wilderness guides and thus escape the need to leave the reservation for wage labor. But this sanguine suggestion was hardly a substitute for a thoroughgoing economic policy that met the economic needs of indigenous nations. In the end Marshall deserves credit for thinking about how to use public lands to benefit native peoples, but like Catlin he was too bound up with his own presuppositions to effectively work on behalf of Indian peoples.

Marshall's fellow scientists, particularly those in the Ecological Society of America (ESA), were another group increasingly interested in wilderness lands. They wished to conserve wilderness areas to ensure functioning natural ecosystems for future study. But many ecologists eschewed politics, fearing it would compromise their scientific objectivity. Other ecologists waded directly into political waters and criticized those colleagues who did not. Victor Shelford, a founder of the ESA, was a vocal member of the ESA's committee on the Preservation of Natural Conditions for Ecological Study. Shelford described their mission as the "preservation of natural places with all their native animals." In a message to the National Parks Association, Shelford chastised his fellow "biologists of our country" who "have been very derelict in their duties toward the preservation of plants and animals."

Park Service employees were reaching similar conclusions. A comprehensive study of wildlife in the parks, the two-volume *Fauna in the National Parks of the United States* was completed in 1933 by Park Service biologist George Melendez Wright (1904–1936), with assistance from Joseph S. Dixon and Ben H. Thompson. Wright, the scion of a wealthy Salvadorian immigrant, funded the project. *Fauna* urged the parks to preserve ecosystem integrity. "Predator control"—that is, removing predator species—was of particular concern. As Wright put it, "an apathetic national consciousness condemned wildlife to walk the plank." Wolves, cougar, and lynx had been exterminated from Yellowstone; Rocky Mountain National Park removed grizzly bears. Preserving ecosystems thus demanded new management policies. Parks should forgo predator control and enhance habitat through such measures as saving dead trees for small wildlife. Wilderness became a tool for ecosystem preservation.

At times wilderness advocates and ecologists had different priorities. But the tentative collaboration between scientists and wilderness advocates was the beginnings of rethinking wild lands in terms of ecosystem viability rather than for human recreation. George Melendez Wright argued that parks violated their mandate if they did not preserve ecosystem integrity. Failure to maintain wildlife, reasoned Wright, amounted to a "failure to maintain a characteristic of the national parks that must continue to exist if they are to preserve their distinguishing attribute."

For her part Rosalie Edge simply combined both views, arguing that parks should "be preserved for . . . recreation" and as "laboratories for the study of ecology."

The idea of ecosystem integrity began to transform the way conservationists understood the value of wild lands. A good example of this transformation is the reappraisal of wetlands by the great Florida conservation activist Marjory Stoneman Douglas (1890–1998). Born in Minnesota to a family that disintegrated in divorce when she was six, she moved with her mother to Massachusetts. Her unsteady childhood continued as her mother, suffering from mental breakdowns, was repeatedly committed to a sanitarium. Later in life Douglas credited the night terrors she occasionally endured (neighbors might find her wandering at night, delirious, barefoot, and dressed in only a nightgown) to her tenuous upbringing, but she also valued her childhood for making her "a skeptic and a dissenter." Despite her misgivings about leaving her mother, she enrolled in Wellesley College in 1908, graduating with a degree in English in 1912.

After graduation, Douglas moved to south Florida to begin a career in journalism with the *Miami Herald*. Her intelligence and skepticism of the social order quickly manifested itself, despite the *Herald* confining her early work to the society pages. "Action without intelligence," she wrote, "is nothing but idiocy." She was a suffragist, religious skeptic, and social reformer. She combined social and environmental consciousness in the service of reform. Douglas was appalled, for example, at the polluted public well and lack of running water and sewers endured by the residents of a poor, segregated neighborhood (known as Colored Town) in Coconut Grove, Florida. She joined the Coconut Grove Slum Clearance Committee, which lobbied for and won a local ordinance requiring that all housing in the Miami area come equipped with toilets and bathtubs. No longer would the city services of Coconut Grove stop at the edge of black neighborhoods. During the two years that it took to pass the ordinance, Douglas and like-minded friends set up an interest-free loan program so that black residents of Coconut Grove could access the capital needed to improve their houses. Every loan was fully repaid. "Child welfare," Douglas later wrote, "ought really to cover all sorts of topics, such as better water and sanitation . . . [as well as] clean streets and public parks and playgrounds."

Douglas's interest in the Everglades grew in the 1920s after she joined the Florida Federation of Women's Clubs, which pursued an active conservationist agenda. That agenda was often utilitarian; while working to protect the everglades from market hunters, Douglas also supported reclaiming Everglades lands for agricultural purposes. After leaving the *Herald* to enjoy the freedom of a freelance writer, she began, in the 1930s, to publish articles in defense of the birds in the Everglades. This focus eventually resulted in her landmark 1947 book, *The Everglades: River of Grass*.

In an era when wetlands were mostly dismissed as dangerous and unsightly swamps—Sloughs of Despond destined to be "improved" through draining—Douglas found ecological value in the complex, wandering network of forests and wetlands. Even the very metaphor of the title—that the Everglades was a river—transformed how her audience conceived of wetland ecology. Unlike Yellowstone or the Grand Canyon, the Everglades, she wrote, will be "the only national park in which the wildlife, the crocodiles, the trees, the orchids, will be more important than the sheer geology of the country." Parks and wilderness were becoming less about scenery and transcendent values and more about ecosystem integrity. In 1947, President Harry Truman signed the bill that established the Everglades National Park.

The comparatively small protected area—the park safeguarded only about 20 percent of the Everglades ecosystem—faced continued threats including the population boom in southern Florida and water diversion projects initiated by the Army Corps of Engineers. In 1969 the threat of a proposed Everglades Jetport (an airport five times the size of John F. Kennedy airport in New York City) would, in the words of the Interior Department, "inexorably destroy the south Florida ecosystem and thus the Everglades National Park." Environmentalists turned to the passionate and seemingly tireless Douglas to fight the project; to do so she founded Friends of the Everglades in 1969. Made up of mostly female activists, Friends of the Everglades defeated the jetport. Today the proposed jetport's lands belong to the Big Cypress National Preserve.

The experience enabled Douglas to reassess the limits of her earlier, use-based environmental worldview. "Conservation is now a dead word," she argued in 1982; "you can't conserve what you haven't got." Like other environmentalists, Douglas learned to deploy ecological truths to support her goals. Wilderness helped; in 1997 roughly 86 percent of Everglades National Park received greater protection when it was designated the Marjory Stoneman Douglas Wilderness. Beyond

Figure 5.2 Like Aldo Leopold, Marjory Stoneman Douglas championed both wilderness and the renewal of debased lands—what we now call restoration ecology.
Courtesy of State Library and Archives of Florida

wilderness, Douglas helped pioneer yet another way to think about wild nature when she lobbied for the renewal of debased lands—what we now call restoration ecology. Her work paid off in 1983 when Senator Bob Graham of Florida won one hundred million dollars to "Save Our Everglades." In 1991, the Florida Legislature passed the Marjory Stoneman Douglas Everglades Protection Act to provide water management districts with guidelines for improving the water quality of the Everglades. In 2000, two years after Douglas's death at age 108, President Bill Clinton signed the Comprehensive Everglades Restoration Act. Stewardship of wilderness meant not just protecting nature from development, but preserving ecosystem integrity and restoring abused landscapes.

Despite the successes of National Park Service and Forest Service designated wilderness areas, midcentury wilderness advocates bemoaned that the nation still lacked a formal mechanism for government to permanently preserve lands as wilderness areas. Conservationists needed a law that would allow them to agitate using a mechanism that could designate specific lands as wilderness. "Let's make a concerted effort for a positive program that will establish an enduring system of areas where we can be at peace and not forever feel that the wilderness is a battleground," argued Wilderness Society Director Howard Zahniser (1906–1964). They achieved that law with the Wilderness Act of 1964. Fittingly, given the way wilderness has always been bound up with the real world of give and take politics, it was the consummate manager, institution builder, and inside the beltway political operative Howard Zahniser who both wrote and persuaded Congress to pass the Wilderness Act.

Before the Wilderness Act, the Forest Service could declare lands as "primitive areas" under the "L-20" regulations it adopted in 1929 and as wilderness under the "U-Regulations" of 1939. These regulations—adopted due to pressure from wilderness advocates such as Leopold and Marshall—enabled the Forest Service to set aside wild lands, which the agency did from the 1930s through the early 1960s. The regulations contained language that road building would be prohibited in wild areas. However, the Forest Service could simply reduce the size of the primitive areas or even reverse the designation to allow for more timber harvesting. Wilderness Society advocates argued that the Forest Service directors had too much personal discretion over the classification of public lands. They wished for permanent protection of wilderness areas through statutory law—the great achievement of the Wilderness Act.

That achievement came from Howard Zahniser, who transformed both wilderness politics and the Wilderness Society itself. Despite the brilliant achievements of its founders, a decade after its founding the society employed only one person and its membership was increasingly frustrated with the Forest Service's administrative fiat over wild lands. In 1945 Zahniser left a secure government position to accept the job as the society's executive secretary. At the same time the Wilderness Society hired the artist and Alaskan wildlife biologist Olaus Murie as executive director. Murie was a passionate ecologist who as director could advocate for policy but remain in his Moose, Wyoming, cabin. Zahniser, as executive secretary, directed day-to-day operations. It was Zahniser who most fully understood that wilderness would be won in the halls of Congress, not in the wilds of Alaska. Wilderness advocates needed to appreciate the political geography of Washington, District of Columbia, in much the same painstaking way they might traverse a crevasse-ridden glacier.

No one was more suited for the task than Zahniser. Careful, quick-witted, and considerate, Zahniser—"Zahnie" to friends—was such a persistent wilderness advocate that he had a Georgetown tailor customize a special suit with several inside pockets. Those pockets—his son Edward called them "fabric file cabinets"—contained versions of the wilderness bill, editorials, articles, speeches, congressional procedures, as well as books by Zahniser's favorite writers: Thoreau, Blake, and Dante. A walking library, whenever he bumped into a congressman he could summon the proper piece of literature to help him press for one more vote.

Zahniser lobbied for the wilderness bill from 1956 to 1964; it ended up being his life's work. He was also keenly aware of the many competing commercial and recreational uses of public lands. "We earnestly wish to be able to cooperate with livestock, lumber, mining, and all interests in the development of a truly rational and enduring wilderness preservation program," he wrote in 1958 in the *Salt Lake Tribune*. "I trust there will be no bitterness in the discussion of this program." Corporate opponents of wilderness were not so generous and immediately propagandized that wilderness areas were an elitist sop to special interests.

Zahniser's lobbying acumen and persistence were matched by his skills as a writer. As part of his duties to the Wilderness Society he edited and wrote for its flagship publication, *The Living Wilderness*. He championed wilderness in both spiritual and ecological terms. He wrote the initial draft of the Wilderness Act in January 1956 in such a way as to affirm and expand existing policies rather than create wholly new ones that would surely be controversial. One persistent problem was how to define wilderness. When wilderness advocate Pauline ("Polly") Dyer used the word "untrammeled" to describe the Pacific Ocean near Olympic National Park, Zahniser liked it immediately. But some of his friends and colleagues worried about it. One wrote to him that "the opposition are viewing it sarcastically among themselves and that it feeds their contempt for us 'softies' who belong to the 'daffodil' wing of the conservationists."

Zahniser ignored such misogynistic contempt for the word. The bill defined wilderness as "an area where the earth and its community of life are untrammeled by many, where man himself is a visitor who does not remain." Zahniser's political skills and otherworldly perseverance finally paid off in 1964 when President Lyndon Baines Johnson signed the bill into law. "If future generations are to remember us with gratitude rather than contempt," remarked Johnson, "we must leave them something more than the miracles of technology." Support for the bill was overwhelming. The House had passed it 373-1; the Senate 73-12. Zahniser did not witness the culmination of his life's work. He died on May 5, 1964, just months before the bill became law. His widow, Alice, attended the September 3, 1964, signing ceremony along with the great Alaskan wilderness advocate Margaret "Mardy" Murie, wife of the late Olaus Murie.

By almost any measure the Wilderness Act has been a stunning success. The act designated fifty-four wilderness areas, 9.1 million acres of land, in the new National Wilderness Preservation System, most coming from national forest lands. Wilderness has grown almost every year since. Today America preserves more than 750 wilderness areas totaling over 109 million acres in forty-four states and Puerto Rico; about 5 percent of the United States is protected as wilderness. Excluding Alaska, however, the United States has just about the same amount of pavement as it does wilderness. Despite the relatively small amount of wilderness, it attracts over twelve million visitors each year. Most profoundly, wilderness helps move our society and culture toward understanding that nature is not a commodity we possess but a community to which we belong.

The Wilderness Act was hardly the only pivotal law passed in 1964; that year witnessed the passage of the Civil Rights Act as well. Few commentators have connected the two laws but in fact they share two essential traits. Most obviously, they both grew out of Lyndon Johnson's "Great Society"—the raft of liberal reforms that defined his domestic policy. But a deeper connection joins the two laws. Both are reforms of private property. The Civil Rights Act freed all Americans to occupy not just lunch counters and buses, but schools, swimming pools, parks, hotels, theatres, and universities. No longer could private or public interests exclude Americans from participating in our common civic infrastructure. The Wilderness Act similarly assured the democratization of our civic wild lands. Some of the nation's most beautiful and valuable landscapes would be preserved for all—and for perpetuity. No longer would national forests mostly serve the exclusive interests of the timber industry; they could serve the people, and even the larger biotic community as well. Both laws expanded the spaces the American people claimed as civic and communal.

Nor did the notion of "untrammeled" land prevent historically abused lands from entering the wilderness system. In fact, some lands that became wilderness areas were almost comically compromised by human activity. West Virginia's Dolly Sods wilderness protects part of the Allegheny Plateau, a high-altitude rocky plain featuring upland cranberry bogs, open vistas, and grassy fields—called "sods" by the area's early sheep ranchers. Designated a wilderness in 1975, foresters in the late nineteenth and early twentieth centuries had nearly clear cut the spruce, hemlock, and black cherries that comprised its woodlands. The area was subsequently grazed by sheep and cattle, and during World War II served as a staging ground for mountain maneuvers and artillery practice. Afterward, ordnance teams grid-searched the area to remove unexploded bombs. Live shells were found as late as 1997.

Dolly Sods Wilderness was created by passage of a 1975 law known as the Eastern Wilderness Act (technically Public Law 93-622). The Forest Service was reluctant to declare lands as wilderness that were not, in its words, in "pristine" or "untouched" condition. Few eastern lands qualified to that standard. Happily, Congress did not accept that argument. Washington State Senator Henry "Scoop" Jackson warned of the "serious and fundamental misinterpretation of the Wilderness Act" that attempted to define wilderness as "pristine." Congress directed the Forest Service and the National Park Service to find eastern lands appropriate for a wilderness designation. The resulting Eastern Wilderness Act designated the Dolly Sods as one of sixteen new wilderness areas.

Emphasizing recent campaigns for wilderness is important to understand the broad scope of environmental politics in recent years. Wilderness activism over the last forty years undermines common misunderstandings of environmental politics. Scholars of the wilderness idea have criticized it as implying the bifurcation of humans and nature: the wild is where humans are not. This split leads to pernicious ends, those critics charge, because it has focused environmentalism's energies on wild nature at the expense of human well-being. Hence most histories of environmentalism, to account for the great concern with human health that has animated environmental politics—notably the fights for clean air and water and against toxic pollutants—situate the politics of wilderness as coming before the modern, more inclusive environmentalist movement. And yet wilderness has continued to animate environmental politics, often drawing upon the same constituency that has fought for clean air and water. Moreover, recent wilderness victories have confounded notions that wilderness comes at the expense of social concerns.

The protection of the Dolly Sods wilderness resulted from an impressive coalition that wilderness advocates put together by the mid-1970s. Local activists representing more than fifteen hundred affiliates of about a dozen key national organizations were crucial voices in a political machine that included professional lobbyists and high-level policy directors. Following the election of 1976, the Carter administration and a Democratic Congress were sympathetic to wilderness. The confident coalition turned its eyes to the biggest wilderness goal in the United States: the wildlands of Alaska. United under the banner of the Alaska Coalition, local and national organizations advocated for the protection of the glorious wilds of the forty-ninth state. "Alaska must be allowed to be Alaska, that is her greatest economy," testified Alaska conservationist Mardy Murie in 1977. "I hope that the United States of America is not so rich that she can afford to let these wildernesses pass by—or so poor that she cannot afford to keep them."

In 1970 the federal government oversaw 97 percent of Alaska's lands. By 1981 much of that land would be in the control of the state, Alaska's native peoples, and federal land management agencies. How much would be wilderness? The question seemed especially urgent given the rapacious consumption of Alaska's bountiful resources, exemplified by the oil-transporting Trans-Alaska Pipeline. Environmental groups, opposed by resource extraction industries and a growing right-wing anti-environmental backlash, put together a broad and tenuous coalition, one often held together by the formidable qualities of Celia Hunter, a longtime activist with the Alaska Conservation Society. The Alaska Coalition felt that Alaska was an opportunity to get wilderness right—"the last chance to do it right the first time," in the words of one supporter. Ecosystem science was part of doing it right—wilderness advocates wished to protect habitats, watersheds, and migratory corridors. Representative Morris "Mo" Udall introduced the plans of the Alaska Coalition as House Resolution 39 on the first day of the ninety-fifth congress in 1977.

Doubling the size of the Arctic National Wildlife Refuge was part of the plan. Designated a refuge by the Eisenhower administration, the Arctic National Wildlife Refuge supported a riotous abundance of life in the summer—163 bird species and forty-four mammal species, including marten, wolves, lynx, black bears, grizzly bears, and the massive (numbering between sixty thousand and 165,000) Porcupine caribou herd. The native peoples of the area were suspicious, however. The inland Athapascan Indians and coastal Inupiat Eskimos worried that a wilderness designation would restrict their subsistence resource use and force them to leave their homelands as had happened to native peoples living in lands that became parks in the lower forty-eight states.

But the Alaska Coalition supported native peoples continuing to use the lands for subsistence activities, and included such provisions in HR 39. An uneasy coalition was born. The coalition also included the Tlingit people of southeastern Alaska. They too wanted to ensure traditional subsistence and have their native corporations—Alaskan native peoples were incorporated by the Alaska Native Claims Settlement Act of 1971—exploit the region's timber. A 1975 canoe trip with Sierra Club leaders secured the Tlingit people as part of the Alaska Coalition.

Native Alaskans turned out to be savvy political players. They used their image as people living gently with nature and their corporate power to further their interests. Their inclusion helped environmentalists tremendously in lobbying and publicity efforts. But the Alaska Coalition encountered fierce resistance from Alaska's oil-funded home state senators and an emboldened and aggressive conservative political movement. Following so closely the oil crisis of 1973/1974, environmentalists also had a difficult time countering demands for greater energy resource extraction from public lands. The Alaska bill was reduced from protecting 119 million to ninety-three million acres of park lands, and from sixty-six million to thirty-eight million acres of wilderness. Yet conservative publications still lambasted the bill as "the big federal land grab." When the anti-environment Ronald Reagan won the presidency in 1980, the Alaska Coalition used the lame duck congressional session before Reagan took office to secure passage of a replacement to HR 39—the less ambitious Alaska National Interest Lands Conservation Act of 1980.

If the Alaska Coalition lost millions of acres to development, they still won massive protections: the Alaska National Interest Lands Conservation Act protected over 157 million acres of land—more land than the State of California—including national parks, national wildlife refuges, national monuments, wild and scenic rivers, recreational areas, national forests, and conservation areas. And, remarkably, park lands in Alaska have accommodated the subsistence economies of native peoples. Fishing and subsistence hunting that is "customary and traditional" is allowed in nine out of ten Alaska's national parks. In addition, 9.4 million acres of "preserves" allow both sport and subsistence hunting. The wildlife refuge lands also allow for subsistence hunting and fishing. These practices are consistent with wise ecological management. Native (like all human) hunters are simply another predator in the food chain. Wild lands also support the larger economy of Alaska: in 2015 outdoor recreation generated 9.5 billion dollars of spending in Alaska, supporting ninety-two thousand direct jobs and providing 711 million dollars annually in state and local tax revenue.

Despite successes, the alliance between native peoples and the Park Service is full of tensions and misunderstandings. Denali National Park—earlier named Mount McKinley National Park—attempted to control subsistence uses through regulations and permitting. Residents chaffed at the restrictions, and juries regularly freed convicted poachers. The situation improved under the Alaska National Interest Lands Conservation Act when the Park Service invited local residents to shape the rules that governed use of their park. Such power sharing is likely the key to a meaningfully inclusive future. Historian Theodore Catton concluded that National Park Service policy "was evolving toward a greater sharing of power . . . [with] resident peoples" in ways that create land management procedures and invoke the ongoing construction of the meaning of wilderness. The relationship between environmentalists and native peoples is as fraught as with native peoples and any other segment of American society. But in inhabited lands environmentalists have devised a more inclusive approach to native peoples that far surpasses what most other American institutions have achieved.

The inhabited wilderness of Alaska returns wilderness to its roots—to the inclusive and welcoming pronouncements of Muir and others who invited all Americans to experience the wild. It even returns wilderness all the way back to the Puritan settlers who viewed wilderness as inhabited—if, in their view, by people they disregarded and feared. Despite these achievements, balancing wilderness values and ecosystem integrity with the desires of tourists and needs of subsistence users will surely remain a difficult, even unsolvable, challenge. But in integrating wilderness into the social matrix wilderness advocates can call upon a proud tradition of pragmatic political actions that attempted to serve some of the American people's most transcendent aspirations.

CHAPTER 4

PROGRESSIVE PUBLICS AND THE SOCIAL NATURAL ORDER

The movement for the conservation of wild life and the larger movement for the conservation of all our natural resources are essentially democratic in spirit, purpose, and method.

—TEDDY ROOSEVELT, *A Book-Lover's Holidays in the Open* (1916)

IN THE winter of 1873 Mrs. Etta Wheeler, a New York City charity worker, received a tip about an abused child in Hell's Kitchen, a working-class Irish-American neighborhood. Wheeler discovered that an orphan named Mary Ellen Wilson suffered from horrific cruelty at the hands of her foster family. "Mamma has been in the habit of whipping and beating me almost every day," the child later testified. "She used to whip me with a twisted whip—a rawhide." The family rarely included her in domestic life. The child was forbidden to go outside, except at night and then only in her small yard. She slept on the floor, was infrequently fed, and was often locked in a dark room. When Etta Wheeler first saw her, Mary Ellen Wilson was covered with welts and scars and dressed only in rags.

Etta Wheeler immediately sought relief for the child, but in an age of "spare the rod, spoil the child" neither New York City nor the federal government had much power to intervene on the child's behalf. Frustrated, Wheeler turned to a superficially unlikely ally: the American Society for the Prevention of Cruelty to Animals (ASPCA). It proved to be a shrewd move. The ASPCA hired a renowned attorney, Elbridge Gerry (grandson of the politician who bestowed his name to gerrymandering), who employed a novel use of habeas corpus to emancipate the child. Mrs. Wheeler eventually adopted Mary Ellen and raised her on the outskirts of Rochester, New York. Mary Ellen married at age twenty-four, adopted an orphaned child of her own and lived to be ninety-two. Mary Ellen's case prompted Gerry and other philanthropists to establish the New York Society for the Prevention of Cruelty to Children. Similar agencies proliferated, and many of them were "dual" agencies—organizations that worked for both animals and children.

The crucial involvement of the ASPCA into Mary Ellen Wilson's case highlights the profound changes in American society that birthed the stunning array of reforms we now know as the Progressive Era. Moral concern for innocents included both children and animals. Both were oppressed sufferers. And contrary to the laissez faire state of the early nineteenth century, following the Civil War federal authority to intervene in social life gained legitimacy. The same government that can free slaves can set aside forest reserves, abate pollution, and protect children. Given a government more willing to intervene for the social good, reformers could now push it to pass legislation making cruelty a crime. "As many reformers sought to create a society free from suffering," writes historian Susan J. Pearson, "they adopted a theory of violence that linked cruelty to animals with cruelty to human beings." The natural world finally began to find a place in the moral consideration of American society.

Linking of the rights of nature with human well-being infused almost every area of progressive reform. The Progressive Era was profoundly environmental. Whether tenement slums or deforested watersheds,

Americans at the turn of the twentieth century believed that impoverished environments impoverished the populace. Reforming environments for the better affected every major institution in American life. City and country were united as progressives fought for clean air, healthy forests, and productive farmyards. Schools were used to instill a love for nature. Government became a tool to achieve environmental improvement. Finally, progressives sentimentalized landscapes and animals while at the same time believing that technological innovation could solve environmental problems. In this, they created the complex and sometimes contradictory commitments that make up the environmental movement.

Progressivism was built on an American tradition of everyday people linking the welfare of nature to their own well-being. As shown by Richard Judd in his history of conservation in New England, rural people were conservationists. Three major assumptions about the land dominated popular thought. First was the idea of a natural commons, in which citizens held democratic access to resources such as forests, wildlife, waters, and fish. The second belief was in the value of manipulating nature for human ends. But rather than domination, manipulations such as agriculture were to serve human needs within the balance of nature. The third widely shared idea was a veneration of nature, a sense that it had its own purposes beyond its usefulness to humans. When weighing bird protection efforts, local farmers spoke of the "right to life of the animal races" and even the "harmonious balance of nature, disturbed by the destruction of former forests." Vermonter George H. Perkins summed up a lot of common wisdom when he averred that, "It is better not to meddle at all with nature's arrangements, than to interfere without sure knowledge of what should be done."

Growing industrialization and commercialization forced older attitudes and practices to adapt to new circumstances. Conservation was a tool for that adaptation, but it required many compromises. Rural people, for example, generally supported the restoration of common use resources such as fisheries. But industrialists resented the costs of providing spawning fish (mostly salmon, shad, and alewives) with ladders or channels for their upstream migrations. A compromise of sorts was reached when locals allowed the fishing industry to be dominated by wealthy sport-casting tourists, rather than commercial harvesting. But they did so with the expectation that sport angling would enrich them with tourist dollars. Similarly, lobstermen supported conservationist size limitations on harvested lobsters to ensure a healthy lobster population and also to prevent competition from other economic interests. State Representative Charles E. Davis reasoned that limits and other policies would allow lobsters to "increase in number" which in turn would mean that "the Lobster Fisherman will earn a better living." Sustained yield management replaced the informal contracts of an earlier era.

Progressives focused on urban as well as rural nature. In 1888 a small group of urban planners and architects launched *Garden and Forest* magazine. Its aim was to help Americans, in the words of historian Shen Hou, "promote an integrated landscape, one where nature and culture were seen as one, where cities and countryside were joined in a common effort, where both gardens and forests were able to thrive." Part of the impetus was that America was rapidly urbanizing—Frederick Law Olmsted called it a "strong drift townward." At the time of the Civil War, just under 20 percent of Americans lived in cities. Well over a third of Americans were urban by the time the twentieth century dawned. As urban life began to define the American environment, city parks advocate Sylvester Baxter used *Garden and Forest* to argue that cities must not overwhelm "the natural features of the landscape" with "a vast desert of houses, factories and stores." Cities must be vital living spaces, not just warehouses of workers. The city must be made natural.

A natural city that included open spaces and urban parks meant planning and the confident use of professionals to design beautiful and inclusive civic spaces. Founded in 1891, the Boston Metropolitan Park System helped pioneer citywide integrative planning. In 1893 its purview extended regionally, establishing a park system that served an entire metropolitan region. It protected ten thousand acres of open space and open water systems (a total now doubled) known as the area's "Emerald Necklace." The system was used for recreation and for the preservation of natural features such as the Waverly Oaks—a stand of old growth in Belmont, Massachusetts. Nor did the preservation of urban features mean neglect of the wilder landscape. National parks, claimed *Garden and Forest*, should imbue Americans with "a deep interest and national pride." Indeed, it was wild landscapes that reached the "nobler part of man's nature." Municipal parks and national parks were both, as editor William A. Stiles asserted, "essential to health and comfort."

Gardening was one way to bring nature and creativity to urban life. Mabel Osgood Wright (1859–1934), founder of the Connecticut

Audubon Society, championed gardens as a means of personal development and environmental reform. In her 1901 novel, *The Garden of a Commuter's Wife* (a novel suffused with gardening tips and digressions into natural history), Wright advised that "{Ext}Gardening is the most cheerful and satisfactory pursuit for women who love the outdoors. . . . In a garden one's personality can come forth." Gardens were both utilitarian (growing vegetables) and aesthetic (if planted with flowers). They represent the kinds of integration of nature and culture that attracted so many progressive reformers.

City gardens would also attract birds. In her hometown of Fairfield, Connecticut, Mabel Osgood Wright founded the Birdcraft Museum and Sanctuary, named after a classic field guide she authored in 1895. She envisioned the ten acres of native plants as providing visitors with "an oasis in a desert of material things." Beyond its service to humans, Wright conceived Birdcraft as "a place where [birds] can nest in peace, or rest in their travels. *People must be considered only as they fit in with this* scheme" (emphasis in original). Though the reserve was home for the thirty-two different species of birds that nested there, many people visited: within ten years of its opening in 1914 Birdcraft received over ten thousand visitors. Rather than traipsing off to the wilderness, people could appreciate birds in a natural habitat close to home.

The careers of other Progressive Era reformers, such as Mira Lloyd Dock (1853–1945) of Harrisburg, Pennsylvania, also demonstrate the intertwined interests in urban and rural environments. Following her mother's death, Dock's early adulthood was devoted to care for her father and younger siblings. When her father passed in 1895, she enrolled, at age forty-two, at the University of Michigan to study botany. After graduating she studied forestry in Germany then returned home to Harrisburg.

Described by one traveler as "one of the ugliest cities in the state," Harrisburg had dirty, unpaved streets and used its waterways, Paxton Creek and the Susquehanna River, as open sewers. Dock immediately threw herself into the cause of urban reform. Working with J. Horace McFarland, popularizer of the City Beautiful Movement, Dock helped establish the Harrisburg Plan that called for paved roads, sewage treatment, city-managed parks, summer playgrounds, and a water purification system. Such improvements would help the economic future of the city and ensure the "physical rest and moral uplifting" that

Harrisburg residents deserved. Harrisburg's park acreage increased more than twenty-fold, and the city installed water and sewage systems. Dock and other women reformers also lobbied for health clinics and endowed scholarships for poor girls.

In 1901 the governor of Pennsylvania selected Dock to fill a vacancy on the State Forestry Commission. She served the commission for thirteen years. Local newspapers acknowledged her appointment as "a recognition of the invaluable aid which the women of Pennsylvania have given [to forestry]." The first woman appointed to a Pennsylvania state government position, Dock spent her time on the commission educating citizens about scientific forestry and inspecting forested lands to recommend whether the state should purchase them. She also pushed the use of forests as recreation for "persons of moderate means" so they "can enjoy scenery and opportunities for quiet inexpensive recreation." In 1903 she began teaching botany at the newly opened State Forestry Academy at Mont Alto, a school she had helped found. Dock taught there until 1929, emphasizing to her students a working knowledge of the state's native trees. "What we need here in the United States" wrote Dock, "is better housekeeping out of doors." That housekeeping was both municipal and rural.

A well-kept house entailed battling the pollution that befouled not just Harrisburg but most of urban America. Investigating Pittsburgh's housing for the Russell Sage Foundation in 1908, social worker Frances Elizabeth Crowell encountered "sluggish clouds of thick smoke over the roofs . . . the air was full of soot and fine dust." The byproduct of incomplete coal combustion, smoke, and soot were pervasive throughout urban America. The amount of soot was appalling. In 1912 the Mellon Institute measured Pittsburgh's share, concluding that two thousand tons of factory-produced soot fell annually on some working-class neighborhoods; overall, 42,683 tons of soot blanketed the city. The soot was filthy—it clung to clothes, drapes, rugs—and also a dangerous health hazard, part of what historian John Opie terms a "negative infrastructure"—the pollution, waste, and overcrowding that plagued cities such as Pittsburgh.

The negative infrastructure consisted of intertwined environmental hazards. Beyond soot and air problems, backyard privies leaked waste into neighboring drinking wells, fouling water and spreading diseases such as typhoid fever. Even when Pittsburgh water was drawn from upstream sources, it was still polluted by what Russel Sage researchers described as "oils and other carbon compounds" as well as the human sewage produced by 350,000 people that flowed untreated into the Allegheny and Monongahela rivers. Those waterways were also subject to the same pollutants as Ben Franklin's Dock Creek. Investigators found "flesh-disintegrated and putrescent" dead animals as well as the "off-scourings of iron and steel mills, tanneries, [and] slaughter houses" in the rivers that supplied Pittsburgh's drinking water. An anonymous worker described Pittsburgh as "hell with the lid clamped on."

In 1909 the Pittsburgh Civic Commission recommended many of the reforms subsequently suggested by the Russell Sage Foundation: smoke and dust abatement, improved water quality, building codes, public utilities, and strict regulations that would prevent future abuses. But the muckraking Russell Sage Foundation report went further, accusing Pittsburgh of a "double standard of civic morality." Business was given nearly free reign. Wealthy people were taxed at far lower rates than the working classes. It was the working poor who suffered most severely from environmental abuses. Most importantly, the report argued forcefully that pollution was not simply a cost of doing business, but an unjust hazard inflicted on the working-class citizens. Though Pittsburgh was the focus of the foundation's report, it emphasized that "We did not turn to Pittsburgh as a scapegoat city" but rather studied it because it "exhibits national tendencies." The problems were not just Pittsburgh's but the nation's.

As with so much of Progressive Era environmental reform, women led the charge to clean up cities. Often called "municipal housekeeping" women worked for improvements in urban environments, because, as one activist put it, "A woman's place is Home, but Home is not contained within the four walls of an individual house. Home is the community." In this sense women's public activism was an extension of their social roles as wives and mothers.

In 1884 a group of New York City women became appalled with the "foul odors" emanating from a massive manure pile—it was two hundred feet long and thirty feet high—adjacent to their toney Beekman Hill neighborhood. They formed the Ladies Health Protective Association which successfully sued for garbage removal. Emboldened by their success in court, they promptly lobbied the mayor for school sanitation, cleaner streets, restricting slaughterhouses, and other municipal improvements. Tackling one problem at a time was their strategy; the president of that association declared that, "We deal with the little things that make up the sum of universal misery." By the 1890s similar women's sanitary organizations appeared across the country, in every large city and many smaller ones.

The problem of water pollution was attacked by one of the pioneering environmental chemists in the United States, Ellen Swallow Richards (1842–1911). The first woman graduate from the Massachusetts Institute of Technology, Richards returned to the school as an unpaid lecturer and then in a paid position and eventually as a faculty member of sanitary chemistry working at the Lawrence Experiment Station. In the 1880s the problem of water pollution occupied Richards. She was put in charge of an extensive sanitary survey of Massachusetts's inland waterways. For two years Richards and colleagues analyzed water and sewage samples, some forty thousand in all. A key problem was to understand chlorine as indicator of pollution (it occurs naturally as well as being suspended in sewage). Richards did not just record the results of her experiments, but plotted them geographically. The result was "Richard's Normal Chlorine Map," which determined inland water pollution based upon chlorine content. Based on Richards's work, Massachusetts established the nation's first statewide water quality standards.

Richards's environmental interests followed waterways into the home and school. In 1897 she delivered a biting commentary at the annual meeting of the American Public Health Association in which she charged the city of Boston and "the great tax-paying public" with the "murder of some [two hundred] children per year." The murders derived from inadequate school infrastructure. The open sewer pipes, filthy toilets, and unclean, unventilated school buildings facilitated the spread of fatal diseases among the students. Boston politicians failed to act on her assessments, so she lobbied the National Education Association and her fellow citizens. A number of improvements were eventually implemented, and they became a model for similar reform efforts nationwide.

Her reforms in Massachusetts presaged other important national reforms of the Progressive Era. Her 1885 book *Food Materials and Their Adulturations* led to the passing of the first Pure Food and Drug Act in Massachusetts. The Massachusetts law set the stage for national action. Building from success at the state level, in 1906 President Roosevelt signed two vital pieces of legislation that protected public health: the

Meat Inspection Act, which regulated meat packing, and the Pure Food and Drug Act, which regulated adulterations in food and drugs. It established the federal government's ability to regulate contaminants, which included biocides. The Pure Food and Drug Act thus became one of the most important precursors to modern environmental regulations.

The reforms achieved by Richards and by women's sanitary organizations served as impetus for the creation of modern systems of municipal garbage collection and disposal. In 1894 New York City hired Colonel George E. Waring (1833–1898), a former Union cavalry officer, as its sanitation commissioner. Between 1895 and 1897 he attacked garbage as if were a military foe. Waring formed a paramilitary-style force of twenty-seven hundred organized street cleaners. His employees donned white suits and pith helmets and thus became known Waring's White Wings. His admirers proclaimed that Waring was the "Apostle of Cleanliness."

The white wings recycled much of the garbage they collected (they instituted the practice of separating different kinds of refuse into different bins), and their work became the basis for modern street cleaning and garbage collection systems. Waring and his charges briefly made garbage collection a glamorous profession. His outreach included a separate Juvenile Street Cleaning League. Children in the league wore badges proclaiming that, "We Are for Clean Streets." They recited a "civic pledge" and were ranked according to their level of involvement. Upon his untimely death in 1898, *The New York Times* proclaimed that "There is not a man or a woman or a child in New York who does not owe [Waring] gratitude for making New York, in every part, so much more fit to live in than it was when he undertook the cleaning of the streets."

In New York City Waring removed garbage as a government employee; in Chicago, activists Jane Addams (1860–1935), Mary McDowell (1854–1936), and Dr. Alice Hamilton (1869–1970) had to fight not just garbage but political hostility. Addams was a pioneer of the settlement house movement, in which middle-class reformers moved into working-class neighborhoods to bring education and social services to neighborhood residents. In 1889, Jane Addams and her friend Ellen Starr founded Hull House on south Halstead street in Chicago. Improving the sanitary conditions of the neighborhood was an immediate need. "The streets are inexpressibly dirty," Addams wrote in her memoir *Twenty Years at Hull House*, "the number of schools inadequate, sanitary legislation unenforced, the street lighting bad, the paving miserable and altogether lacking in the alleys and smaller streets, and the stables beyond description. Hundreds of houses are unconnected with the street sewer." A local women's club, working through Hull House, documented over one thousand violations of health department codes, to no avail: garbage collection was a patronage job with little expectation that those selected would actually do the work for which they were contracted.

Frustrated with political corruption and indifference to her working-class neighbors, Addams bid to remove the garbage herself. Her bid was not selected, but she was hired as the ward's garbage inspector. For a year Addams and her colleague Amanda Johnson awoke early to follow garbage collectors on their rounds, using Addams's position, reported the *Omaha Bee*, to "burden . . . the garbage collectors" of Chicago. Though resented by politicians and city employees, her work meant "a great deal in the way of cleanliness and health to a people who are greatly in need of both." Not only did she make sure that the garbage collectors performed their jobs, she reported landlords who failed to provide trash receptacles for their residents and convinced city hall to increase the number of sanitation workers. It was classic progressive reform: Addams formed a class alliance with her working poor neighbors to force government to respond to the needs of all its citizens. As Mary McDowell wrote, garbage collection "should not be carried on for the benefit of a political party, but for the welfare of human beings."

Mary McDowell formed an even more impressive class alliance as she tackled an even more intense Chicago sanitation problem. A former Hull House volunteer, McDowell founded the University of Chicago settlement house, Back of the Yards, in Packingtown, a neighborhood that abutted Chicago's slaughterhouses. She moved there to partner with neighborhood residents: "settlement residents do not go to the people with a plan, a policy, or a proposition; they go as friends, as neighbors with a keen sense of the commonness of all that is best in all."

Air and water pollution plagued Packingtown. Empty lots were given over to piles of garbage, some of which was imported from the city's wealthier quarters. A small creek—"once a little innocent stream with willows and wild flowers along its banks," wrote McDowell—was now a "cesspool" known as "Bubbly Creek" due to the gases that emanated from the putrid matter decaying beneath its oily surface. Packingtown smelled horribly due to Bubbly Creek, nearby garbage dumps, and the animal wastes and belching smokestacks of the stockyards.

McDowell organized her neighbors to lobby city hall for systematic changes. She convinced local women's clubs to establish waste committees. She even accepted the chair of the City Waste Committee of the Women's City Club, which sent her to Europe to study best practices in waste management. She returned with many new ideas, but lobbying of city leaders went for naught until July 1913 when women won the franchise in Chicago. Suddenly the city council responded to citizen pressure and created the Chicago City Waste Commission, which recommended city-owned garbage collection "without deference to either personal interest of local prejudice." Its waste dumps removed, life in Packingtown immediately improved and its high death rate dropped significantly. The city eventually established Packingtown as a manufacturing district, filled in Bubbly Creek, and installed modern sewage systems.

Dr. Alice Hamilton moved environmental reform from public spaces to inside the factory walls. Raised in Ft. Wayne, Indiana, Hamilton overcame her lack of early science education to enroll in the University of Michigan Medical School, graduating in 1893. In medical school, she developed an interest in public health, knowing that "I could be of use anywhere." But as Hamilton explained in her 1943 autobiography, *Exploring the Dangerous Trades*, "it was also my experience at Hull House that aroused my interest in industrial diseases. Living in a working-class quarter, coming in contact with laborers and their wives, I could not fail to hear tales of dangers that workingmen faced, of cases of carbon-monoxide gassing in the great steel mills, of painters disabled by palsy, of pneumonia and rheumatism among the men in the stockyards." During a 1902 typhoid epidemic that struck the Hull House neighborhood, Hamilton demonstrated that open, undrained privies allowed flies to spread the disease.

One disease that intrigued her was "phossy jaw," a dreaded plague among workers in match factories. Hamilton described the disease as arising "from breathing the fumes of white . . . phosphorus, which penetrates . . . to the jawbone, killing the tissue cells which then become the prey of . . . germs from the mouth. . . . The jaw swells and the pain is intense." After encountering a labor leader concerned with the problem,

Figure 3.1 Jane Addams and Mary McDowell were leaders in cleaning up the urban environment. Typical of Progressive Era reformers, they were interested in a wide range of issues; here they march for peace.
Photo Courtesy of the Chicago History Museum

she worked with him to publicize the issue. The campaign led to legislation in 1912 that effectively eliminated white phosphorus—a substance easily replaced by manufactures—through taxes and regulations. Hamilton thought such reforms were straightforward, but in America she "gained the impression that [occupational safety] was a subject tainted with Socialism or with feminine sentimentality for the poor."

Hamilton's formal investigations into industrial diseases began in 1910 when she was appointed by reformist Illinois Governor Charles Deneen as managing director of a survey on industrial illness in Illinois. The Illinois Commission on Occupational Diseases was the first such body in the United States. Hamilton visited households, neighborhoods, and factories while also poring over medical records, searching for connections. It was "shoe leather" epidemiology. Hamilton focused her painstaking research on lead, which she was (rightly) convinced was a dangerous toxin. Because her work came before an established diagnostic standard for lead poisoning, she relied upon a rigorous self-imposed standard. "I would not accept a case as positive," she wrote, "unless there was a clear 'lead line' . . . a deposit of black lead sulphide in the cells of the lining of the mouth, usually clearest on the gum along the margin of the front teeth." Armed with the information she gathered, Hamilton overcame her natural shyness to attempt to persuade factory owners and managers to remedy dangerous conditions.

Hamilton proved the connection between occupation and illness. As a result, in 1911 the Illinois legislature passed an occupational disease law that required employers to implement safety procedures that limited exposure to dangerous chemicals, provide monthly medical examinations for those laborers in contact with hazardous substances, and to report illnesses directly to the Department of Factory Inspection. Hamilton went on to investigate carbon monoxide poisoning in steelworkers, mercury poisoning in hat makers, and "dead fingers" syndrome among workers using jackhammers.

Hamilton noted that industrial chemists were using workers as "laboratory material" by exposing them to substances "about whose effects on human beings we know very little." Her success in Illinois led to a variety of similar posts. From 1911 to 1920 she served as a special investigator for the U.S. Bureau of Labor Statistics, where she performed a landmark study on the manufacture of white lead and lead oxide, substances commonly used as pigments in the paint industry. Hamilton subsequently pushed for safer working conditions. She eventually became the first female member of the Harvard University Medical School. She is widely credited with founding occupational health as a profession.

Activists such as Waring, Addams, McDowell, and Hamilton were establishing that pollution arose largely from institutionalized processes, not individual habits. Transportation by horse was a great example. New Yorkers made millions of trips each year by horse car; by 1880, there were at least 150,000 horses living in the city. Each one produced, on average, twenty-two pounds of manure each day. Horses deposited at least forty-five thousand tons of street manure each month. This is surely what Colonel Waring meant when he described Manhattan as stinking "with the emanations of putrefying organic matter." He was not alone. One traveler wrote that the streets were "literally carpeted with a warm, brown matting . . . smelling to heaven."

The problem was not unique to New York City. Horses dropped 133 tons of manure on Milwaukee's streets each day. Health officials in Rochester, New York, calculated in 1900 that the cities' fifteen thousand horses produced enough manure to make a pile 175 feet high coating an acre of ground. One way the manure was removed was by local farmers who carted the rich fertilizer to nearby fields. But they could only remove a small portion of the manure and could not cart away the horses that died in the city. In 1880 alone, some fifteen thousand dead horses—the animals were often overworked and otherwise mistreated—were removed from the streets of New York City. In 1866, *The Atlantic Monthly* described Broadway as being clogged with "dead horses and vehicular entanglements."

The solution to the pollution problems caused by horses came not from citizen activists, government agencies, or new regulation. It arose from technological innovation, particularly modern methods of sanitation, electric-powered transit (the "horseless carriage"), and by the 1920s, internal-combustion automobiles. Such technologies had many advantages, not least that they polluted far less than horses: "The horse in the city is bound to be a menace to a condition of perfect health," warned Dr. Arthur R. Reynolds, superintendent of the Chicago Department of Health in 1901. By 1912, automobiles outnumbered horses in New York City, and in 1917 the city's last horse-drawn streetcar made its final run. Today automobiles are rightly excoriated for the incredible environmental damage they inflict, but in the early twentieth century they contributed to environmental reform, making urban life vastly less noisy and polluted.

Such technological solutions to social problems greatly improved environmental quality and contributed to the notion that efficiency and better tools could solve problems that were as much social as mechanical. A good example comes from smoke reform. Coal had powerful friends; it was essential to the industrial economy. But its combustion created much of the pollution that was pervasive in American cities. The debate over how to combat smoke was fierce. Nuisance laws were cumbersome and difficult to enforce—how could people know which smokestack was causing them difficulty in breathing or soiling their clothes? Industry successfully challenged the ability of cities to regulate them—usually a state legislature needed to pass enabling legislation before a city could outlaw pollution. Protecting citizens against smoke, the Women's Club of Cleveland allowed, was a "steady, though perhaps slow progress."

Two groups vied to lead the progress. The first were progressive reformers who worked to clean up the urban atmosphere. In Cincinnati, Dr. Julia Carpenter and her partners in the Cincinnati Women's Club helped establish the Cincinnati Smoke Abatement League in 1906. It quickly became one of the most influential civic organizations in the city. Membership included a "Who's Who" of Cincinnati, including a dues-paying membership from President William Howard Taft. The league won a 1907 Smoke Ordinance that created the Office of the Smoke Inspector, which was staffed with four employees. Smoke Inspectors used an umbrascope, a monocular tube with gray-tinted glasses, to determine violations of the ordinance. If smoke was visible through the gray lenses of the scope, then the smokestack was deemed in violation of the city ordinance. In 1910, the League's most active year, citizen inspectors made 12,137 separate observations of smokestacks, sent out 477 notices to proprietors with darkly smoking chimneys, and arrested forty-four offenders. Seven of those arrested received fines. The Smoke Abatement League continues to operate as the Air Pollution Control League of Greater Cincinnati.

Technical experts comprised the second group of reformers. Many were professionals armed with scientific skills who worked within government bureaucracies. They were public health officials, sanitarians, efficiency experts, and especially engineers. Their main role was to design systems to combat health hazards and pollution. To do so they integrated social and natural thinking. "One cannot get far in a discussion without taking account of environment," wrote sanitary engineer George Whipple in *Scientific American*. "In fact, it is difficult to conceive of man apart from his environment. . . . The environmental factors, however, are especially of interest to sanitary engineers."

Engineers exhibited great confidence in solving environmental problems through technological innovation. Technological innovations sprang from the heart of one of the key tenants of progressive ideology: efficiency. Smoke could be understood as a nuisance and a health problem; it also embodied gross wastefulness. Smoke was at its worst when boilers were overfed with coal. Thick black smoke pouring forth from an industrial chimney was no longer an indicator of bustling prosperity but a hallmark of profligate waste. Technology allowed reformers the double win of abating smoke and, due to increased energy efficiency, saving money over time. As engineers came to dominate discussions of smoke pollution, the issue was seen less as a moral and health problem, and more a problem of mechanical failure.

Progressive conservationists were so successful to a large degree because the president, Theodore ("Teddy") Roosevelt (1858–1919), was himself a passionate conservationist and wildlife defender. Roosevelt had long been a conservation activist. In 1887 he and George Bird Grinnell, editor of *Forest and Stream* magazine, founded the Boone and Crockett Club, a collection of hunter-conservationists dedicated to preserving game species. They were hardly alone. Following the Civil War hunting clubs proliferated; by 1891 there were nearly a thousand. Such clubs, working to ensure plentiful game, constituted a powerful lobby for wildlife conservation.

The elite origins of the Boone and Crockett Club affected its conservation concerns. The club supported hunting as a leisure pursuit, but railed against commercial hunters conscripted by market forces, the "trout hogs," "night hunters," and "pseudo-sportsmen" who took game for a living. More productively, the Boone and Crockett Club advocated for game laws, bison protection, and forest reserves. Grinnell also worked diligently to bring women into the conservation movement.

Born to a wealthy businessman, Roosevelt was an asthmatic, sickly, and nearsighted child. To improve his physical health and, later, to buttress his public image as a rough and tumble outdoorsman, he spent time in nature. It turned him into a genuine nature lover. He was a rancher, camper, explorer, big game hunter, lover of trees—especially pines—amateur entomologist, and enthusiastic birder. Disdained by the Republican establishment of his day—President McKinley's right-hand man Mark Hannah bluntly called him a "madman"—Roosevelt is the most important environmental president in American history.

Roosevelt was dedicated to using nature wisely by ensuring the long-term viability of the nation's natural resource base. The fate of resources preoccupied Roosevelt. In his first message to Congress, he argued that "forest and water problems" were "perhaps the most vital internal problems of the United States." He articulated his concerns in an opening address before the 1908 White House Conference on the Conservation of Natural Resources—one of seven Conservation Conferences and Commissions he convened:

> We have thoughtlessly, and . . . unnecessarily, diminished the resources upon which not only our prosperity but the prosperity of our children must always depend . . . the time has come to inquire seriously what will happen when our forests are gone, when the coal, the iron, the oil, and the gas are exhausted, when the soils shall have . . . washed into the streams, polluting the rivers, denuding the fields, and obstructing navigation.

Roosevelt responded programmatically to such concerns. Most importantly he created and then greatly expanded the U.S. Forest Service. When Roosevelt entered office, the United States had forty-one forest reserves totaling about forty-one million acres; when he left office, there were 159 national forests (many later consolidated) encompassing 150 million acres.

The idea of professional management of forests had been circulating through government and conservation circles. President McKinley appropriated funds for forest management in 1897. Known as the Forest Organic Act, it charged forest reserves with "securing favorable conditions of water flows" and with supplying the United States with "a continuous supply of timber." In 1898 Gifford Pinchot became chief of the Division of Forestry, then housed in the Interior Department. In 1905 Pinchot and Roosevelt succeeded in transferring the newly named Forest Service—a designation that emphasized that forests were to be used for the national benefit—to the Department of Agriculture where they thought forests could be managed in the public interest. Pinchot was the first chief of the Forest Service.

Like Roosevelt, Gifford Pinchot (1865–1946) came to conservation from a patrician background but dedicated his career to public service and social reform. Like many environmentalists he developed a love of the outdoors as a child. A man of strong convictions, he was selected deacon for the Yale class of 1889, and was deeply involved in what was known as "muscular Christianity"—a movement of Christian life that embraced robust physical activity. He worked in the University Settlement House in New York's Lower East Side: "There I came into operating contact with the other half and learned something of how it lived and thought and why, whereby my conservative opinions were greatly changed, to my very marked advantage." He thought seriously of becoming a minister before deciding on a career in forestry. After graduating Yale, he studied forestry in France and Germany. Armed with this education, he helped establish professional forestry to the United States, working to manage forests with the utilitarian philosophy of the "greatest good for the greatest number for the longest time."

Pinchot embodied the idea of conservation as the judicious use of resources managed for long-term public benefit. Orderly, rational management would prevent resource scarcity. For Pinchot, scientific management was also about equity: no longer would public forest lands merely profit the already wealthy. In his 1910 book *The Fight for Conservation*, Pinchot argued that "conservation is the most democratic movement this country has known for a generation. It holds that the people have . . . the right . . . to control the use of natural resources . . . it regards the absorption of these resources by the special interests . . . as a moral wrong." In the end "conservation is the application of common-sense to the common problems for the common good." Pinchot managed the nation's forests with great success in part because he decentralized decision making. Policy was set in Washington, but implemented locally in response to specific conditions. In theory, those decisions were made in accordance with the Forest Service's thick *Use Book*. In practice, local customs often won out over federal policy.

Other environmental issues had no engineering solution, only the possibility of new morals informing laws and customs. In the late nineteenth century that meant campaigning against the popular women's fashion of adorning hats with birds. Egret plumes, owl heads, warblers—sometimes as many as eight or ten on a single hat!—joined whole hummingbirds, and, in the 1890s, entire terns or pheasants as fashionable decor. "The extremely softening effect" of birds that adorn a hat, advised one fashion magazine, "is ever desirable, especially for ladies no longer young." Observing the many birds used in the 1897 winter fashion season, *Harper's Bazaar* wondered if there was "an owl or ostrich left with a single feather." A Chicago reporter grumbled that "it will be no surprise to me to see life-sized turkeys or even . . . farmyard hens, on fashionable bonnets before I die."

Supplying such fashion decimated wild bird populations. Conservative estimates put the number of birds sacrificed to the millinery trade at over five million each year. Large colony nesters were most vulnerable. *Good Housekeeping* reported in 1887 that "At Cape Cod, [forty thousand] terns have been killed in one season by a single agent of the hat trade." Ornithologist Frank Chapman, originator of Christmas bird counts, described heron massacres in which hunters "Mercilessly . . . shot down at their roosts or nesting grounds, the coveted feathers are stripped from their backs, the carcasses are left to rot, while the young in the nest above are starving." In an era when the loss of passenger pigeons was still a freshly embittering wound, millinery hunters demolished heron, tern, gull, and egret rookeries along the entire eastern seaboard.

Bird-hat fashion coincided with the emergence of one of the major social developments of the late nineteenth century: the rise of the "woman movement" (or "organized womanhood"), especially the Woman's Club movement. Drawing mostly from the middle and upper classes, Women's Clubs combined often-conservative views of gender with social activism. The General Federation of Women's Clubs became a leader in conservation, maintaining that "conservation in its material and ethical sense is the basic principle of womanhood." Women's Clubs were particularly active from the 1890s through World War II. In 1911, the *Ladies' Home Journal* echoed such sentiments, instructing its readers that as housekeepers "you have been practicing conservation all your life, doing on a small scale what the Government is beginning to do on a huge one." Conservationist Lydia Adams-Williams explained that it was women who needed "to educate public sentiment to save from rapacious waste and complete exhaustion the resources upon which depend the welfare of the home, the children, and the children's children."

The fight to save birds engendered a strong coalition of conservative and liberal women who challenged the masculine idea of unending resource exploitation. Naturalist Ella Higginson accused men of being so obsessed with profits that they "tear down our forests, rip open our mountain sides, blow out our stumps . . . [and] dam up our water ways." Women's Clubs were joined in their efforts by the Audubon Society, which was rapidly organizing at the state level. The national journal *Club Woman* endorsed the Audubon campaign, reminding its readers that "A dead bird's body . . . on a fashionable hat . . . is positively repulsive."

The great majority of Audubon founders were women, including prominent Boston socialite and social reformer Harriet Lawrence Hemenway, who established the first state Audubon Society in Massachusetts in 1896. (Its bylaws charged it with "protection of our native birds" and, more specifically, with "discouraging the buying and wearing for ornamental purposes the feathers of any wild bird.") But conservative notions of gender also restrained these activists. In state after state women founded Audubon clubs and then asked male scientists or civic leaders to assume leadership.

Women employed economic and ecological reasoning, not just moral suasion, to argue for bird preservation. The ecology-minded Marion Crocker, for example, warned of damage to crops if insectivorous birds are no longer able to check insect propagation. "If we do not follow the most scientific approved methods [of resource use] . . . the time will come when the world will not be able to support life." Crocker continued by emphasizing that "This is not sentiment. It is pure economics." Crocker was amplifying arguments used by the American Ornithologists Union. Leading ornithologist William Dutcher put the matter succinctly: "have the milliners, with their petty interest any right to jeopardize the safety of the agricultural interests"?

Some politicians resisted the idea of bird protection. Missouri Senator James A. Reed wondered, "Why should there be any sympathy or sentiment about a long-legged, long beaked, long-necked bird that lives in swamps and eats tadpoles?" Such birds should be used "for the only purpose that the Lord made it for . . . so we could get aigrettes for the bonnet[s] of our beautiful ladies." Many women rejected such trivialization of women's social concerns. "I believe it is woman's sacred mission to be the conservator of beauty, and not its destroyer," asserted Iowa club woman Margaret T. Olmstead.

Figure 3.2 The most significant environmental president, Teddy Roosevelt established fifty-five bird reservations and game reserves and over 150 million acres of national forest land. Library of Congress Photo Archive

The campaign to stop bird-hat fashion—sometimes known as the "feather wars"—met with remarkable success. Local efforts included Harriet Lawrence Hemenway and her cousin Minna B. Hall hosting bird-consciousness-raising tea parties that persuaded about nine hundred of their acquaintances to forgo bird hat fashion. In western Massachusetts, a Smith College student, Florence Merriam (1863–1948), founded the Smith College Audubon Society and persuaded her classmates to reject birds on hats. Local milliners were overwhelmed with requests to have the birds removed. Merriam went on to an important career as a nature writer and conservation advocate authoring books using her married name, Florence Merriam Bailey.

National legislation followed. In 1900, Congress effectively ended unregulated commercial hunting by passing the Lacey Act which outlawed the transportation across state lines of wildlife killed in violation of state laws. In 1913, the Weeks-McLean Act unified the patchwork of state game laws by prohibiting the spring hunting of migratory birds as well as the importation of wild bird feathers for women's fashion. In 1918, the Migratory Bird Treaty Act made it unlawful "to pursue, hunt, take, capture, kill or sell" migratory birds. These were major achievements. As historian Nancy C. Unger writes, "Prior to achieving suffrage . . . women were able to wield legislative influence and, by preserving millions of birds, protect complex and vital environmental relationships from ruin by a powerful American industry."

The success was also due to President Roosevelt's abiding passion for wildlife and its protection. In 1899, two years before he became president, he wrote a letter about bird conservation to ornithologist Frank Chapman. Roosevelt explained that, "I would like to see all harmless wild things, but especially all birds protected in every way. . . . When I hear of the destruction of a species I feel just as if all the works of some great writer had perished." Roosevelt and Chapman teamed up to save birds from the millinery trade. The first step was to preserve Pelican Island, a stunningly vibrant islet rookery on Florida's Atlantic coast. President Roosevelt established Pelican Island as the first federal bird reservation in 1903. The land was federal, and no statute prevented Roosevelt from creating the new designation. It was a watershed moment in conservation history: Pelican Island was the first public land set aside solely for the benefit of wildlife. The action birthed what we now know as the Wildlife Refuge System. During his presidency Roosevelt designated nine more reservations in Florida and a national total of fifty-five bird reservations and game reserves.

The establishment of Pelican Island did not end the feather wars. Instead, violence erupted. Roosevelt appointed local conservationist Paul Kroegel as the Pelican Island game warden; because the Department of Agriculture had not budgeted money for game wardens, the Audubon Society supplied his modest salary. A second warden, another local and former plume hunter named Guy Bradley, was added in 1902. Bradley was a convert to conservation; he disdained his old profession of plume hunting as "a cruel and hard calling." Three years after taking the job, Bradley confronted a plume hunting team comprised of a father and two sons as they were loading dead birds onto their boat. Bradley had previously arrested one of the sons and had squabbled with the father. Tensions roiled as the warden prepared to arrest the poachers. One of the men suddenly shot Bradley in the chest; he was left to bleed to death. Three years later in 1908, poachers killed another Florida game warden, Columbus G. MacLeod. Later that same year unknown assailants ambushed and killed Pressly Reeves, an employee of the South Carolina Audubon Society. All of the murderers went free. The deaths infuriated Roosevelt and his Audubon allies, who redoubled their bird protection efforts.

Roosevelt's dedication to using public lands for conservation resulted in a stunning array of achievements: six national parks, fifty-one bird sanctuaries, four national game preserves, and eighteen national monuments. Many of these designations resulted from Roosevelt's robust deployment of the Antiquities Act of 1906. This act arose in response to extensive pillaging of archeological antiquities in the southwest. It authorized the president to preserve as a "national monument" any "historic landmarks, historic and prehistoric structures, and other objects of historic or scientific interest." Congress intended the law to protect small areas near Indian ruins such as Chaco Canyon. But the ambitious Roosevelt realized the law failed to constrain executive authority in any meaningful way. He took the law's language as a license to do good as he saw fit.

The first monuments he declared were relatively small, such as New Mexico's El Morro and Gila Cliff Dwellings National Monuments. Roosevelt changed the equation when he used the Antiquities Act to declare the 806,400-acre Grand Canyon National Monument. Businesses and private builders were exploiting the canyon. Roosevelt used the Antiquities Act to protect the canyon for the public good. He wasn't finished. On his last day in office he deployed the act to reserve more than 630,000 acres of the Pacific northwest for the Mount Olympus National Monument—later, like the Grand Canyon, to become a national park. The pattern of monument to park became a common one; nearly a quarter of the units currently in the national park system originated in whole or part from the Antiquities Act, one of the most powerful weapons in the conservationist arsenal.

Just as progressive conservationists transformed public lands, they also transformed public schools. Progressive Era reformers were appalled by the ways that modern life deprived urban children of contact with nature. Fannie G. Parsons, a pioneer of school gardens in the United States, described urban children as living "encased amid bricks, stone, concrete, trolleys, trucks, and automobiles . . . the blue sky overhead is seldom seen. . . . City children are alienated from their human birthright of trees, fields, and flowers." The effects of this alienation were both physical and psychological. Parsons reasoned that lack of contact with nature made children "hard and unfeeling."

A key programmatic answer to the problem of creating a society in which children could thrive was using the study of nature to bring children into contact with the outdoors. Nature study became an integral part of school curricula nationwide. It used plant identification, animal life histories, and school gardens to cultivate spiritual growth and promote the scientific skills needed to succeed in industrial life. Nature study classes bred animals, raised chickens, learned to identify birds, and watched tadpoles develop into frogs. They planted, grew, and tended gardens whose products they sometimes sold. All nature study adherents agreed that children needed to leave the schoolroom to encounter nature rather than merely read about it in books.

Contact with nature meant that people would develop a "sympathy" with it. Once sympathy is cultivated, explained Margaret W. Morley in *Outlook* magazine, people understand that "there is a duty owed by us to the trees, and through them to our fellow-men." This attitude cultivated conservation in later life: "A love for trees, and a knowledge of the reasons for preserving them" will ensure that "there will be no difficulty gaining advocates for forest laws." Sympathy thus tied nature study to other conservation achievements. "In our great National Parks we have an unrivaled outdoor school that is always open; in it is a library, a museum, a zoological garden," argued Colorado's effusive national park advocate Enos Mills. "In this school-children are brought into contact with actual things, and become personally acquainted with useful facts, instead of merely reading about them." For Mills, as for other nature study advocates, "the wild gardens of Nature are the best kindergartens."

More than any other figure, Anna Botsford Comstock (1854–1930) embodied the nature study movement. Comstock grew up in upstate New York where she spent her childhood exploring its forested wilds. She married her entomology professor at Cornell and later joined him on the faculty. She was an outstanding illustrator; her gorgeous engravings

Figure 3.3 Anna Botsford Comstock argued that nature study should "give the child a sense of companionship with life out-of-doors and an abiding love of nature."

helped make her husband's 1895 *A Manual for the Study of Insects* a favorite in the field. Anna Comstock's professional world expanded greatly as she became actively involved in the nature study movement. She wrote dozens of books and articles on nature study, and lectured widely to rural schoolteachers during her summer travels. Comstock argued that nature study should "give the child a sense of companionship with life out-of-doors and an abiding love of nature." In Comstock's ideal world of popular nature study, "even those who never come to universities" would "be able to go out into the fields and without the aid of books or teachers read the lessons in God's great laboratory." In 1911 she published the massive *Handbook of Nature Study*, an immensely popular guide to nature study that remains in print to this day.

The enthusiasm for nature and nature study extended widely across many social locations. The educator and social reformer Booker T. Washington (1856–1915), for example, enjoyed a lifelong love of nature. He had "always been intensely fond of outdoor life," a quality he attributed to having "had many close and interesting acquaintances with animals" during his enslaved childhood. In *Up from Slavery*, his 1901 best-selling autobiography, Washington described his family outings on Sunday afternoons as an enjoyable escape

> Into the woods, where we can live for a while near the heart of nature, where no one can disturb or vex us, surrounded by pure air, the trees, the shrubbery, the flowers, and the sweet fragrance that springs up from a hundred plants, enjoying the chirp of the crickets and the songs of the birds. This is solid rest.

For Washington, contact with nature was not to be an occasional or weekly event but a daily practice. Gardening was the best way to get dirt under one's fingernails. "I do not believe that any one who has not worked in a garden can begin to understand how much pleasure and strength of body and mind and soul can be derived from one's garden," explained Washington. When a garden thrived, "a feeling of kinship [arose] between the man and his plants." Nature study was a central part of the curriculum at the Tuskegee Institute, the school Washington built.

But the study of nature was much more than a pleasure and a science. Washington used nature study as a means of social change. His emphasis on the pleasures and possibilities of rural life led him to an ecological critique of tenant farming and monoculture. Lack of property encouraged shortsightedness, an attitude that extended to the land itself: "Instead of returning the cotton-seed to the ground to help enrich the soil, [the tenant farmer] sold this valuable fertilizer. The land, of course, was more impoverished each year. Ditching and terracing received little attention." According to Washington, tenant farmers treated tools and animals poorly as well.

In contrast, wise farming methods could exert a positive effect on race relations. Washington famously believed that the key to social equality was for "the Negro, when given a chance, to help himself, and

Figure 3.4 Class in Nature Study held at the Tuskegee Institute. Washington used the study of nature to instill a love of country life in his students, and to help them prosper by using sound agricultural methods.
From Booker T. Washington, Working with the Hands (New York: Doubleday, Page and Company, 1904)

make himself indispensable to the community." Knowing how to prosper was a sure way to make oneself indispensable. To illustrate, Washington wrote about black sweet potato farmers who gained great yields, and hence hefty profits, by applying the methods of scientific agriculture developed by George Washington Carver. "The deep interest shown by the neighboring white farmers has been most gratifying," reported Washington. "I do not believe that a single white farmer who visited the field to see the unusual yields ever thought of having any prejudice or feeling against this colored man . . . there were, on the other hand, many evidences of respect." Washington's attitude entailed much more than capitulation to the dominant social order. It embodied the progressive belief that schools regenerated the social order and hence could be key institutions in the democratization of society.

Washington's concerns over rural culture and economy were typical of many progressive reformers and manifested themselves in a variety of rural reform initiatives. Responding to such concerns, Teddy Roosevelt created a presidential delegation, the Country Life Commission, to investigate the problems faced by rural America. The nature study movement was intimately bound up with these expressions of rural reform. Educators felt that nature study held the answer to economic quandaries by imparting scientific methods of agricultural production that would increase yields and hence profits. Nature study could also assuage the cultural crisis of agrarian America by instilling a love of nature in rural children, encouraging them to appreciate their surroundings and develop a lasting commitment to rural life.

To make his commission work, Roosevelt turned to Liberty Hyde Bailey (1858–1954). Although Bailey was a prominent intellectual who was widely known and widely read during his lifetime, he is now largely overlooked in the history of progressive conservation. Dubbed by one historian the "philosopher of country life," Bailey was a remarkable figure—perspicacious, wide ranging in his academic interests and achievements, a passionate philosopher of not only country life but also conservation and nature study. Bailey tied cultural and environmental reform together. The farmer who sees in his crops "only clods and weeds, and corn," wrote Bailey, leads an "empty and a barren life." Conversely, the "knowledge of soil and atmosphere, of plant and animal life that makes [the farmer] an intelligent producer, puts him in sympathetic touch with these activities of nature." For nature study advocates, such sympathy created happiness. Bailey emphasized that the countryman needed an "intellectual horizon. He needs something else [besides money] to think of. He needs to have a real personal sympathy with the natural objects in his environment. He needs the nature study outlook." Country life advocates championed the study of nature as a means to modernize the agricultural economy and revitalize rural culture.

To gain knowledge about the country life crisis, the committee sent out questionnaires to roughly 550,000 rural residents; more than 115,000 responded. The commission also encouraged rural people to hold meetings to examine rural problems and then forward their ideas to the commission. Thousands of such meetings were held. Bailey wanted rural people to lead the reform of their lives and institutions, and the commission's report reflected his democratic orientation. The commission emphasized that "The forces that make for rural betterment must themselves be rural."

Congress did not accept the report; they had not been consulted on creating the commission and had grown tired of Roosevelt's moralizing.

Despite the lack of congressional response, the Commission on Country Life prompted legislation that led to the U.S. Parcel Post System (which delivered, usually via railroad, large and heavy packages), federally funded rural electrification, and a nationwide extension service. The report is also an overlooked classic of progressive conservation. It called for a "system of self-sustaining agriculture." Conservationist agriculture would consist of "diversified and rotation farming, carefully adapted in every case to the particular region. Such systems conserve the resources of the land." Conventional agriculture was wasteful due to its "lack of appreciation of our responsibility to society to protect and save the land."

The findings of the report did not remove conservation from social conditions; rather, the commission viewed conservation and other social reforms as intertwined. Writing about the "monopolistic control of streams," which it perceived as a "real and immediate danger," the commission recommended the founding of a new governmental body charged with "protecting the people in their ownership" of water. The body would reserve appropriate amounts of water "to agriculture." Such a body would combat "Waterlordism," which "is as much to be feared as landlordism." The role of the government was to help farmers own "both the land and the water," which was crucial if the farmer "is to be a master of his own fortunes."

Such policies were pragmatic, grounded in the real world of solving pressing problems. They embodied progressive ideas about the moral standing of nature and the wise use of resources. Conservation sprang not just from the concerns of elites like Teddy Roosevelt, but the common morality and problem solving of everyday Americans. Pragmatic problem solving defined progressive conservation.

CHAPTER 5

A GREEN NEW DEAL

It is time that the nation insists on the preservation of the national forests. . . . They should be a haven for wildlife. . . . They should be laboratories for the study of ecology. . . . Above all the forests should be preserved for the recreation of those whose need impels them to withdraw from time to time from conventional life.

–ROSALIE EDGE, "Roads and More Roads in the National Parks and National Forests"

ADVOCATING in 1937 for a national law to combat soil erosion, President Franklin Delano Roosevelt (FDR; 1882–1945) emphasized that "The nation that destroys its soil destroys itself." But why was the nation destroying its soil? The honest answer pointed to the very fundamentals of American social structure. The nation destroyed soil for the same reason it suffered from the crazy quilt economic problems of overproduction and underconsumption. It destroyed soil for the same reason that the country suffered massive unemployment—as much as 40 percent in some regions. It destroyed soil for the same reason its displaced citizens were forced to recycle tin, planks, and cardboard into the shantytowns they angrily named "Hoovervilles."

Soil loss, overproduction, unemployment, destitution: all these problems had the same root cause. The people of the nation destroyed the soil because they obeyed the economic logic that governed everything from the investment of capital to the ways that farmers plowed their fields. The Great Depression and ecological destruction—particularly the Dust Bowl—highlighted the two great, intertwined crises of capitalism: its collapse and failure to provide material security for the majority of the country and its destruction of the natural world. We can't fully appreciate one problem, or the New Deal responses to it, without understanding the other.

FDR understood the connection. "Natural resources," he wrote, are "not static and sterile possessions . . . a thing apart." Instead they are "interwoven with industry, labor, finance, taxation, agriculture, homes, recreation, [and] good citizenship." FDR's program to combat the Great Depression, his much-vaunted New Deal, was a massive economic intervention and an attempt to create a new American relationship with the natural world. Roosevelt's critics went so far as to claim that he considered all policy problems in terms of conservation; "I must plead guilty to that charge," he replied. Many New Deal agencies and programs—the Civilian Conservation Corps (CCC), the Tennessee Valley Authority (TVA), soil conservation, and farm security—were attempts to reform rural life through conservation. New Dealers felt that one cause of the depression was the economic imbalance arising from the fact that rural people had little capital compared to their urban counterparts. Their crops were too fertile—hence overproduction—but the prices for those crops were so low they were poor—hence underconsumption. The New Deal set out to rehabilitate the capitalism of rural life and the nature that defined it. The New Deal was a green deal.

FDR was the president to enact a green New Deal. Like his cousin Teddy, he loved trees. When asked his profession, he often replied "forester" or "tree grower" instead of "lawyer" or "politician." Upon inheriting his family's Springwood estate, he began to plant trees to help repair its worn-out soil. Once he started, he was hooked—he planted thousands of trees each year. After polio claimed the use of his legs in 1921, Roosevelt had his staff build wheelchair-accessible paths so he could continue his beloved forest sojourns. It is thus no surprise that Roosevelt connected conservation with economic prosperity. In his "Green Pastures" speech of 1936, he spoke of being "convinced that the long road that leads to green pastures and still waters had to begin with reasonable prosperity. It seemed axiomatic to me that a cotton farmer who would get only five cents a pound for his crop could not be in a position properly to fertilize his land, or to terrace it or to rotate his crops." FDR could just as easily have pointed out that a reasonable economic system would reward the cotton farmer for being green: infertile, gullied, exhausted soils don't produce future prosperity. The utopian promise of the New Deal was that the reasonable economy and ecologic health could improve together.

Taking America's political helm during the grimmest economic crisis in history, FDR's first message to Congress claimed that "Nature still offers her bounty" but the economy had failed to harvest it "because the rulers of the exchange of mankind's goods have failed." The first response to those problems came in the form of the CCC, which Roosevelt implemented just over one month into his presidency. The idea behind the CCC was simple: the government could put the unemployed to work performing the socially necessary tasks of conservation. FDR initiated a similar, if considerably less ambitious, reforestation project in 1931 when he was governor of New York. Roosevelt's New York program— he called it the Temporary Emergency Relief Administration—created ten thousand jobs converting abandoned farmlands into public forests. When lobbying for the CCC's passage, FDR moved beyond job creation to define the idea of forest rehabilitation in ecological terms: "the forests are the lungs of our land [which] purify our air and give fresh strength to our people."

In proposing forestry reform Roosevelt tapped into longstanding concerns over the quantity and quality of American forests—the problem of "timber famine." Government agencies noted that existing forest reserves were in numerical decline and in poor ecological health. One resounding voice in these matters belonged to the venerable Gifford Pinchot who had been sounding the alarm over the state of forestry for decades. In 1928 Pinchot charged that logging companies were fooling "the American people into believing that . . . industry was regulating itself and had given up the practice of forest devastation." To investigate such claims, Congress commissioned *A National Plan for American*

Forestry, colloquially known as the Copeland Report. It concluded that "the forest resources of this country were being seriously depleted" and recommended that the government purchase 240 million acres of privately owned woodlands. Pinchot seconded the Copeland Report, noting that neither "the crutch of subsidy nor the whip of regulation" had reformed timber company practices. The solution, therefore, "was large-scale [public] acquisition of private lands."

The idea to tie forest health to employment came from several sources, including Robert Marshall. Asked by Pinchot and Roosevelt to summarize the massive (1,677-page) Copeland Report into a brisk six pages, Marshall "stressed two things: a huge [public] land acquisition program; and use of the unemployed in an immense way for fire protection, fire-proofing, improvement cuttings, plantings, erosion control, improvements (roads, trails, fire towers, etc.) and recreation developments." Roosevelt had also long admired the Boy Scouts and used them as inspiration for the CCC. In the 1920s Roosevelt created the Franklin D. Roosevelt Conservation Camps for Boy Scouts that taught forestry and wildlife management. Roosevelt particularly wished that poor young men from the inner city be able to take advantage of the camps. The scouts believed in the twin moral benefit of hard work and exposure to nature. By combining conservation with Scout morality, the CCC, argued Roosevelt, could simultaneously improve forests and the country's young men. To save capitalism Roosevelt would enhance both natural and human capital.

Unions initially opposed the CCC, fearing it would depress wages. But FDR appointed union officials to run the program and stipulated that the young CCC workers had to send home almost all their wages of thirty dollars a month. The CCC provided lodging, meals, and basic medical care, so the enrollees had little immediate need for their pay. The workers thus helped their families and stimulated spending back home. Between twelve and fifteen million Americans directly benefited from enrollee checks. The CCC was open to any unmarried U.S. male citizen between the ages of eighteen and twenty-six; most enrollees were poor, many were minorities, and many came from immigrant families. Once enrolled, the young men—fewer than 10 percent of whom had graduated high school—not only worked but took classes in "Forestry," "Soil Conservation," and the "Conservation of Natural Resources." The work itself was likely a better teacher than the classes. "Our work is very

Figure 4.1 Franklin Roosevelt turned his own deep love of forests into social reform when he created the Civilian Conservation Corps. The Corps employed 3.5 million young men during the Great Depression.
Courtesy Franklin D. Roosevelt Presidential Library & Museum

interesting," declared enrollee James Brandon in 1935. "Being out in the open most of the time, we learn more about nature and the natural resources we are striving to conserve."

The CCC lasted from April 5, 1933, to June 30, 1942. Overall, nearly 3.5 million men worked in forty-five hundred different camps. Enrollees built 125,000 miles of road, thirteen thousand miles of hiking trails, developed eight hundred state parks, developed another fifty-two thousand acres of public campgrounds, and planted between two and three billion trees—half the trees planted in all of U.S. history. They also fought fires, stocked fish, controlled mosquitos, revegetated rangelands, and otherwise engaged in erosion control. Given that stunning workload, enrollees unsurprisingly rejected the bureaucratic moniker Civilian Conservation Corps in favor of the more poetic "Colossal College of Calluses," "Roosevelt's Tree Army," "Tree Troopers," "Soil Soldiers," and even "Woodpecker Warriors." Early admirers of the CCC noted its transformative effects on both young men and the forests in which they labored. "They are making a new kind of American man out of the city boy in the woods," declared novelist Sherwood Anderson after visiting a camp in Pennsylvania. "And they are planning at least to begin to make a new land with the help of such boys." The CCC began calling its transformation of young people "human conservation."

Anyone who has visited a national forest or a state or national park has likely benefited from projects completed by the CCC. The CCC's success in building American infrastructure is impossible to deny—and it usefully (if inadvertently) helped train the soldiers who would fight World War II. As the *Alaskan*, a CCC publication from Juneau, noted, the program transformed "baffled, furtive, tough, city youngsters" into "bronzed, clear-eyed, well-muscled soldiers in waiting." As economic relief it surely ranks as one of the great American success stories. But was the CCC good for the earth?

The answer, despite the profound successes of the CCC, is mixed. The CCC often replanted trees in well-ordered rows, which was not only visually unappealing but fashioned more of a tree plantation than an actual forest. The CCC also did not always reforest with native species, a pronounced habitat alteration that provoked a cascade of ecological problems. Among the most notorious mistakes made by CCC conservation was its planting of a Japanese invasive weed—kudzu (*Pueraria lobata*)—as a way to control soil erosion. Lee Brown, a black CCC enrollee in Georgia, quipped that his unit was "like the Johnny Apple-seeds of kudzu." Though widespread, the negative effects of kudzu have been overblown—it is not "the vine that ate the South." It is nevertheless true that kudzu smothers native species—what botanists call "interference competition"—and displaces others. Part of the reason for Kudzu's outsized reputation is that it grows well in disturbed environments such as roadsides and is hence more visually prominent than its ecological impact would suggest.

More broadly, the CCC considered "fire, insects, and disease" the "Three Horsemen" of forest destruction, and attempted to eradicate them with apocalyptic fervor. Fire was their special concern. To combat it the CCC cleared brush from forest floors—ruining valuable wildlife habitat. They also constructed "fire breaks"—cleared strips of land within forests. The longest of the strips extended an astonishing six hundred miles along the base of the Sierra Nevada mountains. When fire did break out, CCC enrollees fought it. It was a rough, exhausting, and dirty job—and dangerous too; twenty-nine enrollees died fighting fires. We now know that fire suppression damaged many of the forests it meant to help. In the 1960s ecologists began to uncover the ecological necessity of fires; now land management agencies allow fires to burn where appropriate. In retrospect, CCC fire suppression harmed the ecosystems by changing forest composition and reducing biodiversity.

Along with these missteps, the CCC also engaged in some truly forward-thinking ecological work. In the desert southwest, the magnificent saguaro cacti were suffering from bacterial infections; CCC enrollees removed dying cacti and saved thousands of others. The CCC repaired infrastructure in thirty-six national wildlife refuges—and many young men trained to rehabilitate wildlife directly. Enrollees planted native flora in wildlife refuges such as Blackwater in Maryland and Saint Marks in Florida. In other refuges such as Aransas in Texas, the CCC built freshwater ponds and stocked them with suitable prey for migratory ducks, geese, and cranes. The CCC even engaged in important archeological work in places such as Chaco Canyon National Monument, stabilizing pre-Columbian architecture. Overall, the CCC conserved more than 118 million acres of American land—an area larger than California.

The CCC operated several camps in the Tennessee River Valley, the lunular watershed of the Tennessee River that begins in Knoxville, Tennessee, dips south into northern Alabama and Mississippi, before turning north to join the Ohio River at Paducah, Kentucky. It was an area of extreme poverty and environmental degradation. Its per capita income was a mere $263, less than half the national average. A total of 3.5 million people lived in the region, but only three hundred thousand had electricity. About 70 percent of the area's farm families worked land that was severely and actively eroding. Uncontrolled lumbering led to dangerous erosion, and the region's farmers stubbornly persisted with row cropping techniques that abused the soil. By one contemporary estimate, erosion had damaged four-fifths of the region's land; the final fifth was in even worse shape, as it was deemed irreparably gullied. The area leapt into political consciousness due to debate over a dam in the Tennessee River town of Muscle Shoals, Alabama. Should the dam be part of a regional public power initiative, or be sold to a private operator?

New Deal regional planners saw the dam and the valley as an opportunity to implement their notion of New Conservation: the integration of social and environmental well-being. Poor land, argued the New Conservationists, produced poor people. Sociologist Lewis Mumford defined the New Conservation as "permanent agriculture instead of land-skimming, permanent forestry instead of timber mining, permanent human communities dedicated to life, liberty and the pursuit of happiness, instead of camps and squatter settlements." New Deal thinkers correctly viewed the Tennessee River Valley as the victim of a colonial economy in which raw materials were exported from the region, leaving its residents poor and the region underdeveloped. New Conservation development by the TVA, a government corporation created to uplift the area, was the New Deal's answer to these pressing problems.

The TVA got to work in 1933, building sixteen dams that generated hydroelectric power for millions of users. "We wanted those dams to have the honest beauty of a fine tool," wrote TVA board member David Lilienthal, because the TVA "was a tool to do a job for men in a democracy." TVA-generated electricity enabled many small, farm-based enterprises that could not have existed without it; TVA dams generate much of the region's inexpensive electricity to this day. The TVA also set about reforesting hillsides and rehabilitating abused farm lands. Though it did not achieve the grandest aspirations of New Deal regional planners, the TVA nevertheless enacted an impressive list of environmental reforms. It eliminated malaria from the region and established a state park system in Tennessee. It taught farmers to use nitrogen-fixing cover crops like vetch and clover to fertilize fields, freeing them from having to purchase expensive and polluting nitrate fertilizers. It sponsored many agricultural demonstration projects.

TVA dams became embroiled in an environmental controversy in the mid-1970s. The TVA wanted to build a new dam named "Tellico" on the Little Tennessee River near Lenoir City, Tennessee. It was unneeded—it barely generated electricity—and unwanted; local property owners opposed it, along with environmentalists. In helping prepare the environmental impact statement for the project, a University of Tennessee professor discovered the presence of a small, endangered relative of the perch—the snail darter (*Percina tanasi*)—which he quickly dubbed "the fish that will stop the Tellico dam." Given the protections of the Endangered Species Act, it appeared it would, especially as the project was widely recognized as a pork barrel boondoggle to begin with.

But proponents of the dam cleverly worked bureaucratic channels to further their plan. They amended the Endangered Species Act to include a cabinet-level committee whose charge was to weigh species preservation against the economic costs of doing so. Nicknamed the "God Committee," the group shocked dam proponents by favoring the snail darter and thus opposing the dam. Once again it appeared the dam was finished. But in June 1979 dam proponents sneaked a rider into an appropriations bill exempting the Tellico dam from environmental regulations. The Tellico dam was built that year. Happily, scientists discovered more snail darter populations in nearby rivers. The species remains "threatened" but is no longer "endangered." But the damage to the Endangered Species Act—it was weakened by Tellico dam proponents just five years after congress had updated and strengthened it—remains acute.

As with the varied and down-to-earth approach to social and ecological problems embodied by the CCC and TVA, New Deal conservation was pragmatic and civic in its orientation. Less frequently acknowledged is that this is also true of the wilderness values expressed by New Deal planners. Wilderness was less about transcendent notions of the divine and more about enacting the often-conflicting values and commitments of human communities. To see pragmatic New Deal conservation exist hand in hand with local communities, visit the most renowned footpath in the United States: the Appalachian Trail. Extending 2,180 miles from Springer Mountain in Georgia to the (in Thoreau's words) "cloud factory" that is Mt. Katahdin in Maine, the Appalachian Trail is partially hiked by two to three million people each year. (About two thousand people attempt to "thru hike" the entire trail; most don't make it.) Combining recreation with community development and the preservation of nature, the Appalachian Trail represents New Deal conservation at its finest.

The idea for a fourteen-state footpath connecting Georgia to Maine was first proposed by the conservationist, Wilderness Society co-founder, and regional planner Benton MacKaye (1879–1975). He claimed to have come up with idea while sitting in a tree atop Vermont's Stratton Mountain. He formalized his notion in a 1921 article entitled "An Appalachian Trail: A Project in Regional Planning." In the article MacKaye lauded the national parks as "playgrounds for the people" but noted that most were in the west—a far journey for the majority of Americans who lived in the urban east. Fortunately, a short excursion from big eastern cities revealed "a fairly continuous belt of under-developed lands" that were ripe for purposeful recreation.

But MacKaye did not have a park in mind as he proposed the trail. Rather, the trail constituted part of a larger vision of nature preservation and a reform of social and political community that was nothing short of a "new approach to the problem of living." Visitors to the trail would find "health and recuperation" and "real living"—by which MacKaye meant a regaining of perspective on one's life and labor. The trail would also foster adjacent "community groups" and "farm and food camps," offering opportunities for productive labor driven by real need rather than market imperatives, "a retreat from profit." Camps along the trail could offer craftwork, farming, and "reposeful study"—alternatives for Americans suffering from the "invasion of an over-wrought mechanized civilization." In short, the civic purpose of MacKaye's trail resembled the individual purpose of Thoreau's Walden Pond: it would allow people to live deliberately. Community development along the trail would allow them to live cooperatively. The trail would combine local action with federal authority, a trait that turned out to be one of its greatest innovations—and a source of continuing struggle.

MacKaye vigorously recruited allies to make his vision a reality, and in 1925 helped found the private, nongovernmental Appalachian Trail Conference (ATC) to create the trail. It was a superhuman effort. Led by the enthusiastic Washington, District of Columbia, lawyer Myron Avery (who in 1937 became the Appalachian Trail's first successful thru-hiker), the ATC received easements and right of ways from property owners along the trail. In 1937 the ATC announced completion of the continuous footpath. The trail proved popular, especially during the explosion of outdoor recreation in the postwar decades. To help manage the crowds, Congress passed the National Trails System Act in 1968, giving the Appalachian Trail federal protection as a national trail. The Park Service began overseeing the Appalachian Trail, and the Federal Land and Water Conservation Fund was used to purchase lands adjacent to the trail. What began as a private and independent effort became part of the federal land management bureaucracy.

The popularity of the trail triggered many of its difficulties. As the number of hikers increased, landowners balked at allowing the trail to cross their property. The *Washington Post* reported in 1975 that the trail was "in jeopardy precisely because it has become too popular." Increased use led to problems such as erosion and more trash along the trail. By the late 1970s, the growing anti-environmental conservative backlash in the name of property rights and anti-federalism led to the formation of groups such as Citizens Against New Trail when the ATC proposed a new trail route for Pennsylvania's Cumberland Valley. In response, the ATC created the Appalachian Trail Location Advisory Committee, a productive group that worked to ensure local citizens had full voice in determining the future of the trail. In the end, the trail followed a compromised route that neither the ATC or Citizens Against New Trail initially envisioned. The history of the trail shows the promise and the difficulty of conservation simultaneously operating at the federal, state, and grassroots levels.

Sometimes a vibrant personality could ease the interactions between federal officials and local citizens. This is the case with Hugh Hammond Bennett (1881–1960) and his New Deal mandate to end soil erosion. Born to a North Carolina farming family, Bennett graduated from the University of North Carolina and began work for the Bureau of Soils, then a division of the Department of Agriculture. In 1905 Bennett discovered that erosion occurred not just in gullies or rills, but could remove soil in a sheet of more or less uniform runoff. Bennett coined the term "sheet erosion"—now an accepted geologic concept—to describe this phenomenon. During the New Deal Bennett was promoted to lead the Soil Erosion Service. He hated the name—it accentuated the negative, and he wished the agency to be called the Soil Conservation Service (SCS). Despite his reservations with the name, Bennett preached and practiced the gospel of soil conservation with evangelical fervor.

Emphasizing the limits of natural resources went against the grain of the longstanding American tradition of assuming the inexhaustibility of nature. Rather than a paean to inevitable progress, Bennett summarized the American story as "Having cut down our trees, killed off the buffalo, and plowed up our grasslands of the plains, we began to exploit the soil." For Americans, progress was "not how long you can keep a thing, but how quickly you can economically scrap it." Soil exhaustion was a particularly difficult sell. Milton Whitney, an admired soil scientist who helped pioneer the federal government's soil surveys, argued in his 1909 *Soils of the United States* that, "The soil is the one indestructible, immutable asset that the Nation possesses. The soil . . . cannot be used up." It wasn't easy to overcome such prejudice. For years Bennett preached that both "scientific agriculturalists" and "practical farmers" could benefit from using soils "more in accordance with their adaptations and requirements."

America's barren farms testified to the necessity of Bennett's message; the Dust Bowl proved it to be an absolute imperative. Named after the bowl-shaped area of the southern plains that suffered from the worst dust storms, the Dust Bowl was more than a drought. It was a drought combined with capitalist farming: that is, a social system that rewarded (through greater short-term yields) the farmers who cultivated as much land as possible, thereby removing the root systems that hold the earth in place. As historian Donald Worster writes, the Dust Bowl resulted from a culture "operating in precisely the way it was supposed to," which was "deliberately, self-consciously . . . dominating and exploiting the land for all it was worth."

The result was one of the greatest ecological disasters in human history. Stripped of its defenses against drought and high winds, the soil blew up into storms of almost unimaginable intensity. "Black blizzard" dust storms rose seven thousand to eight thousand feet above the plains, accompanied by thunder and lightning, or, even spookier, an eerie silence. One dust storm in 1934 carried off over three hundred million tons of fertile topsoil. Not only did "Kansas dirt" blow onto residents of New York, it settled onto ships three hundred miles out to sea. Beginning in 1935, at least forty storms each year were serious enough to cut visibility on the wide-open plains to less than a mile. Caroline Henderson of Eva, Oklahoma, wrote in 1935 of "dust covered desolation" where "visibility approaches zero." Even inside the home "everything is covered again with a silt-like deposit which may vary in depth from a film to actual ripples on the kitchen floor." Some of the world's most fertile farmlands turned to desert.

In 1935, Congress was debating a bill to make the SCS (Bennett's preferred name) a permanent agency within the U.S. Department of Agriculture. Called to testify for the bill on April 2, 1935, Bennett knew beforehand that a major dust storm was blowing toward Washington, District of Columbia. During testimony Bennett detailed the intricate facts of soil erosion. He belabored points, adding broad but nuanced answers to questions meant to elicit a concise response. The delaying tactic served two goals. First, Bennett needed to emphasize the facts of conservation and the causes of the Dust Bowl. In 1934, *The New York*

Times editorialized that the "explanation of the storms is quite simple . . . the soil from the West is drier than usual." The ways farmers used the soil was of secondary concern. Second, Bennett knew the storm, and the dramatic impact it could have on the Senate, was on its way. Eventually the sky darkened; one senator wondered if a rainstorm had descended upon the capital. Many senators walked over to the window where they witnessed not the sodden thunderclouds of a rainstorm, but a thick blanket of dust settling over the capital city. The bill passed Congress unanimously and was signed into law by FDR on April 27, 1935.

The SCS offered residents of the plains the hope of regaining working farms. The SCS readily used CCC enrollees to perform its tedious labor. That number expanded greatly as fighting the Dust Bowl became a national priority. As noted by CCC historian Neil Maher, from March 1935 "until Congress terminated the CCC in 1942, the Soil Erosion Service supervised approximately 30 percent of all Corps camps nationwide." The SCS taught farmers new methods of plowing and planted shelterbelts of trees (about 217 million of them) to designate property lines and to stabilize loose soil.

Between 1937 and 1942, the SCS rehabilitated millions of farmland acres; it restored over a million acres of damaged soil in the Amarillo, Texas, area alone. Conservation allowed farmers to remain on the land. Bennett and his SCS thus embraced the philosophy of the New Conservation: "Eroded soils," he wrote, "make for eroded people." Conservation produced the precise opposite: it "has stabilized the people *on* the land and well as the land itself."

Bennett saw the fundamental problem the SCS faced as needing to "penetrate the wall of a traditional, exploitative, erosion-inducing farming system and introduce an ever-widening wedge of scientifically sound, modern, conservation agriculture." The best way to do this was to demonstrate to farmers the successes of new methods, then allow them to implement the needed changes. Demonstration farms allowed farmers to see for themselves: "The results of an applied program of erosion control," wrote Bennett, "taken from a large number of demonstration projects . . . will illustrate the relation of this kind of work to the alleviation of rural difficulties caused by excessive soil erosion." After witnessing such demonstrations, "farmers themselves decide what they want to do to improve their land and water resources, and how they go about doing it."

Demonstration also granted democratic credibility to conservation agriculture: "Soil Conservation Districts are, of course, essentially democratic mechanisms," argued Bennett. "They are the farmers' own governmental units—of, for and by the farmers." Land use capability surveys were one tool put into the hands of farmers. The survey was a map, usually color-coded, which described, "No more than about five land classes. These classes range from land of such favorable quality as to require no special treatment for proper cultivation . . . through land that requires a variety of treatments . . . to land that should never be cultivated under any circumstances." Government could suggest reform, but farmers had to implement it.

While Bennett was successful at reform, the larger question of capitalism and its relationship to nature remained unanswered. Still, the New Deal engaged this most profound question in a meaningful way. In 1936 Roosevelt empaneled a group of experts, the Drought Area Committee, to make recommendations for plains agriculture. Its report, *The Future of the Great Plains*, charged "plowing and overcropping" with causing the Dust Bowl; it argued that the "Plainsman . . . must realize that he cannot 'conquer nature'—he must live with her on her own terms." Living with nature on her own terms meant that the number of plainsmen mattered greatly. The government must "consider how great a population, and in what areas, the Great Plains can support." Too many people employing the wrong farming techniques amounted to "an attempt to impose upon the region a system of agriculture to which the Plains are not adapted." Humans must conform to nature's limits.

Bennett preached the same sermon: "Man may for a time attempt to impose artificial and economic consideration on the use of land. But ultimately the inexorable influence of physical laws will prevail and man will come face to face with the utter necessity of cooperating—not competing—with nature in the use of land." Recognizing the limits of nature was a consistent theme of Bennett's speeches. Addressing the "Engineering and Human Affairs" Conference at the Princeton University in 1946, he argued that, "We cannot dig deeper into the Earth and find new productive soil. We cannot pump it from wells, plant it with seeds, or dig it from mines. We must keep what we have or do without, for when soil has been washed or blown into the oceans it is not recoverable." For civilization to thrive, it can't treat soil like dirt.

One driving force behind the forceful conclusions of *The Future of the Great Plains* was Lewis Cecil Gray (1881–1952). With a University of Wisconsin doctorate in economics, Gray left academics for a career in government. He started with the Land Economics Division of the Bureau of Agricultural Economics, then became an assistant to Rexford Tugwell in the Resettlement Administration. His writing spanned his academic and governmental careers; in 1932 he published an important history, the *History of Agriculture in the Southern United States to 1860*. In his work as an historian and as a policy innovator, Gray argued that the problems of American land use arose from unfettered capitalism. Capitalism was particularly destructive on the Great Plains, Gray asserted, because the United States prized individualism, unlike Europe which had "social or collectivist" impulses that restrained individual acquisitiveness.

Like most New Dealers, Gray did not want to repudiate capitalism, but rather use conservation as a means "to find an intermediate ground between laissez-faire capitalism and socialism." Gray was not just a philosopher. He pushed for the Taylor Grazing Act of 1934, which declared most of the unappropriated grasslands left in the United States—about eighty million acres—as a common grazing resource managed by local livestock growers. He also pushed the federal purchase of submarginal lands—officially the Land Utilization Project—that removed 11.3 million acres (of an originally proposed seventy-five million acres) of Appalachian hillsides, cut over Midwestern forests and Great Plains grasslands, from production. Most significantly, Gray also proposed a decentralized committee of county planners that would nudge "the recalcitrant individual" farmer who failed to engage in wise conservation measures toward more sound practices.

Americans have yet to follow Gray's wise counsel, though some reforms have helped the plains. The Conservation Reserve Program, revitalized in the 1985 farm bill, allows the U.S. Department of Agriculture to make voluntary agreements with farmers to exclude environmentally sensitive lands (usually erodible croplands) from production. But far from adapting to the Great Plains, farmers have avoided the problem of limits by mining fossil waters from the Ogallala Aquifer. But that water has run out in some areas and has become cost prohibitive to pump in others. As Jim Casey, deputy chief of planning for the Bureau of Reclamation, put it, "no aquifer [such as the Ogallala] can sustain this rate of pumping. There goes your whole economy. This corner of the world is going to be Appalachia without trees."

The draining of the aquifer is severe enough that in 2015 the *Kansas City Star* reported that "the days of irrigation for western Kansas seem numbered." Farmers responded to the lack of water by enlisting advanced technologies to extend the use of what water was available and by creating voluntary pacts with neighbors not to irrigate. "It's not that I can say, 'Oh, this is the next people's problem,'" Kansas farmer Brant Peterson told the *Star*. "No, this is my problem. It's happening now." The problem is dire enough that Kansas Governor Sam Brownback, a hard-right antagonist of government involvement in the economy, proposed diverting water from the Missouri River via a 360-mile aqueduct to western Kansas. But such plans are fraught with environmental, political, and economic challenges. One likely future for the Great Plains is a large increase in dry land farming, with concomitant decreases in production and profitability.

The ideology of New Deal agricultural reform—that poor land produces poor people—had been advocated for decades by a variety of progressive agricultural reformers. Prominent among these was George Washington Carver (1860s–1943), the soil scientist at the Tuskegee Institute in Macon County, Alabama. Often reductively misremembered as a mere champion of the peanut, Carver was in fact a proponent of social betterment through agricultural reform. "Wherever the soil is wasted," wrote Carver in 1938, "the people are wasted. A poor soil produces only a poor people—poor economically, poor spiritually and intellectually, poor physically." Despite many such pronouncements seemingly so congruent with the New Deal's New Conservation, Carver, a black man working in the South, was on the outside of the larger political conversation. Carver also eschewed politics, instead espousing a vision of humanity united by adherence to the golden rule and informed by scientific agriculture.

Carver's outsider status should not detract from his conservation legacy. Carver grew up in Iowa but made his career among the abused soils of the Alabama Black Belt. His vision of agriculture was conventional, with two important exceptions. Carver defined agriculture as "the cultivation or the manipulation of the soil in such a way as to bring about the greatest possible yields of products useful to man." Crucially, his definition continued by asserting that those yields must be gained "with the least injury to the soil and at the least expense." Soils and expenses were vital. Carver felt that educated farmers, and especially poor black farmers, could harvest nature's bounty and thus improve their social and economic standing. "It is a source of regret," lamented Carver, "that we do not appreciate what Nature has so lavishly provided for us." Vegetables were a good example. "Nature has provided us with an almost innumerable variety of wild vegetables," a bounty that serves "not only as food, but as medicine."

Teaching others, especially farmers, to properly appreciate nature's lavishness was Carver's calling. Most broadly, the smart farmer and informed citizen should appreciate "the mutual relationship of the animal, mineral, and vegetable kingdoms." More specifically, Carver advocated enriching soil via crop rotation and manuring, and argued that farmers should fulfill needs through efficient reuse of waste and byproducts. Carver promoted the cultivation of nitrogen-fixing cowpeas (*Vigna unguiculata*)—they were "indispensable in a wise crop rotation"—and green manuring, the plowing under of green crops for soil enrichment. The soil experiment stations so beloved by Hugh Hammond Bennet were also greatly admired by Carver, who called them the best things that ever happened to America's rural poor.

Nor did Carver believe that interaction with nature was simply a matter of expediency. For Carver, as with his fellow nature study proponents, the study of the natural world "encourages personal investigation, stimulates originality [and] awakens higher and nobler ideas." An appreciation of flowers, for example, provides "never ending delight to the lovers of the beautiful." Carver taught these ideas at the Tuskegee Institute, but also through his many publications, at the annual Negro Farmer's Conference and even (early in the twentieth century) though the Jessup Agricultural Wagon, a school-on-wagon-wheels that reached out to rural farmers. Carver summarized his advice with a subtle jab at Jim Crow: "Be kind to the soil" he implored his readers, "unkindness to anything means an injustice done to that thing." And though most people considered such golden rule morality as a guide for social relationships, Carver emphasized that it applied "with equal force to the soil."

National parks could also be used to teach people about nature's lavishness, and one underappreciated legacy of FDR's New Deal is his expansion and democratization of public lands. One reason for FDR's success with national parks was due to the influence of his Secretary of the Interior Harold Ickes. Ickes was a progressive Republican so appalled at the do-nothing response of Herbert Hoover to the depression that he led an exodus of liberal Republicans (including FDR's secretary of agriculture and future Vice President Henry A. Wallace) into the Democratic party. The brusque Ickes, who christened himself "the old curmudgeon," was the staunchest and most effective advocate of parks that the Interior Department had ever seen. Under his visionary leadership and ruthless political maneuvering, the number of national monuments increased from thirty-three to eighty-six. These include such treasures as Cedar Breaks, Zion and Capital Reef in Utah, Jackson Hole in Wyoming, Organ Pipe in Arizona, and the George Washington Carver National Monument in Missouri. The amount of lands in national parks and monuments increased from fourteen million acres in 1933 to twenty million acres by 1946.

Roosevelt established seven new national parks. He declared 1934 the "Year of the National Park." Parks also figured into his relief efforts. CCC enrollees built the campgrounds, visitor centers, fire watchtowers, and roads of Shenandoah and the Great Smokey Mountains National Parks, which FDR designated in 1935 and 1934, respectively. Locals enthusiastically backed the projects, knowing that the parks would bring tourist dollars to their region. The New Deal also offered conservation employment to locals who were married or too old to enroll in the CCC. Knowing the importance of resident support for a project, the CCC hired "local experienced men" to instruct the "green" enrollees how to work.

FDR enlarged the Park Service with new nature parks and by expanding its mission to include historic preservation. Historic sites such as the Civil War battlefields Gettysburg, Vicksburg, and Shiloh needed preservation. The Park Service, which already managed such historic and archeological sites as Bandolier in New Mexico, was the natural home for a system of unified federal preservation that included historic and wilderness parks. Roosevelt backed and won the Historic Sites Act of 1935, which made the conservation of historic sites a National Park Service obligation. Historic preservation was now understood to be a government duty, something hinted at but unexpressed in the Antiquities Act of 1906.

Establishing parks continued to involve some social dislocation. To create Shenandoah National Park, the Roosevelt administration relocated about 450 families from the Blue Ridge. Unlike the native peoples removed from western parks, these families were compensated for their troubles. But one can't help but wonder how their status as poor rural people fed into their treatment by government. Locals could and did push back. Their success depended upon their political organization. The small township system of Vermont, for example, allowed locals to influence outcomes in regional planning decisions. But the large, dispersed areas governed by counties in Virginia granted individuals only a tenuous connection to federal decision making. Rural Vermonters thus influenced the federal government's decisions about their local lands more than their Virginia counterparts.

A more salutary legacy of New Deal public lands was the anti-racist work undertaken by New Deal planners. Two New Deal leaders were particularly important for these efforts: Harold Ickes and Robert Marshall. Before accepting a cabinet position, Ickes was a longtime civil rights advocate and president of the Chicago chapter of the National Association for the Advancement of Colored People. Ickes enlisted the well-publicized "Black Kitchen Cabinet," an informal group of African-American public policy experts, to advise him on civil rights matters. In 1933, Ickes abolished segregation in the cafeteria and rest rooms of the Interior Department. When queried about Jim Crow segregation in the National Parks by Walter White of the National Association for the Advancement of Colored People, Ickes replied that "everyone, regardless of creed, color, or race, who conforms to the rules and regulations, is invited to visit the national parks and monuments." But at the same time, Ickes allowed that "it has long been the policy" of the parks "to conform generally to the State customs with regard to accommodation of visitors." Ickes was not yet willing to combat Jim Crow in the southern parks.

Ickes's attitude changed in part due to William J. Trent Jr., a black graduate of the Wharton School of the University of Pennsylvania who became Ickes's advisor on Negro affairs. Trent described his job as "securing maximum Negro participation" in New Deal programs. Trent emphasized not only the unjustness of segregation, but that the larger purposes of the parks in terms of education and recreation should not be denied to any American. Ickes was on board, but the politics were tricky. He had clashed with segregationist senators such as Carter Glass of Virginia, who had publicly denounced him for "openly" advocating for "the repeal of all segregation laws." Southern senators chaired many key Senate committees; how much political capital could Ickes spend?

Ickes settled on a strategy of desegregating specific facilities instead of the parks as a whole. The "Sexton Knoll" picnic area in Shenandoah National Park was desegregated in 1938 and renamed the "Pinnacles Picnic Ground." No one noticed, let alone protested, and the strategy was set. The Lewis Mountain campground was similarly desegregated. The strategy worked especially well after World War II erupted. The Interior Department issued no press releases, but quietly removed segregationist facilities under the cover of wartime patriotism. The strange but comparatively brief career of Jim Crow in the national parks was over.

Trent was not the only voice in Ickes's ear that demanded desegregation. Robert Marshall was a civil rights activist concerned with segregated campgrounds. "Negroes are scared to use our campgrounds," observed Marshall; hence they are "used only by white people." Were segregated campgrounds the answer? Some progressives thought so; theoretically they would at least allow for more use of the parks by blacks. But Marshall worried that segregated campgrounds involved "having the government openly recognize the principle of discrimination." The only answer seemed to be a nondiscrimination policy.

Marshall had little influence with the Park Service, but had real effect on Forest Service policy. He was a great believer in the public mission of the service; in 1933, he published *The People's Forests* which made a passionate case for the public ownership of the nation's forests in the face of generations of ecologically devastating lumbering. For Marshall, the forests were a storehouse of natural resources and a place for "the happiness of millions of human beings." But all Americans couldn't be happy if the Forest Service allowed openly discriminatory private operators to use its lands. Anti-Semitism was an important issue: the Sahnaro Lake Ranch of Arizona advertised "the patronage of Gentiles only is desired"; Lairds' Lodge in Montana refused "guests of the Jewish faith"; the H.F. Bar Ranch in Wyoming advertised their broad policy of not accepting guests "against whom there can be the slightest racial, moral, physical or social objection." Marshall fumed and advocated that the Forest Service refuse to permit any private group that practiced discrimination. The recreation policy committee initially refused; they worried that the policy was unenforceable in the South and that southern congressmen would cut their funding. But in 1938 Marshall earned a victory when the Forest Service issued a nondiscrimination policy for its permittees.

Battles over segregated campgrounds and other discriminatory practices emphasized that no matter how serene or remote, nature was no escape from society. And that fact helps us understand with greater precision why nonwhite people rarely used campgrounds. To do so we can visit the first national park in the east: Acadia National Park. Among its many charms are its incredible shoreline, a mosaic of rocky coves, cobblestone shores, and intertidal pools. The great sociologist and civil rights activist W.E.B. Du Bois loved it: "God molded this world largely and mightily off this marvelous coast," wrote an astonished Du Bois in his essay "Of Beauty and Death." He sounded a great deal like John Muir. "In the tired days of life men should come and worship here and renew their spirit." The Maine coast evoked in him a powerful "human awe." For Du Bois, it was the "glory of physical nature" that evinced the "divine."

Nature's glory brought to Du Bois's mind a key question: "Why do not those who are scarred in the world's battle and hurt by its hardness travel to these places for beauty and drown themselves in the utter joy of life?" The answer for black people was straightforward: "Did you ever see a 'Jim-Crow' waiting room?" They had "no heat in winter and no air in summer." Purchasing a ticket was a "torture" of rudeness and ignorance. Seats for blacks were old, dirty, and grimy. The conductor was disrespectful and bossy. The toilets were gross ("don't" use them advised Du Bois—but what was the alternative?), and "lunch rooms either don't serve niggers or serve them at some dirty and ill-attended hole in the wall." Maine was beautiful, even transcendent, but was it worth bearing such awful circumstances to get there?

For Du Bois, Jim Crow not only explained the low number of blacks in parks and other wild lands, but also the reason blacks were (ostensibly) slower to adopt progressive farming methods. In his celebrated book *The Souls of Black Folk*, he explained that black tenant farmers "are careless because they have not found that it pays to be careful; they are improvident because the improvident ones of their acquaintance get on about as well as the provident." Land ownership and accruing value was key. Blacks "cannot see why they should take unusual pains to make the white man's land better." Conversely, the white landowner shows "the scarred and wretched land" to a northern visitor and then proclaims,

"This is Negro freedom!" Du Bois thus understood that racial animosity obeyed a circular and self-perpetuating logic. Debased people debased the land.

Even those not facing segregation and able to consume faced unknown dangers. One of the great muckraking books of the 1930s was *100,000,000 Guinea Pigs: Dangers in Everyday Foods, Drugs and Cosmetics* by Arthur Kallet and F.J. Schlink. *100,000,000 Guinea Pigs* levied a broad indictment of products sold to the public—particularly pharmaceuticals and food products—that were either untested or known to be dangerous. The book clearly struck a deep chord. It went through thirteen editions in its first six months and became one of the best-selling books of the decade. Kallet and Schlink ascribed the problem to a society that had "sanctified the fastest acquisition of the greatest number of dollars" as the only achievement, a situation that enabled "misrepresentation and exploitation" to be "the unfailing handmaidens of success."

In the fall of 1937 a chemical tragedy emphasized the need for reform. At least seventy-one adults and thirty-four children died after they were prescribed the drug elixir sulfanilamide. Researchers had shown that the compound's active ingredient, sulfanilamide, protected against bacterial infections in mice. The S.E. Massengill Company used the compound as part of a fluid—they mixed it with diethylene glycol—and aggressively marketed it as a treatment for ailments ranging from sore throats to gonorrhea. They were free to do so. Government approval was not required to market new drugs; the 1906 Pure Food and Drug Act only required the U.S. Food and Drug Administration to police claims against adulterated drugs. After doctors established the toxicity of elixir sulfanilamide, Massengill initially did little to prevent further prescriptions then helped government agents in a mad rush to find and safely destroy remaining supplies of the drug.

100,000,000 Guinea Pigs developed a number of ideas central to the environmental critique of chemical commercialism. Synergy effects are the greater outcomes of multiple substances mixed together. American consumers are not only exposed to individual chemicals, but to different individual chemicals reacting together. The authors also advocated the precautionary principle in which manufacturers should demonstrate the safety of a product before releasing it to the market. Over a hundred Americans would have lived if Massengill had to demonstrate the efficacy of elixir sulfanilamide before they sold it. The success of *100,000,000*

Guinea Pigs and the elixir sulfanilamide debacle led to the passage in 1938 of the Federal Food, Drug, and Cosmetic Act.

Other critiques of New Deal conservation arose from an ecological mindset. The orgy of road building by the CCC provoked concerns about the necessity of protecting large swaths of comparatively untouched nature. As America urbanized, more and more Americans were learning about nature through leisure, rather than through the labor of farm work or the lumber camp. But would they still find wild nature on our public lands? Conservationist Leonard Wing, writing in *American Forests* in 1936, worried that "we shall look upon the early days of the CCC as a crowning blunder in conservation." The reason was that CCC enrollees, armed with "saws, axes and shovels," removed "deciduous growth." But in removing snags and fallen logs, the CCC removed the "browse for deer [and] buds for grouse . . . [and] drumming logs for partridges." What was needed instead was the counsel of the "conservation biologist" who could recommend "the better application of biological and ecological principles."

Many activists agreed with Wing, and conservation began to reform from within. Among the most effective reformers was Rosalie Edge (1877–1962), who lamented that our national forests were "honeycombed with roads." "The lumberman walks softly behind the roadmaker," explained an exasperated Edge, "computing the profit to be gained from trees which were already old when Columbus discovered America." Even more shameful, wrote Edge in 1934, was the "teaching of our CCC boys to poison harmless and valuable wild creatures." Five years later she evoked the "profound study of ecology" to denounce predator control as violating "the balance of all living things." Prompted by Edge, the Audubon Society engaged in a decade-long campaign to reform the CCC along more ecological grounds. Environmental activists were charging that the Corps was ecologically reckless. In doing so they were evoking the science of ecology in ways that demanded the reform of not just conservation, but of society as a whole.

Edge was an unlikely radical, as she was born into the privilege of a Fifth Avenue high-rise that overlooked Central Park. But after first becoming involved in suffragist politics—she worked with the Equal Franchise Society and with Carrie Chapman Catt in the New York State Women Suffrage Party—Edge moved into conservation, mostly inspired by her love of birds. Though not herself religious, she held that

Figure 4.2 The "indomitable hellcat" of conservation, Rosalie Edge reformed both staid conservation organizations and helped Americans see the value of predators. Courtesy of Hawk Mountain Sanctuary Archives

in viewing a bird, "we see not the inspiration of God filtered thorough human agency, but the very handiwork of the Creator himself." She was an avid birdwatcher and accumulated an impressive "life list" of 804 species viewed. After finding out about overhunting on lands managed by the National Association of Audubon Societies (now the National Audubon Society), she embarked on reform from within by speaking up at meetings and in exerting outside pressure through her Emergency Conservation Committee.

Edge supported hunting, even of birds, but only if well regulated; she opposed indiscriminate killing and use of poisons. In 1934 she founded

Hawk Mountain in Pennsylvania, the first sanctuary for birds of prey in the United States. "Man hates any creature that kills and eats," reasoned Edge; "He does not take into account the millions of rodents and insect pests that hawks consume." Edge thus became an important figure in the popular reappraisal of predator species. Her lasting work was not just for wilderness on Forest Service lands, but in expanding the national park system as well. Edge campaigned to enlarge Crater Lake, Sequoia, and Yellowstone National Parks to include lands biologically critical to the surrounding ecosystems. Her fellow Audubon reformer Willard Van Name dubbed her "the only honest, unselfish, indomitable hellcat in the history of conservation." Historian Stephen Fox appropriately included her as a key example of a "radical amateur" who continually challenged the complacency of "conservation professionals" such as those men employed by the Forest Service.

No writer-activist was more important to the ecological reform of conservation than Aldo Leopold (1887–1948). Like Edge, Leopold initially supported the CCC, but soon criticized it on ecological grounds: "The abstract categories we have set up as conservation objectives may serve as alibies for blunders." As evidence Leopold cited the "CCC crew which chopped down one of the few remaining eagle's nests in northern Wisconsin, in the name of 'timber stand improvement.'" His critique extended from the local to the national. The CCC had drained "the whole Atlantic tidal marsh from Maine to Alabama" forgetting, or not ever knowing, that such wetlands are key "wintering ground for many species of migratory waterfowl and the breeding ground of others." The CCC lacked the ecological understanding to gauge the impacts of their actions on the larger ecology.

Leopold's criticism reflected his own changing appreciation of how to manage nature. Born in Burlington, Iowa, Leopold received a nature study childhood. "Bird study" was his favorite subject and he spent hours outside, writing and drawing the natural world. He attended the Yale School of Forestry and after completing his master's degree pursued a career with the Forest Service. In 1909 Leopold, then a young man "full of trigger itch," shot a wolf he encountered in Arizona's Apache National Forest. This was not unusual. Like many conservationists Leopold was an avid hunter and "predator control" dominated conservationist thinking. After firing he scrambled toward the animal, just in time to witness "a fierce green fire dying in her eyes." It startled him into a fundamental ecological realization: if wolves were exterminated—something "state after state" was doing—deer will overpopulate, overgraze the mountain (making it look "as if someone had given God a new pruning shears"), and then starve to death on the denuded hillsides where wolves once hunted. "I now suspect that just as a deer herd lives in mortal fear of its wolves, so does a mountain live in mortal fear of its deer," wrote Leopold.

The ecological consequences of predator control dramatically emphasized Leopold's point. For example, predator control on the Kaibab Plateau, a heavily forested highland bordering the Grand Canyon, caused a mass deer starvation. When the area was incorporated into the Grand Canyon Game Preserve in 1905, deer hunting was prohibited while government hunters simultaneously worked to extirpate wolves, mountain lions, coyotes, and other predators from the area. Soon the deer population "irrupted" and overgrazed plateau flora—thus reducing the carrying capacity of the ecosystem—which led to their mass death by starvation.

Leopold cited the starvation of the Kaibab deer as a classic example of game mismanagement. The story was of course more complicated than an easy morality tale of misguided predator control. Domestic grazing animals had also been removed from the area—did that account for the rise in deer populations?—and how reliable were estimates of deer populations anyway? But recent scientific surveys of the area's historic vegetation patterns support the basic structure of Leopold's deer irruption story. The Kaibab deer irruption has been widely used to illustrate how ecological understanding must be part of wildlands management. Species must be understood in the context of their environment. These and many other insights led Leopold to publish in 1933 his now classic textbook on managing and restoring wildlife populations, *Game Management*.

What makes Leopold a central figure in American environmental history is that he did not stop at applying science to the comparatively narrow issues of public lands management. Leopold understood that scientific information alone could not guide human interaction with complex ecological realities; Americans must also rethink economics and ethics. His insights have been profoundly influential on environmentalists ever since. For Leopold, economics did not have a satisfactory way of handling concepts like wilderness or beauty or even the basic health of the land. As early as 1934 Leopold decried the "too narrow" limits that confine our "political and economic law and custom." Economics

Figure 4.3 Aldo Leopold remains an enormously important prophet of environmentalism. He worked for wilderness, for ethical reform that would include the land as an object of human ethical concern, and was an early restoration ecologist.

dominated the relationship between people and the land, even for conservationists. But econometric valuations did not work and even fostered environmental degradation: "The land-relation is still strictly economic," wrote Leopold, "entailing privileges but not obligations." We must "quit thinking about decent land use as solely an economic problem."

Bound up with rethinking the economy demanded by real conservation was a thoroughgoing rethinking of ethics. "Conservation is getting nowhere," argued Leopold, "because it is incompatible with our Abrahamic concept of land." In the most famous passage of his 1949 classic *A Sand County Almanac, and Sketches Here and There*, Leopold called for a new ethic that incorporated the insights of ecological science to enlarge human ethical consideration to include the land itself. "The land ethic," explained Leopold, "simply enlarges the boundaries of the community to include soils, waters, plants, and animals, or collectively, the land." Most profoundly, humans can no longer consider nature as a mere backdrop to society or a resource to be exploited. Rather, the land ethic "changes the role of Homo sapiens from conqueror of the land community to plain member and citizen of it." The good or right, then, is determined not by utilitarian values or economic measure, but by whether a thing "tends to preserve the integrity, stability, and beauty of the biotic community. It is wrong when it tends otherwise." In keeping with the democratization of land under the New Deal, Leopold held that such ethics were not only for scientists or professional land managers, but must be internalized by American society as a whole.

But the land ethic held especially true for land managers such as Leopold. The green fire within the wolf's eyes haunted Leopold, and his ethics incorporated the predator as a key to ecological health. In his essay "Round River," Leopold concluded that

> Harmony with land is like harmony with a friend; you cannot cherish his right hand and chop off his left. That is to say, you cannot love game and hate predators, you cannot conserve the waters and waste the ranges, you cannot build the forest and mine the farm. The land is one organism.

As with the Dust Bowl, if humans failed to recognize these ecological limits, they endangered their own health and even survival. Leopold's thought was public and practical, emphasizing that all citizens share a vital interest in ecological health.

The land ethic also highlighted a driving force for many environmental activists—the fascination with and love for the wild things of nature. Many people are greatly moved by the sheer magic of what Charles Darwin called "endless forms most beautiful and most wonderful." John Muir observed how "Any glimpse into the life of an animal quickens our own and makes it so much the larger and better every way." Leopold built on this heritage by beginning *A Sand County Almanac* with the simple observation that, "There are some who can live without wild things, and some who cannot. These essays are the delights and dilemmas of one who cannot." Understanding humans as part of the natural world enlarged human morality to account for nature in ways that pretending nature is separate from people cannot.

Like any real ethics, the inclusion of wild things into human consideration required change. "Wild things were taken for granted," observed Leopold, "until progress began to do away with them." Beyond being delighted by wild things, their preservation was of utilitarian value. Humans have little understanding of nature, but we must interact with it. Basic humility and common sense, then, require us "To keep every cog and wheel" of nature, which Leopold designated "the first precaution of intelligent tinkering." Leopold was no Luddite; it was not technology per se, but the lack of ecological and social restraint, the belief in "salvation by machinery," that drove the culture into harmful relationship with wild nature.

Insofar as the New Deal pushed Americans into a more intelligent tinkering with nature, it must be measured as a profound success. Another success was the New Deal's combining of social and environmental reform—as Leopold's criticism of economics demands that we do. New Deal conservation, and Leopold's criticism of it, also set the stage for what we today call "sustainable development": incorporating long-term environmental planning into the fundamentals of civil society. Both the New Deal's real achievements and the social and ecological criticisms of its faults enabled many of the most important environmental reforms of the postwar era.

The New Deal also proved to be a valuable precedent for innovative contemporary conservationists. Following the 2008 financial collapse, many environmentalists called for a "New Green Deal" that addressed the economic collapse and dire ecological problems such as climate disruption. The lawyer and political activist Van Jones, for example, "came to understand that the answer to our social, economic and ecological crises can be one and the same: a green economy strong enough to lift people out of poverty." To create the green economy Jones called for a "New Green Deal" brought about by a political coalition he dubbed the "Green Growth Alliance." The alliance would consist of labor, social justice activists, environmentalists, students, and faith organizations. "Their goal," writes Jones, "would be straightforward: to win government policy that promotes the interests of green capital and green technology over the interests of gray capital (extractive industries, fossil-fuel companies) in a way that spreads the benefits as widely as possible." Like FDR's New Deal, Jones's Green Growth Alliance would solve economic deprivation through environmental reform.

Jones's call for a New Green Deal was unquestionably smart given the dramatic social pain inflicted by the 2008 financial crisis and the systematic environmental challenges such as climate disruption that the nation desperately needed to address. Alternative energy sources really can generate clean energy and put millions to work in fulfilling, socially necessary, good-paying jobs. But the larger question embedded in such proposals—how much can an economy grow given the limits of nature?—remained unresolved. It is a question that would repeatedly and forcefully animate environmental politics in the postwar years.

6

DAMMING THE ARID WEST

Whiskey Is for Drinking;
Water Is for Fighting Over.

–Western Adage

LIKE THE Zen Buddhist gardens they sometimes resemble, the vast desert landscapes of the American West provoke many people into serious contemplation about the relationship between people and nature. On a float trip—one of the last—through Utah's Glen Canyon, the desert environmentalist Edward Abbey mused that "From the mortally human point of view, the landscape of the Colorado [River] is like a section of eternity—timeless. . . . Men come and go, cities rise and fall, whole civilizations appear and disappear—the earth remains, slightly modified . . . [a] heartbreaking beauty where there are no hearts to break." Abbey made the high desert plateaus and meandering red rock canyons of the American southwest his home place, but he always questioned its prospects for maintaining civilization. He was hardly the first American to do so. Perhaps it comes from the stark contours of the landscape itself. The austerity, the impression of vacancy, and all the possibilities that implies—deserts seem designed to elicit basic questions about the relationship between humans and the rest of nature. The deciduous forests of the humid east replaced themselves comparatively easily. The desert offered few if any second chances. If people are to thrive there, they must account for the land in ways that other environments allow them to ignore.

The battles over how the desert might house American civilization are some of the most profound in American history. Beyond marveling over the parched landscapes of the southwest, the question of adapting to their limits included the problem of the political organization of those lands. Referred to as the Great American Desert by some map-makers in the nineteenth century, many Americans concluded the southwest did not receive enough rain to permit large-scale agriculture or high population densities. American deserts were not places to live, but places to cross, a dangerous bridge to more habitable terrain. Others found in the desert a chance to remake democracy along ecological lines, a laboratory for testing the notion that environments shaped the course of civilization. Still others found aridity a challenge to overcome. For them, deserts were an invitation to irrigation and a future of green prosperity. For useful cranks such as Abbey, the desert was the last retreat, a place to escape from an overbearing society, from intrusive government, from industrial civilization itself. If the New World offered Americans the promise of a democracy based upon abundance, deserts promised the end of the eternal frontier.

The most revolutionary early appreciator of deserts and democracy was John Wesley Powell (1834–1902). When Powell encountered the desert, he pondered how society might fruitfully adapt to its arid limits. His solution was to organize society along the topographies of natural watersheds instead of through the political geographies that governments artificially imposed upon the landscape. His proposed West was not just shaped by the watershed, but one of organically organized communities devoted to democratic control and conservation of the inhabited landscape. Settlement should occur through the ground truth of river basins and stream drainages, rather than the abstract rectilinear acres of the government surveyor. For Powell, private property, individualism, competition, and 160-acre agriculture were maladaptive to life in the arid west.

Powell was born in New York, but grew up farming the open prairie lands of Ohio, Wisconsin, and Illinois. The son of abolitionist Methodists, Powell eagerly volunteered for Civil War duty. At the Battle of Shiloh, a Confederate Minié ball shattered his right forearm; surgeons amputated the limb two days later. Powell later returned to active duty, commanding artillery batteries at Vicksburg as well as during the Atlanta campaign and the Battle of Nashville. Following the war, he became a professor of natural sciences before leading two daring scientific explorations of the Colorado River. Those extraordinary adventures made Powell a national figure. Following the Utah canyons of the Colorado River, Powell's expedition encountered new, unnamed places. One he christened Glen Canyon was full of "wonderful features—carved walls, royal arches, glens, alcove gulches, mounds and monuments." Beyond new canyons, Powell met many native peoples. Their lifeways and languages fascinated him. Paiutes named Powell "Kapurats"—he who is missing an arm. Powell detailed both expeditions in his 1875 book *Exploration of the Colorado River of the West and Its Tributaries* (reprinted in 1895 as *Canyons of the Colorado*). Powell also produced the first comprehensive linguistic survey of North America's indigenous languages, *Indian Linguistic Families of America, North of Mexico* (1891).

Upon returning east, Powell carved out an important career as an institution builder in Washington, District of Columbia. In 1879, he was appointed the first director of the U.S. Bureau of Ethnology. During his tenure, he championed native interests and attempted "to organize anthropologic research in America." Powell held the post until his death; he also served as director of the U.S. Geological Survey from 1881 to 1894. These policy-making positions, as well as his explorations, helped him see the folly of how the desert west was being settled.

There were mountains of folly to be seen. Lured west by the Homestead Act and, more specifically, the Desert Lands Act of 1877, settlers struggled to farm under harsh desert conditions. The Desert Lands Act offered settlers unsurveyed 640-acre lots at $1.25 per acre if they irrigated the land within three years. But single individuals or families did not have the capital, infrastructure, or expertise to irrigate hundreds of acres; for them the promise of land proved to be a cruel hoax. One such investor was Pat Garrett, the lawman famed for killing outlaw William

Figure 6.1 John Wesley Powell argued that the U.S. government should respect native American treaty rights, and that settlement of the West should follow the natural contours of the watershed—not the arbitrary political boundaries imposed on the land.
Courtesy National Archives

"Billy the Kid" Bonney in 1880. Despite discovering a basin of water near Roswell, New Mexico, Garrett's repeated attempts to capitalize on the resource all failed. He was not alone. By 1902, 90 percent of irrigation companies were in or near bankruptcy. Beyond the inability of small investors to make a go of irrigation, the Desert Lands Act also provoked an orgy of land speculation from large corporate investors. Many were livestock grazing syndicates that used the flimsiest definitions of irrigation to expropriate huge tracts of the public domain into private hands.

Powell, a populist wary of corporate power, wished to settle the west in a vastly different manner. For Powell, forests should protect river headwaters. Communities would manage them, and timbering would be limited to careful harvesting. Meadowlands below the forests would be open to grazing, again with communal rules to abrogate overgrazing and to protect soils from erosion. Homesteading would occur along bottomlands where individual farmers could irrigate their crops. Only local control that adapts to local conditions could make the system work. Thus Powell urged the North Dakota legislature in 1890 to "fix it in your Constitution that no corporation—no body of men—no capital can get possession and right to your waters. Hold the waters in the hands of the people." Watersheds required local, democratic control—the real constituents of resource development.

Social systems that controlled and allocated water in ways similar to what Powell envisioned already existed in the West. Hispanic settlers brought a method of water control from Spain to the New World where it comingled with Native American practices. The fundamental principle was that water was owned communally and distributed as a shared resource. A series of community ditches or *acequias* allocated water among the *acequia* members. A *mayordomo*, or "ditch boss," worked to ensure equitable water distribution and resolved disputes as they arose. It was a very successful system with some *acequias* functioning well to this day, some four hundred years after their founding. The early Mormon settlers of the desert southwest adopted similar strategies. They managed their lands as a common resource and ensured that every farmer received an agreed upon amount of water. At a time when the rest of America was hell bent on an orgy of laissez faire acquisition, these successful societies demonstrated that communal practices could thrive in the American desert.

Not just North Dakotans but the rest of America failed to heed Powell's vision of watershed democracy. He knew that failure would lead to social and political malfunction. Speaking in 1893 to a group of farmers and developers in Los Angeles, Powell warned that "there is not enough water to irrigate all the lands. I tell you gentlemen you are piling up a heritage of conflict and litigation over water rights, for there is not enough water to supply the land." Few statements have ever been as prophetic. A cliché of the twentieth-century west holds that water flows uphill—toward money. While western water developers did not follow Powell's democratic vision, they did adopt, at least rhetorically, some of his principles. Americans recognized that solving the problem of aridity required more than private capital and individual initiative.

The programmatic answer came in 1902, the year of Powell's death, in the form of the Newlands Reclamation Act, named after Nevada Congressman Francis G. Newlands. The Reclamation Service (later renamed the Bureau of Reclamation) embarked on a vast project of damming, diverting, channeling, and otherwise controlling western water. Reclamation would capture water in dams, store it in massive reservoirs, and then reroute it to needy farmers. In a bid to follow Powell's vision of a smallholder west, the bill limited the size of farms that received the bureau's irrigated water to 160 acres. It was classic Gifford Pinchot-style progressive conservation: trained and dispassionate experts (in this case hydraulic engineers) would apply their expertise for the benefit of the broad public. But nowhere did the law mandate local control of water, let alone the inclusion of forest and grazing lands into an integrated system of local resource governance.

The Bureau of Reclamation proved to be technically excellent. Among its key advances was economic long-distance power transmission, which made big dams on big rivers such as the Hoover, Grand Coulee, and Glen Canyon economically feasible. Dams themselves created a new resource: stored water that could be diverted for irrigation or released through turbines to generate hydroelectric power. But reclamation often benefited speculators and industrial-sized farmers at the expense of yeomanry. Reclamation projects were funded by the sale of public lands, but frequently required copious infusions of federal funds to square the books. Small farmers received loans at generous terms, but could rarely repay them; repayment schedules stretched from ten to twenty to fifty years. Western congressmen quickly learned to lobby for reclamation projects in their districts, flooding local constituencies with federal money. While some benefits of reclamation were widely distributed, the corporations, land speculators, and large-scale operators that Powell feared would undermine western democracy were as firmly in place on the landscape as the dams that stored water for them.

If reclamation embodied one powerful strain of progressive conservation—dispassionate technological and scientific expertise deployed in service of the public good—other visions of conservation also arose from the desert. The writer Mary Hunter Austin (1868–1934) articulated one of them. Encouraged by the Homestead Act, Austin moved with her family to the San Joaquin Valley, north of Bakersfield, California, in 1888. The landscape profoundly affected her, as did the people who made it their home. Her vision, most popularly articulated in her 1903 book *Land of Little Rain*, shared some key elements with Powell's. "The earth was the right and property of those who worked it," asserted Austin; "its values should accrue to them if to anybody." Like Edward Abbey who would come to the desert southwest twenty years after her death, Austin found that desert wilderness "brings the first hint of human impotence." Indeed, the desert undermined "the subdued hum of domestic life," forcing people to confront the illusion of "man's dominance of the earth." Austin loved the wild desert, but was also moved by its often-overlooked human inhabitants: native peoples (particularly the Inyo), Hispanics, women. The desert and its human inhabitants made each other; Austin found regional culture to be the "sum, expressed in ways of living, of mutual adaptations of land and people."

Given her appreciation of harsh landscapes and marginalized peoples, it's not surprising that Austin opposed the grand-scale water control projects favored by the Bureau of Reclamation. A powerful feminist, Austin disparaged the "Bitch-Goddess, bigness." She opposed the City of Los Angeles's diversion of water from the Owens Valley because of the political underhandedness of the deal—Los Angeles had laid its "greedy, vulgarizing hand" on the valley—and because it undermined "natural beauty" for the sake of "purely material culture."

Feminist language also informed her protest of the Colorado River Compact (CRC) that apportioned Colorado River water among the southwestern states. The State of Arizona dissented from the deal, feeling it should control the lower river rather than losing water to Los Angeles. Siding with Arizona, Austin decried what she saw as "the rape of the natural resources of one State against that State's consent, for the advantage of another State." The whole project was another example of business and government "woozy with speed and goggle-eyed with [the] infatuation of size." Rather than big dams that allowed for big industry, Austin championed local desert folkways as a means to overcome the psychological alienation of industrial society. In a fitting irony to her legacy, the lands she loved most dearly are now protected under the California Desert Protection Act of 1994, which established Death Valley and Joshua Tree National Parks as well as the Mojave National Preserve.

Those reserves grew in part from the efforts of another desert environmentalist, Minerva Hamilton Hoyt (1866–1945). A genteel southerner transplanted by marriage to Pasadena, California, Hoyt immersed herself in local charities and became a popular leader with the Garden Clubs of America. Her attention to plants led her to value the beauty and inventiveness of desert flora—especially Joshua trees, named by Mormon settlers who saw in their somber, gnarled limbs the uplifted arms of the Old Testament prophet. Hoyt wrote that "the [Mojave] desert with its elusive beauty . . . possessed me and I constantly wished that I might find some ways to preserve its natural beauty." To do so she organized exhibitions of desert flora in such cities as Boston, New York, and London, and in 1930 she founded the International Deserts Conservation League, to, she said, "respond to an urgent demand for the protection of desert life and conservation of desert beauty spots."

Tapped by Frederick Law Olmsted Jr. (like his father a noted landscape architect and also a wildlife conservationist) to serve on the California State Park Commission, she advocated for protected parks in Death Valley, the Anza-Borrego Desert, and for the Joshua tree forests. In June 1933, she took her advocacy all the way to the White House where she charmed and badgered Harold Ickes and Franklin Roosevelt into creating Joshua Tree National Monument in 1936. She also took the international mandate of her organization seriously. She helped convince the government of Mexico to set aside ten thousand acres near Tehuacán for cactus preservation; Mexican President Pascual Ortiz Rubio anointed her the "Apostle of Cacti."

Desert preservation remains an underappreciated legacy of New Deal Conservation. Though FDR did not favor the desert—he preferred the verdant forests of the east—his administration set aside large tracts of land to preserve key desert species. The first was bighorn sheep. Numbering nearly two million when Europeans arrived in the West, overhunting, habitat loss, and introduced diseases reduced their numbers to the thousands. But in 1936 FDR established the 1.5-million-acre Desert Game Range that protected bighorns by protecting the Mojave and Great Basin ecosystems. (The area was renamed the Desert National Wildlife Range in 1966.) It remains the largest refuge in the contiguous United States. One year later FDR established the 330,000-acre Organ Pipe Cactus National Monument to help its namesake octopus-armed cacti. Bordering the Tohono O'odham Indian Reservation, the reserve retained the rights of the Tohono O'odham to harvest the fruits of the organ pipe and other cacti. Roosevelt also established the desert reserves Cedar Breaks National Monument in Utah and Big Bend National Park on the Texas-Mexico border.

Despite these important achievements, grand-scale federal intervention in the west most often took the form of reclamation, not habitat preservation. The great age of dam building in the west—what historian Marc Reisner rightly identified as the "go-go years" of the Bureau of Reclamation—began in the late 1920s under the presidency of Herbert Hoover. Hoover was a curious mix of contradictions regarding conservation. He was an avid fisherman whose very few emotional effusions were reserved for his time in nature. This passion informed his belief that purposeful outdoor recreation made people into better citizens. At the same time, he was a technocrat bent upon "improving" an irrational natural world. "Some waterfalls are in the wrong place," he explained to a reporter in 1924. "We could save water and we could have waterfalls in better locations if we handled the subject of waterfalls with the aid of human intelligence." But for Hoover that intelligence would not be federal; he opposed federal control of resources and generally felt that improvement should be undertaken by private business or local government—the challenges of aridity be dammed.

Hoover broke his commitment to localism when as president he signed in 1928 the Swing-Johnson Bill that created what would become the world's largest dam—initially called the Boulder Dam, now the Hoover Dam—on the Colorado River. It took the failure of private initiative to irrigate arid California and the need for federal adjudication of water sharing among the southwestern states for Hoover to act. The story begins in the early 1900s in the Mojave Desert, which averages a mere 2.4 inches of rainfall per year. Entrepreneur Charles Rockwood and irrigationist George Chaffey built a canal into an area then known as the Valley of the Dead. The irrigation worked and the area, soothingly rechristened "Imperial Valley," boasted two towns, two thousand settlers, and an impressive one hundred thousand acres of crops. But the notoriously turbid Colorado River quickly silted the first canal. (The rich soils of the Imperial Valley are made in part from the deposits the Colorado River eroded away as it formed the Grand Canyon.) A flood in the spring of 1904 washed the second canal away, along with several houses and thousands of acres of crops.

The railroad magnate (and national park advocate) E.H. Harriman purchased Rockwood's irrigation company and managed to stop the flooding in 1907, but not before flood waters broke diversion canals and emptied into the Salton Sink, a dry seabed, creating the Salton Sea. The Bureau of Reclamation stepped in and built a new canal to supply irrigated waters to the Imperial Valley. Undone by floods and realizing the importance of water to California's future, Imperial Valley farmers joined the bureau in calling for a "unified Colorado River project" that would tame river flooding and distribute its waters among urban and agricultural users.

If an upriver dam on the Colorado that controlled river flow was the solution for Imperial Valley farmers, the question of rights to the river's water remained to be settled. The Colorado River originates two miles above sea level in the mountains of Colorado before cutting through Utah along the eponymous Colorado Plateau and into Arizona. It then runs west into Nevada, turns south along the California-Arizona border before entering Mexico and emptying into the Gulf of California. The drainage area of the river encompasses 244,000 square miles. How much water could each state that borders its meandering route claim? The answer came from the CRC, an agreement brokered among western states in 1922 by Herbert Hoover. The CRC divided the river into two grouped basins, allocating 7.5 million acre-feet of water to the "upper basin" states of Colorado, New Mexico, Utah, and Wyoming, and 7.5 million acre-feet to the "lower basin" states of California, Arizona, and Nevada. (An acre-foot of water is the amount of water needed to cover one acre of land to a depth of one foot.) Mexico (which was not partner to the negotiations) received 1.5 million acre-feet, with the final one million acre-feet allocated to the lower basin states.

But the CRC proved to be another profound folly in the history of western water. Most importantly, when the Reclamation Service estimated the amount of water in the Colorado River, it did so in the unusually wet years of the early 1900s—the wettest years since the 1600s. Rather than the 17.5 million acre-feet the CRC distributed among the states, the Colorado River typically averages about twelve million acre-feet of water each year. The rights to the Colorado's water—its "paper water"—greatly exceed actual flow—its "wet water." Powell's warning of a "heritage of conflict and litigation over water rights" proved correct. Working out the details of allocation took decades more and remains contentious to this day. Disputes will certainly continue, especially given that climate disruption will likely reduce the southwest to a state of severe permanent drought. In most years the Colorado no longer reaches the sea, its waters entirely claimed by upstream users. In 2012, however, the United States and Mexico reached an agreement, known as Minute 319, that mandated flow along the lower river and into the Colorado Delta. But for most of its history what the CRC did promote is reclamation, including such mammoth projects as the Boulder (Hoover) dam.

Congress passed the Boulder Canyon Project Act in 1928, authorizing construction of the giant dam: it stands 726 feet high (about the height of a fifty-five-floor skyscraper) as it straddles the Colorado River southeast of Las Vegas. Construction began in 1931 and employed, at its peak, more than five thousand workers. The nature of heavy construction combined with the blistering heat and deep water to make the dam building dangerous work: 112 laborers died during its building. It's no exaggeration to say that their work transformed the southwest. Workers flocked to the tiny, parched outpost of Las Vegas (which means "the meadows"), transforming it into a city. The dam created Lake Meade, the largest reservoir by volume in the United States (when it is full). It provides flood control and hydroelectric power to California, helping enable the explosive growth of Los Angeles. As western water historian Norris Hundley observed, canals and other water control projects "obliterated any sense of restraint about Los Angeles's capacity to absorb ever more people and industries." Los Angeles grew from a city of five hundred thousand inhabitants in 1920 to two million in 1952. Technology, it seemed, could turn the desert green and make cities bloom.

Hoover Dam set off a flurry of dam construction. The golden age of dam building in the west lasted from the middle of the 1930s to the middle of the 1960s. The success of the Hoover Dam also spurred an intense competition between the Bureau of Reclamation and the Army Corps of Engineers. Both were technically adept, even excellent, but the inevitable bureaucratic rivalry was inefficient. It fragmented resources and made planning more difficult. Irrigation was one reason for dam building; cheap and clean hydroelectric power was another. Both reasons fueled arid lands development. By 1964, nineteen large dams blocked the Colorado. Overall in the United States there are about eighty-one hundred "major" dams—defined as dams at least fifty feet tall that can store five thousand or more acre-feet of water. Worldwide dams are so pervasive that they have changed the speed at which the planet spins.

From the 1930s until the 1950s, conservation in the west generally meant dams, canals, irrigation, and development. The rush of development also initiated a new kind of conservationist counter movement. That movement grew from the environmental consequences of the CRC. Upper basin states envied the surge in lower basin state development fostered by the Hoover Dam. When upper basin state economies stated to boom after World War II, they wanted continued economic growth and to meet the infrastructure needs of their growing populations. The Bureau of Reclamation responded with an ambitious plan known as the Colorado River Storage Project (CRSP). The CSRP consisted of a series of dams and power plants along the upper Colorado River and its tributaries. Central to the CRSP was a dam in Echo Park, just south of the junction of the Yampa and Green rivers in Dinosaur National Monument.

The same qualities that made Echo Park such an extraordinary place are the same ones that made it good for a dam: its narrow valley and high, nearly vertical walls. The resulting reservoir would extend sixty-three miles up the Green and forty-four miles up the Yampa. Conservationists were horrified. The ghost of Hetch Hetchy rose up before them. As in California during the early years of the twentieth century, would postwar development in the west mean sacrificing ostensibly protected lands set aside from industrial development?

Conservationists had many reasons to be worried about the sanctity of public lands. The Army Corps of Engineers planned a dam on Montana's Flathead River that threatened Glacier National Park. Organized opposition from the National Parks Association, the Sierra Club, and the Wilderness Society defeated the dam, only to have the proposal resurrected a few years later. As Rosalie Edge warned, "the despoilers await like hungry wolves the opportunity to exploit our Parks." Proving Edge right, in 1947 timber interests pushed hard to open the less-than-a-decade-old Olympic National Park to logging. Local wilderness advocates such as Polly Dyer (conservation chair of The Mountaineers) and Emily Haig (president of the Seattle Audubon Society) combined forces with Edge to save the park. "What indeed will be left of our national parks," thundered Edge in her pamphlet *The Raid on the Nation's Olympic Forests*, "if small, selfish groups should be allowed to cut out of them all they covet?" The bills that permitted logging in Olympic National Park were defeated, but many other plans for development in supposedly protected lands arose. In 1955, the Sierra Club president reported on the existence of no less than sixteen dam proposals in eight different national parks.

The push for industrial development in parks and other protected areas came from government agencies, coalitions of powerful economic interests (builders, banks, and labor unions), and the congressmen that aggressively pushed development. In congress, the post–World War II era witnessed organized hostility toward public lands. Led by Nevada Senator Pat McCarran, who announced himself as a "states' rights Democrat," a group of western legislators, colloquially known as the Cow Block, agitated to open all western lands, particularly grazing tracks, to resource extraction. Using the slogan "Return the Public Lands to the West" the Cow Block introduced legislation that would enable each state to set up a commission to evaluate all public lands, including parks and monuments, to see if they could be better utilized by the private sector. The federal government, then as now, was a convenient target for demagogues who loved big government if it subsidized private economic interests but hated it when it preserved lands in parks. McCarran in particular railed against the "swivel-chair oligarchy" of Washington, District of Columbia, bureaucrats that enacted environmental protection. "The greatest enemies of our republic," he thundered in 1939, "may not be foreign foes but rather domestic termites."

As the 1940s wore on, McCarran increasingly linked public lands to communism and communism to his own anti-Semitic and racist beliefs. Publicly McCarran criticized Washington bureaucrats; in a private letter to his daughter he simply asserted that "under the Taylor Grazing Act all grazing rights have been allocated to the Jews." McCarran's private sector colleague, J. Elmer Brock, vice president of the American National Livestock Association, went public with his opposition to conservation because conservation was instituted by "Communist-minded bureaucrats." In the *Denver Post* Brock charged that conservationists themselves were "tinged with pink or even deeper hue."

In reality government agencies were favorable to development. The secretary of the interior during the Echo Park controversy, former Oregon Governor Douglas McKay, was known as "Giveaway McKay" for his close ties to development and timber interests. Even the Park Service promoted development projects within the parks. With the Echo Park dam, Newton Drury, director of the National Park Service, signed a secret agreement with the Bureau of Reclamation pledging to not oppose the dam. Drury even quipped that "Dinosaur is a dead duck."

As its name implies Dinosaur National Monument was initially a paleontological site, eighty acres of Mesozoic era fossils that Woodrow Wilson set aside in 1915. The site grew in 1938 when Harold Ickes convinced Franklin Roosevelt to expand the monument to include over two hundred thousand acres of desert canyon wilderness. It was a beautiful place. Rosalie Edge marveled at "the wonders of Dinosaur's lovely rivers, flowing at the base of cliffs that have no superiors in majesty." For conservationists, the battle over the dam was not only about the place itself but the principle of whether lands set aside from development were actually set aside—or, like Hetch Hetchy, only temporarily spared damming. But unlike the battle over Hetch Hetchy where John Muir had comparatively few allies, the burgeoning environmental movement could count on eight national and 236 state and local organizations to fight for the park. David Brower, president of the Sierra Club, Howard Zahniser of the Wilderness Society, Fred Packard of the National Parks Association, and Arthur Carhart of the Izaak Walton League grouped their organizations together as The Conservation Coalition to fight the dam. These generally well-educated white men represented much of the leadership of environmental organizations at the time—"male, Yale and pale" as some ruefully observed.

The Conservation Coalition made two important strategic decisions. First, it gathered a coalition of strange-bedfellow dam opponents that included the Army Corps of Engineers, water users in California, and members of Congress from the east who feared that irrigation would enable western farmers to compete with their eastern counterparts. Most importantly, The Conservation Coalition, especially David Brower, skillfully engaged the national media to rally the public to their cause. They took members of the public and journalists on float trips through the canyon. National publications such as *Time*, *Life*, *The New York Times*, and even *Reader's Digest* featured stories and photographs of the beautiful canyon. David Brower hired filmmaker Charles Eggert to produce *Wilderness River Trail*, a twenty-eight-minute documentary that featured regular people floating the spectacular canyon—a powerful argument against the idea that conservationists aimed to "lock up" the public lands. Brower also convinced publisher Alfred Knopf to produce

This is Dinosaur: Echo Park Country and Its Magic Rivers, edited by the noted writer and historian Wallace Stegner. Each member of Congress received a copy. The media campaign worked. Mail to Congress ran an astonishing eighty to one against the dam.

Dam proponents knew they were beat. One Utah congressman admitted that developers had "neither the money nor the organization to cope with the resources and mailing lists" of the preservationists. When a group of congressmen who hoped to reinsert enabling language for the dam met in Denver in 1955, The Conservation Coalition, tipped to the meeting, took out a full-page advertisement in the *Denver Post* that threatened to undo the entire CRSP if the Echo Park dam was permitted. Dam proponents settled for a compromise. Howard Zahniser negotiated the final deal in which conservationists pledged not to oppose the CRSP in return for the CSRP not violating the boundary of any national park or monument. Dams would be built at Glen Canyon on the Colorado, at Flaming Gorge on the Green River, on the San Juan River in Utah, and at the Curecanti site on the Gunnison River in western Colorado. But rivers in parks and monuments would remain free flowing.

The battle over Echo Park brought David Brower into the national spotlight. David Ross Brower (1912–2000) grew up in Berkeley, California, where his father, laid off from his job as a mechanical drawing instructor at the University of California, worked as a landlord and janitor. The family took frequent camping trips together. When Brower was eight, his mother lost her senses of sight and smell due to a brain tumor. Young David escorted her first around Berkeley, but soon on long hikes, describing the flowers and vistas to her. Forced by financial hardship to drop out of the University of California after his first year, he would later tell his friends that he was "a graduate of the University of the Colorado River." Brower worked odd jobs in Yosemite and developed into an outstanding alpinist; he eventually logged seventy first ascents of mountain peaks, including the first climb of New Mexico's beautiful but imposing Shiprock diatreme. Painfully timid as a child, hiking and climbing helped Brower overcome his childhood reticence.

When he wasn't climbing, Brower worked as an editor at the University of California Press and rapidly moved up the ranks of the Sierra Club. He became executive director of the club in 1952. When he took over it had a membership of seven thousand and an annual budget of seventy-five thousand dollars; in 1969, when he stepped down as director under pressure from members who thought his uncompromising attitude harmed the organization, it had seventy-seven thousand members and assets of three million dollars. Brower certainly was uncompromising. The shy child had become a warrior. "Polite conservationists leave no mark," he grumbled, "save the scars upon the Earth that could have been prevented had they stood their ground." Environmental Protection Agency Director Russel Train once allowed that Brower "makes it so easy for the rest of us to be reasonable." Under Brower's direction the Sierra Club transformed from a group of outdoor enthusiasts into a political organization fully committed to environmentalist activism.

Brower's transformation of a relatively staid conservationist organization into an activist juggernaut happened because it mirrored a larger transformation in American culture. Post–World War II affluence gave millions of Americans from all walks of life the leisure to explore their public lands. Beyond rest and recreation, Americans flocked to public lands due to a widespread romantic critique of their lives. Those Americans who wished "to get away from it all" and experience the American landscape were following, in a less pervasive manner, the advice of Thoreau, the Lowell factory girls, and Muir. The wild was a tonic; for many even sacred. This sense gave fights over public lands a greater meaning than utilitarian arguments about park boundaries or the efficacy of dams. As Howard Zahniser wrote in 1951, "we are part of the wildness of the universe. Our noblest, happiest character develops with the influence of wildness."

The Conservation Coalition did not know it at the time, but their pact to preserve Echo Park surrendered to development some of the most spectacular canyon wilderness on the continent. The sacrificed area was John Wesley Powell's Glen Canyon, the "curious ensemble of wonderful features" that he and his men explored in early August 1869. And what features they were. Glen Canyon was bigger (nearly two hundred miles long), wilder, and more spectacular than Dinosaur, and featured a stunning abundance of Native American archaeological sites tucked into its maze of two thousand side canyons. It was a perfect site for a national park. Filmmaker Charles Eggert wrote to Brower that "to destroy music temple" (a magnificent sandstone grotto within the canyon) amounted to a "crime against the God Almighty." Brower visited the canyon six years after its fate was sealed, but before it was flooded. The stunned

Brower immediately "realized . . . that this was not a place for a reservoir." Blaming himself for what suddenly looked like a foolish compromise, Brower never recovered from the loss. "The magic of Glen Canyon is dead. It has been vulgarized," he lamented. Damming the canyon was akin to "urinating in the crypt of St. Peter's." Brower and many others learned to never decide the fate of an unknown place, and for some, to never compromise.

That passion was needed, for new plans threatened other desert cathedrals. In 1963, just before the floodgates of Glen Canyon Dam closed, the Bureau of Reclamation proposed the billion-dollar Pacific Southwest Water Plan. Its ambitious agenda called for transporting water from northern California and the Columbia River Basin in Washington State to the southwest. And to ensure that it could pump Arizona's share of Colorado River water to rapidly growing cities such as Phoenix, it proposed hydroelectric dams at Marble and Bridge canyons, both within Grand Canyon National Park. Marble and Bridge bookended the park, so their damming would turn the canyon into a reservoir. "If we can't save the Grand Canyon," asked a flabbergasted David Brower, "what the hell can we save?"

It was a surprisingly difficult question to answer. Dam proponents included President Lyndon Baines Johnson and his Secretary of the Interior Stewart Udall, as well as the usual retinue of politicians and business interests eager to capitalize on development funded with federal dollars. The outspoken leader of the dam proponents was Floyd Dominy, the two-fisted, hard-charging, hard-drinking bundle of passion who was commissioner of the Bureau of Reclamation. He was quick-witted, salacious, and a gambler, the kind of man whose cigar remained lit when he rafted through a waterfall. Dominy described the dams as "cash registers," a way to raise funds for the Central Arizona Project that would pump water to Phoenix and Tucson. Dominy badly wanted the dams at Marble and Bridge. Dan Dreyfus of the bureau remembered Dominy as refusing compromise and pursuing the dams like "an utter maniac." Brower and Dominy were classic foils, two forces of nature that seemed to leap from the pages of a Hollywood script. The smart thing to do was to put them together on a raft on the Colorado River. That's what writer John McPhee did, in the final chapter of his 1971 portrait of Brower, *Encounters with the Archdruid.*

Figure 6.2 David Brower fought to preserve the open landscapes of the American West—including the Grand Canyon. "If we can't save the Grand Canyon" grumbled Brower, "what the hell can we save"?

Led by Brower, the Sierra Club responded to the Central Arizona Project with a media blitz. Brower blamed the loss of Glen Canyon on the fact that it was so little known; he had learned well the lessons of Echo Park. Advertisements appeared in the *Washington Post,* the *Los Angeles Times,* and *The New York Times.* The ads were written by Brower and by an advertising agency he hired that featured the work of Jerry Mander, an important intellectual who would go on to pen widely read books on the relationship between consumer-technological society and the natural world, including *Four Arguments for the Elimination of Television* (1977). Brower and Mander would team up again on campaigns to establish Redwood National Park and to fight U.S. Supersonic Transport. The first round of publicity emphasized the grandeur of the canyon. "This time," the ads declared, "it's the Grand Canyon they want to flood, the *Grand Canyon.*" The ads also urged citizen action: "Now Only You Can Save Grand Canyon From Being Flooded . . . For Profit." The ads included a coupon that readers could clip and send to key players in the drama: President Johnson, Secretary of Interior Udall, the reader's Senator and congressional representative. The Sierra Club produced a lavish coffee table ("Exhibit Format") book about the Grand Canyon, *Time and River Flowing.*

The Bureau of Reclamation responded by emphasizing that by volume only a small part of the canyon would be flooded and that it would actually benefit sightseeing vacationers because they could better see its rock walls as they floated near them. That argument was like lobbing a softball over home plate and the Sierra Club promptly smacked it over the fence. Their response simply asked, "Should we also flood the Sistine Chapel so tourists can get nearer the ceiling?" Not only did the reply puncture the bureau's rationalization, it showed yet again the potency of the old idea of wilderness as a sacred space. Thousands of letters poured into Congress, 95 percent of them against the dam. "I never saw anything like it," recalled one official from the Bureau of Reclamation. "Letters were arriving in dump trucks . . . and a lot of them quoted the Sierra Club ads." When the Central Arizona Project was signed into law in 1968, it kept Grand Canyon National Park intact. Floyd Dominy was incensed. He said of Stewart Udall, "my secretary turned chickenshit on me."

Public response was certainly powerful, but the dam also failed because of complex congressional maneuvering in which legislators from the Pacific northwest, especially Scoop Jackson, opposed the diversion of water from the Columbia River Basin to the desert southwest. Whether public outcry or western water politics was the final undoing of the dam, the victory gave the Sierra Club great credibility and was a high point in the history of scenic preservation. Most importantly, it marked the end of the big dam era in the west. Dams were now appraised on their environmental merits rather than being viewed as unassailable boons to economic development. But the victory came at significant cost for Brower and the Sierra Club. The Internal Revenue Service ruled, appropriately, that the club was a political organization, not just an organization of hiking enthusiasts, and summarily revoked its tax-exempt status. For the Sierra Club Board of Directors, the change in tax status was the breaking point in their relationship with Brower. They admired but were also unnerved by Brower's independence and passion; they forced him out as executive director. Brower launched a new organization, Friends of the Earth, with the slogan "Think globally, act locally," the next year. The Sierra Club continued to grow, especially under the leadership of Carl Pope, executive director from 1992 to 2010. Pope came to environmentalism through social justice work; he was an activist in Students for a Democratic Society and a Peace Corps volunteer. Pope brought a "big tent" approach to the organization, working to form coalitions with labor and other organizations.

The strange bedfellow politics of the Echo Park and Grand Canyon dam controversies emphasized the ideological complexities of environmental activism. Surely an admiration for efficiency and economic growth cut across party and ideological lines. But as the 1960s and 1970s progressed, scenic preservation, combatting toxins, and working for the integrity of ecological systems—not to mention the questioning of economic growth—became increasingly identified with liberal politics. Anti-statist conservatives, however, could also be passionate lovers of wild lands, and the entire tradition of wild lands activism featured the use of nature as a standpoint for searing criticisms of bureaucracy and strong commitments to individualism and freedom. The desert seemed to bring forth the most important conservative green thinkers or green activists with a strong libertarian streak. The desert also highlighted the ideological problems of green conservatism—who but the government can ensure democratic access to natural wonders such as the Grand Canyon?

No less a figure than Barry Goldwater (1909–1998), known as "Mr. Conservative" and the Republican Party nominee for president in 1964, struggled with these contradictions. Goldwater lost that election in an overwhelming landslide, spurring many contemporary commentators to foolishly declare the end of conservatism. Instead, conservatives regrouped and with the Reagan revolution have dominated American politics for the last forty years. Several historians have pointed out that Goldwater's libertarian conservatism was at times an uneasy fit with the religious right conservatism that propelled Reagan and his followers into office. Goldwater, after all, supported abortion and gay rights because he did not want government to interfere in an individual's private life. But the more important difference between Goldwater's conservatism and Reagan's may be environmental. In his 1970 book, *The Conscience of a Majority*, Goldwater asserted that "Our job . . . is to prevent that lush orb known as the Earth . . . from turning into a bleak and barren, dirty brown planet." Moreover, it was the government that had to work to achieve that end: "It is my belief that when pollution is found, it should be halted at the source, even if this requires stringent government action against important segments of our national economy."

Goldwater was an avid hiker and skilled nature photographer, and his environmentalism is best reflected by his work for wilderness and public lands. Like so many in the west, he was devastated by the loss of Glen Canyon—he called his vote for the dam the biggest mistake of his political career. "The beauty of the canyons which are now covered by Lake Powell," he told a correspondent in 1982, "are etched forever in my memory, and it saddens me to think that my grandchildren will never see those magnificent creations of God." As a Senator from Arizona, Goldwater was particularly interested in the Grand Canyon and he submitted legislation in 1969 to substantially enlarge Grand Canyon National Park. His congressional colleagues failed to act, so in 1973 he introduced an even more ambitions bill. It was eventually signed into law in 1975 as the Grand Canyon Enlargement Act. During legislative wrangling over the bill Goldwater formed a surprising enemy: the Sierra Club. The conflict arose over enlarging the reservation lands of the Havasupai. Goldwater wanted to increase the size of those lands. The Sierra Club, fresh from victory with Grand Canyon National Park but still bruised and fearful of the precedent of appropriating national park lands for other purposes, opposed the deal. The break was bitter, and Goldwater even took to the floor of the Senate to indict the Sierra Club for failing to understand that his bill meant "to put the Grand Canyon in the state of protection it is going to need in the future."

Despite his bitter break with the environmental community and his increasing belligerence about "excessive regulation"—Goldwater opposed strengthening the Clean Air Act—and his favoring of petroleum-based economic growth, Goldwater continued to use the federal government to achieve environmental ends. He voted in 1978 to strengthen the Endangered Species Act, the bête noire of anti-environmentalists, and supported the "Superfund" bill, a tax on polluters used to clean up toxic waste sites. He also sponsored significant legislation to permanently protect Arizona lands as wilderness. In 1982 Goldwater introduced a bill to protect Aravaipa Canyon, a one-thousand-foot gorge in the Galiuro Mountains 120 miles southeast of Phoenix. He waxed eloquently about the canyon on the Senate floor, concluding that his "very simple" bill attempted to "preserve and protect a magnificent desert sanctuary." Nor was Goldwater done with wilderness. In 1984 he introduced and championed the Arizona Wilderness Act that designated twenty-eight areas in national forest lands as wilderness, about 752,000 acres in total. Reagan signed the bill into law later that year. Goldwater's environmentalism was always in profound tension with his booster instincts, militarism, and hatred of regulation. But it was an environmentalism nevertheless, one that found even a man as skeptical of governmental power as

Goldwater clearly understanding the need for federal protection of his beloved desert landscapes.

Other desert environmentalists shared Goldwater's libertarian commitments, but in radically different form. On March 21, 1981, a three-hundred-foot crack scarred the front of Glen Canyon Dam. It was not an actual fissure, but a crack-shaped plastic banner placed by a new, daring and radical environmental organization: Earth First! Inspired in part by Edward Abbey, whose 1975 novel *The Monkey Wrench Gang* depicted a small group of eco-saboteurs gleefully dismantling bulldozers, chopping down billboards, and, eventually, returning the Colorado River to free-flowing status, Earth First! united under the mantra of "No compromise in defense of Mother Earth." As the plastic crack unfurled on the Glen Canyon Dam, Edward Abbey stood atop the dam, shouting "Earth First! Free the Colorado [River]!" The group had learned much from the radical protests of the 1960s: they put their bodies on the line, directly confronted their adversaries, and exulted in guerilla theatre. The entire history of environmental reform had been remarkably staid, even conservative, working almost entirely within the American reformist tradition. Earth First! upended that history. The primary brainchild behind this radical group was a registered Republican who had spent 1964 working on the Goldwater presidential campaign.

Earth First! co-founder Dave Foreman (b. 1947) exemplified the complex political ideologies that comprised the many strands of environmentalism. Most importantly, Earth First! arose from disgust with conventional environmentalism. Foreman began his environmentalist career working for the Wilderness Society as the southwest regional representative in New Mexico and as its director of wilderness affairs in Washington, District of Columbia. Other founders included Susan Morgan, also from the Wilderness Society, and Howard Wolke, a former Friends of the Earth staffer, as well as the leftist of the founders, Mike Roselle, a former Vietnam War protestor. Foreman remembered the stolid and moderate organized environmental politics of the late 1970s in this way: "We looked like statesmen. They won. . . . When the chips were down, conservation still lost to industry." Where once the indefatigable consensus building of a figure like Howard Zahniser looked like effective political brilliance, for Earth First! it was nothing more than ineffective compromise that gave the wilderness away.

The cultural politics of Earth First! followed a similar trajectory. The group deliberately cultivated an image of rowdy drunken rednecks.

Irreverent and committed to civil disobedience, everything Earth First! did was in defiance of the button-down corporate order, whether that order was the petroleum industry or inside-the-beltway environmentalist organizations. Although this cultural attitude effectively mocked the social order, it also engendered a patriarchal and belligerent ethos. It was also fun. Earth First! advertised its first gathering—its Round River Rendezvous—as a way to "reinvigorate, enthuse [and] inspire wilderness activists in the West." Beyond environmental action, the Round River Rendezvous encouraged "passion, humor and joy" as well as "friendships," and even "a few romances" as wilderness activists got together to "get drunk" and "howl at the moon." As Howie Wolke recalled, the redneck image also reminded Earth First! to not "lose focus and drift into general left wing politics." Earth First! was about nothing more and nothing less than wilderness, public lands, and biodiversity. The movement attracted a large, vibrant, and ideologically diverse group of followers.

The immediate precipitating event to Earth First!'s creation was RARE II, a Forest Service acronym for "Roadless Area Review and Evaluation" completed in 1979. The Forest Service had surveyed its lands and except for a handful of high altitude enclaves—Wolke called them "wilderness on the rocks"—recommended road building for logging, mining, and other forms of resource extraction. As Howie Wolke remembered it, "In a misbegotten effort to look 'moderate,' the conservation movement had compromised away most roadless areas at the outset of the process." Once again roads and road building spurred wilderness activists into action. In this sense, Earth First! was a direct descendant of earlier wilderness activists like Aldo Leopold, Bob Marshall, and Rosalie Edge. The tactics of Earth First! included the familiar—aggressive litigation to protect roadless areas in national forests—and the confrontational—Earth First! activists blockaded bulldozers, sat in trees slated for the axe, and occupied the offices of decision makers. The confrontational tactics were effective, and they also garnered media attention to issues otherwise ignored.

Beyond attention-grabbing theatrics, Earth First! articulated reasons for wilderness defense that went well beyond the recreational, spiritual, aesthetic, and utilitarian justifications found in mainstream environmental thought. Applying the insights of a philosophy known as Deep Ecology, Earth First! defended wilderness for its own sake rather than as having value for people. Earth First! and other Deep Ecologists argued that because humans evolved in a state of wilderness and were part of a larger community of living organisms, they should not have substantially greater rights beyond those enjoyed by any other member of the ecosystem. They termed this worldview "biocentrism"; it amounted to an attempt to grant democratic rights to all living organisms. It was an ethically challenging and daring line of thought. Earth First! confronted not just the tactics of conventional environmentalism, but its moral and intellectual foundations as well.

Given their militant stances and willingness to harm or disable ("sabotage") property—but not living things—it is small wonder that Earth First! attracted the attention of federal law enforcement. On May 29 and 30, 1989, four Earth First! activists, including Dave Foreman, were arrested and charged with several crimes, most importantly with conspiring to topple power lines that ran to a nuclear power plant. All four were convicted; Foreman later pled guilty to a misdemeanor and avoided jail time.

A year after the arrests of the Arizona activists, a suspicious car bomb nearly killed Judi Bari, the most prominent member of an Earth First! campaign to prevent the logging of ancient Redwood forests in northern California. Bari was a feminist and social justice advocate. She expertly directed Earth First!'s effective guerilla tactics: road blockades, "spiking" of trees—hammering nails into them that would harm lumberyard equipment, thus making the forest uneconomic to log—and tree sitting, in which activists lived in the canopies of trees set to be logged. The authorities charged Bari and her companion Darryl Cherney with knowingly carrying a bomb and publicly labeled them "ecoterrorists." The pair was later vindicated, and the Federal Bureau of Investigation was forced to pay a multimillion dollar settlement to Cherney and to the estate of Judi Bari, who had died from breast cancer.

Part of Earth First!'s upending of environmental politics arose from the fruitful mind and devastating pen of Edward Abbey (1927–1989). Abbey's central theme was that an industrial, militarized culture hated and destroyed nature as it simultaneously undermined what it meant to be human. "How can we create a civilization fit for the dignity of free men and women if the globe itself is ravaged and polluted and defiled and insulted?" asked Abbey. "The domination of nature leads to the domination of human beings." Environmental protection, then, meant much more than "preserving forests and rivers, wildlife and wilderness."

Rather, it presaged "keeping alive a certain way of human life." If humans can "force industrialism underground, where it belongs," they can also "restore to all citizens of our nation their rightful heritage of breathable air, drinkable water, open space, family farm agriculture, and truly democratic political economy." As historian Brian Drake writes, "few, if any, [political writers] linked the destruction of nature to the domination of humans as tightly as Abbey did. For him, preserving human freedom went hand-in-hand with protecting the environment." Wilderness was not just a place to revere or a standpoint from which to criticize civilization. Abbey's wilderness was also a place of resistance. Wilderness was freedom.

Abbey formed this worldview not in the deserts of the southwest of which he wrote so affectingly but in the lush forests of Appalachian Pennsylvania. The region's history of brutal ecological and human exploitation by the timber and coal industries shaped his view of government, democracy, and resistance. His father was a socialist of the Eugene Debs style, and Abbey inculcated that passion for democracy and need for critique and confrontation. He served as a military policeman after World War II and later worked as a case worker for a welfare agency in Hoboken, New Jersey. In 1959, he earned a master's degree in philosophy from the University of New Mexico, writing a thesis on "Anarchism and the Morality of Violence." But it was his job as a seasonal park ranger in Arches National Monument (now Park) that generated his best writing, most notably his 1968 collection of autobiographical essays, *Desert Solitaire*.

Desert Solitaire does not contain much appreciation of the government for preserving some of the stunning landscapes of the high southwest, but rather an insightful denunciation of "industrial tourism." For Abbey, the Park Service undermined its mission by building roads and other developments in the name of park "improvement." The improvements were for an unexamined and certainly unneeded but nevertheless overweening notion of "progress." More development, more tourists, more roads equaled not just less wilderness but less ability for people to find what they came for. The tourists were "being robbed and robbing themselves." Abbey's solution? "No more cars in national parks. Let the people walk." Abbey contended that "we are learning finally that the forests and mountains and desert canyons are holier than our churches . . . let us behave accordingly."

At times Abbey could devolve into infantilism, not to mention overt sexism and a "cultural bias" that occasionally crossed the line into racist diatribe. He was blessed, as historian Patricia Nelson Limerick once quipped, with "freedom from politeness." But to only see Abbey's understanding of wilderness as masculine escapism is to miss its grounding in real problems. The domination of nature does require the domination of people, and industrial agriculture has abolished agrarian folkways. Dams can irrigate farms and provide hydroelectric power; they also destroy nature and embed citizens in "an intricate web, a cobweb, of wires, cables, freeways, dams, canals, highways, fences, laws, regulations, taxes." Bureaucracy and hierarchy are hallmarks of American life. As Abbey and Earth First! aimed to "throw a monkey wrench into the gears of the political machine and let the broken pieces fall where they may," they were acting in a tradition of visionaries who found in desert austerity a powerful antidote to a mindless and harmful industrial capitalism.

For Earth First! and many others, no structure embodied the worst of industrial society more than Glen Canyon Dam. Abbey cheered its destruction: "surely no man made structure in modern American history has been hated so much by so many for so long with such good reason as Glen Canyon dam!" In the early twenty-first century, even moderates are beginning to agree. Dams in the southwest have many problems. Most importantly, in a parched land, they lose water; enough, in the case of Glen Canyon Dam, to fully supply Los Angeles. They lose it because water seeps away into the desert substrate, and the water exposed to the sun in a desert reservoir rapidly evaporates. Drought and evaporation in Lake Powell, the reservoir created by Glen Canyon Dam (Abbey summarily christened it "Lake Foul"), have reduced water levels to less than half full. A "bathtub ring" stain of the old high-water mark is easily visible, high above the waterline. Moreover, downriver, Lake Mead, created by Hoover Dam, is also less than half full, greatly reducing Hoover Dam's ability to produce hydroelectricity. Releasing Lake Powell's waters, its advocates argue, would restore the canyon, restore the flow of that portion of the Colorado River, and restore the water level in Lake Mead enough so that Hoover Dam could regain its full ability to produce hydroelectricity.

In recent years, due to environmental and economic concerns, many dams in the west have been removed. The National Park Service teamed with the Bureau of Reclamation to decommission the Glines Canyon

Dam on the Elwha River just outside Olympic National Park. After removing the dam, Coho and Chinook salmon returned to the spawn. Over the last twenty years, nearly 850 dams have been decommissioned and removed; the same agencies that built dams are now decommissioning them. Could Glen Canyon Dam be next?

If deserts and their dams were a laboratory for testing the limits of civilization, beginning in the 1930s the laboratory turned from the American southwest to the globe as a whole. Ecologist Paul Sears's 1935 classic *Desert on the March*, written at the height of the Dust Bowl, understood that "We have no business messing up any other planets if we can not learn to manage this one." Specifically, deserts themselves, or rather, desertification—the expansion of desert or semi-desert landscapes due to human influences—remain a crucial global issue, eating up wildlife habitat and cropland needed for a growing population. More broadly, deserts emphasized the entire problem of population, resources, and biophysical limits. Desertification proved those limits to be a global problem; in effect, the American southwest was globalized. But it was not until the post–World War II world of atom bombs, exploding populations, cross-border pollution, and humans changing the global climate that the question of global ecological limits moved to the forefront of American environmentalism.

CHAPTER 7

THE ATOMIC BODY POLITIC

A society that allows itself to admit and articulate its
nonmaterial human needs, and to find nonmaterial
ways to satisfy them, would require much lower
material and energy throughputs and would provide
much higher levels of human fulfillment.

–DONELLA H. MEADOWS,
The Limits to Growth: The 30-Year Update

HE USE of atom bombs was an earth-shattering
devastation. Worriedly musing about "The Promethean Role of the United States" just two days
after the August 6, 1945, bombing of Hiroshima, Pulit-
zer Prize–winning foreign correspondent Anne O'Hare
McCormick of *The New York Times* noted that the bomb
"has caused an explosion in men's minds as shattering as
the obliteration of Hiroshima." The obliteration would
continue; little could she know that the United States
would explode another bomb on Nagasaki, Japan, the

next day. In the devastation of Hiroshima McCormick could hope that the "bomb makes peace imperative by making war impossible." War must be avoided because the bomb constituted "an unanswerable argument" for the creation of a "community of nations leagued together for self-protection in the pursuit and maintenance of peace."

The bomb also shattered how people thought about the natural world. Atomic explosions emphasized in ways that the limits of deserts or the demise of passenger pigeons could not, that humans could end all life on the planet. The ability to plunder nature was no longer a species, or a regional but a planetary threat. Environmental thinkers immediately connected the nuclear threat with other forms of ecological degradation. Fairfield Osborn (1887–1969), president of the New York Zoological Society and author of the best-selling *Our Plundered Planet*, instructed a group of biology teachers in 1946 that "there are two major threats in the world today. . . . The first is the misuse of atomic energy. . . . The other is the continuing destruction of the natural living resources of this earth." Osborn worried that technological prowess deceived people into forgetting "our essentiality and oneness with the natural world." The human "conflict with nature" was in fact a "cruel and deadly world-wide war." The atomic bomb revealed that human power could destroy not just a species or even an ecosystem, but a small, limited, and fragile planet.

McCormick's "community of nations leagued together" formed in 1945 as the United Nations. Among its first international conferences were two devoted to conservation: the United Nations Scientific Conference on the Conservation and Utilization of Resources (UNSCCUR) and the International Technical Conference on the Protection of Nature (ITCPN). Both were held in 1949. Progressive Era forester Gifford Pinchot, understanding the international dimensions of conservation, had pushed for such conferences for decades. The topic gained particular urgency in the late 1940s because World War II was in part a war of resources. The German fascist dictator Adolph Hitler commented several times that the Germans needed more land and food to survive—he called this idea "Lebensraum." It justified German expansionism as necessary to secure the resources needed for German living. Hitler insisted that hunger would outstrip agricultural improvements and dismissed the idea that science could improve crop yields and standards of living as Jewish propaganda. Lebensraum tied Hitler's war of extermination to nature's limited ability to provide for a materially abundant lifestyle.

Conservation was instrumental to Allied efforts to combat Hitler's expansionism. Because of the imperative of giving first priority to arming, transporting, and feeding soldiers, the homefront conservation of remaining resources became a vital patriotic duty. The War Production Board created a Bureau of Industrial Conservation whose leader, Lessing Rosenwald, called upon Americans "to change from an economy of waste—and this country has been notorious for waste—to an economy of conservation." Americans responded by biking to work—sometimes on "victory bikes" made from nonessential metals and reclaimed rubber tires—to save fuel. Use of public transit rose 87 percent. Homefront Americans recycled everything from toothpaste tubes to cooking grease.

Most prominently, homefront American households grew victory gardens, a centerpiece of the national "Food Fights for Freedom" campaign. Eleanor Roosevelt grew beans and carrots on the White House lawn. Urban high-rise dwellers planted small victory gardens in window boxes; others cultivated rooftop gardens. Overall, Americans planted more than twenty million Victory Gardens that grew between 30 and 40 percent of the nation's vegetables. The greatly successful program even spilled over into an urban beautification campaign in which vacant lots full of trash were cleaned and turned into neighborhood gardens.

The question of resource conservation thus grew directly out of World War II and its atomic ending. But with only a few exceptions, the UNSCCUR was less about conservation and more about cheerleading the unconstrained consumption of nature. Conference speakers and papers were dominated not just by Americans but by American corporate interests. Topics included "Oil from Oil Shale," "Petroleum Production from Continental Shelves," "Treatment of Trees with Toxic Chemicals to Facilitate Removal of the Bark to Reduce Weight," and "Log Transportation in Tropical Forest Exploitation." Other presenters proclaimed their ability to create food from "algae and yeast," "tiny aqueous animals," or, even more unsettling, from "synthetic plastics and fibers." Still others advocated for food produced from the straightforward exploitation of supposedly "underfished" tropical waters.

Some presenters were more useful and invoked the practical idealism that conservationists such as Pinchot hoped could inform the international order. Massachusetts Institute of Technology physicist Maria Telkes championed solar power at the conference. "Solar energy," she asserted, could replace "fossil fuels" as "a new fuel source." She was close to proving that it could. Telkes had already developed a solar salt water still for

Figure 7.1 Conservation was a vital part of the World War II homefront. Movie star Rita Hayworth made conservation sexy and fun by urging Americans to recycle scrap metals.
Courtesy of the National Archives and Records Administration

the U.S. Navy in World War II; it saved the lives of several torpedoed sailors and downed airmen. After the war, she teamed up with architect Eleanor Raymond to build the first solar-heated home. In subsequent writings Telkes emphasized that solar was "the cleanest and healthiest fuel." Given that other sources were finite, "Sunlight will be used as a source of energy sooner or later." So "why wait" to develop it? Solar was not the only renewable energy source discussed at the conference. U.S. Federal Power Commission employee Percy H. Thomas advocated for the possibilities of wind energy, noting that "it leaves no ashes or poison gas" and that demonstration projects had proved successful.

The UNSCCUR was dominated by business interests committed to increasing consumption, but the ITCPN questioned both the limits of resources and the corporate control of them. Fairfield Osborn attended both conferences. He delivered the opening address at the ITCPN and summarized the situation in this way. "The conservation movement," he wrote, "is at the core of the fight for democracy." The typical "American way of doing business," continued Osborn, had led to vast resource destruction; instead, the use of renewable resources such as forests "must be directed solely to the benefit of all the people." The misuse of resources—as "deadly as a time delayed bomb"—was ultimately a problem of "economic and even social and political" conditions.

Osborn was joined at the ITCPN conference by William Vogt (1902–1968), who authored the other environmental bestseller of 1948, *Road to Survival*. In it he worried that "By excessive breeding and abuse of the land mankind has backed itself into an ecological trap. By a lopsided use of applied science it has been living on promissory notes. Now, all over the world, the notes are falling due." Vogt did not just indict "mankind" but squarely confronted the destructive capacities of corporate capital. "One of the most ruinous limiting factors is the capitalistic system," argued Vogt. "Free enterprise—divorced from biophysical understanding and social responsibility . . . must bear a large share of the responsibility for devastated forests, vanishing wildlife, crippled ranges, a gullied continent and roaring flood crests." For Vogt, capitalism destroyed democracy as well as nature: "The manufacturer cashes in," lamented Vogt, "and the American citizen pays the cost." The remedy was to incorporate ecological thinking into the economy. The "search for economic and political solutions that ignores the ecological," concluded Vogt, "is as helpless as a bird with one wing." Aldo Leopold agreed. Writing at the same time of Vogt, he emphasized the need to "quit thinking about decent land-use as solely an economic problem." Instead, the land must be thought of "in terms of what is ethically and esthetically right, as well as what is economically expedient." Thinkers such as Osborne, Vogt, and Leopold were rooting post–World War II environmentalism in a critique of capitalism and the liberal international order.

The bomb and its implications was so shattering to men's minds in part because the environmental ideas it forced upon the thinking person's consciousness—the limits of nature and the ability of humans to foul our own nests—had been debated for more than two and a half centuries. The originator of the discourse of limits was not a modern scientist deploying sophisticated computer modeling about the earth's resources (though we shall see that those people were very important) but rather a parish priest in Surrey, England, writing at the tail end of the eighteenth century. In 1798 the Reverend Thomas Malthus (1766–1834) published a slim volume, *An Essay on the Principle of Population*; his ideas have been central to ecology, economics, and environmental thought ever since.

Malthus had one great insight: species reproduced faster than their food supply. Humans were no different. The earth's resources were finite and human population growth could outstrip them. "Population, when unchecked, increases in a geometrical ratio" explained Malthus. "Subsistence increases only in an arithmetical ratio." Rather than an earth defined by cornucopian abundance, Malthus asserted that "the power of population is infinitely greater than the power in the earth to produce subsistence for man." Because nature was limited, humans tended to outstrip its resources, leading "to a perpetual oscillation between happiness and misery." Thus society should encourage a preventive check on population growth—individual control based on prudence and reason—to minimize the "positive check" of war, famine, and pestilence. No longer would debates about natural resources be only about their ethical distribution, but also their inherit limits.

American Malthusian concern with nature's limits began with James Madison in his 1818 "Address to the Agricultural Society of Albemarle." In his speech to that society, Madison outlined his understanding of the "economy of nature" in proto-ecological terms. As historian Steven Stoll, in his trailblazing book *Larding the Lean Earth*, explains, Madison evinced a "generous and voluminous awareness of nature and human needs." Not only was Madison acutely aware of nature's limits, he offered a complex understanding of the interaction of the physical and biological forces that make nature. He thus noted a balance between "the animal part and the vegetable part of the creation to each other, through the medium of the atmosphere." That relation, asserted Madison, "comes in aid of the reflection suggested by the general relation between the atmosphere and both." If either animals or plants decreased too sharply, the atmosphere would be exhausted, the "breath of life" would come to an end, and the remaining species would perish.

Such observations brought Madison into a Malthusian line of thought. Madison argued that as "closely as agriculture and civilization are allied, they do not keep pace with each other." In nature "no determinate limit presents itself to the increase of food, and to a population commensurate with it" except "the limited productiveness of the earth itself." But humans would attempt to overcome the limits of the earth: "we can scarcely be warranted in supposing that all the productive powers of its surface can be made subservient to the use of man." The alleged result would be a planet "as full of people, as the spots most crowded now are or might be made, and as destitute as those spots, of the plants and animals not used by man."

Such human voraciousness would eventually deplete the vast storehouse of life, replacing it "with the few grains and grasses, the few herbs and roots, and the few fowls and quadrupeds, which make up the short list adapted to the wants of man." Tellingly, this "multiplication of the human race, at the expense of the rest of the organized creation" could eventually end human proliferation: "Were it less difficult to admit that all the sources of productiveness could be exclusively appropriated to the food of man, is it certain that an obstacle to his indefinite multiplication would not be encountered in one of the relations between the atmosphere and organized beings?"

Such thoughts were a hard sell in the land of the eternal frontier. But especially after the official "closing" of the frontier—announced by the Census Bureau in 1890—worry over the finite nature of resources became a regular theme of American life. In 1893 Minnesota populist Ignatius Donnelly averred that "Free land has been the safety valve of Europe and America. When the valve is closed, swarming mankind every day will increase the danger of explosion. Nothing can save the world but the greatest wisdom, justice and fair play." What constituted wisdom, justice, and fair play in the resource and population debate was of course a matter of perspective. At times, Malthusian worry degenerated into ethno-nationalist concerns with race purity. A good example of the later comes from a renowned biologist of the early twentieth century, Raymond Pearl.

Pearl was a leading eugenicist of the early twentieth century—he wrote of the need for those "endowed with the best traits" to outbreed "those stocks whose characteristics are on the whole bad." World War I emphasized to Pearl the base problem of overpopulation as a cause of the world's problems. "What kind of people," asked Pearl, "will then inherit the earth?" However, Pearl was not only a eugenicist, but a scientist who attempted to base his conclusions on evidence. And the evidence led to a great narrowing of those he considered unfit. Indeed, by the late 1920s he was attacking racists for using false science to support their claims. Rather than eugenics, Pearl wrote more and more about the connection between population growth and resource overconsumption. "The volume and surface of the planet on which we live are strictly fixed quantities," wrote Pearl. "This fact sets a limit." Pearl retained eugenic beliefs, but was careful to distinguish them from his concerns with population and the limits of resources.

Pearl was building on a eugenicist tradition within the progressive conservation movement. Teddy Roosevelt, in many ways a race progressive, also worried that Anglo-Saxons were committing "race-suicide" by not breeding enough. Gifford Pinchot was a supporter of the Race Betterment Foundation of Battle Creek, Michigan. Passionate wildlife conservationist William Temple Hornaday, working as a curator in the Bronx Zoo, created an exhibit featuring a living man from Africa, Ota Benga, as part of a human anthropology display. Benga's quarters were part of the monkey house. Most notoriously, Madison Grant, a founder of the Bronx Zoo and author of the racist screed *The Passing of the Great Race* (which chastised Americans for not being racist enough), clearly connected the preservation of key species such as Redwood trees with the "preservation" of the white race. As with every other part of American society, racist thought wormed its way into the Progressive Era conservation movement.

Pearl was a biologist, and thus not trained in social thinking. But leading economists, among others, were also engaging with Malthusian ideas. One noteworthy thinker is the great economist John Maynard Keynes (1883–1946), who grappled with Malthus in a substantive and prolonged fashion in the interwar years. (Keynes's students responded to his obsessions by dubbing him "Jeremiah Malthus.") How did trade—that is, importing resources from other places—affect thinking about population and resources at the nation-state level? Keynes noted that trade could overcome local resource shortages, but "the problem of food supply . . . is made much worse and far harder of solution by having become, since Malthus's time, cosmopolitan." In this sense economics drove the planetary consciousness of environmental thinkers—resources were not confined to the areas in which they were found, but traded all over the globe.

Keynes also credited Malthus with discovery of the "principle of effective demand" that became the central tenet of his *General Theory* and subsequent advocacy of government spending on public works to combat the problem of unemployment. That rising populations could create demand and hence employment growth was central to Keynes's economic thinking. But rising populations demanded more resources, thereby pitting the solutions to the twin "Malthusian devils" of population and unemployment against each other. It was and is a problem not solved by Keynes—or any other mainstream economist.

Keynes did not live to see nuclear proliferation. But atomic blasts emphasized the limits of resources and the environmental damage wrought by technology because nuclear radiation affected the entire planet. Following World War II, the American military chose Bikini Atoll, a ring-shaped set of coral islands along the equator in the Pacific Ocean, for Operation Crossroads, the testing of its fourth and fifth nuclear bombs. Biologists soon discovered a significant residual radioactivity in the surrounding ecosystem. Tuna, for example, absorbed radiation in their fatty tissues, which would then transfer to anyone who ate them. A young physician who took part in the experiments, David Bradley, detailed the effects of radiation in a best-selling book of 1948, *No Place to Hide*. From 1946 to 1958, the United States conducted twenty-three nuclear tests on Bikini. During the military's Castle Bravo thermonuclear weapons tests, the crew of a Japanese fishing trawler, the *Fukuryū Maru* (*Lucky Dragon*), was inadvertently irradiated by fallout. One crewmember died a few months later, and the rest suffered from radiation illnesses. Such events made the American public wary of nuclear power.

Nuclear issues became embedded in public life in part because defense industry research drove the larger economy: the aircraft industry, nuclear power, computers, the space industry, and semi-conductors all grew from defense industry research. Thousands of spinoffs, such as the microwave oven, which developed from the invention of radar, also spurred economic growth. In 1939 the federal government allotted fifty million dollars for scientific research. By the end of World War II that number grew to five hundred million dollars; by 1955 it was 3.1 billion dollars. In 1953 President Eisenhower delivered his "Atoms for Peace" speech before the United Nations, which committed the United States to commercial nuclear energy development. In 1957 Eisenhower signed the Price-Anderson amendment to the 1954 Atomic Energy Act, which limited the liability of nuclear utilities, thereby making them a more attractive investment.

Nuclear fears coexisted with a belief in nuclear-fueled cornucopian abundance. In 1954, Lewis Strauss, chairman of the U.S. Atomic Energy Commission, spoke to the National Association of Science Writers. "Our children will enjoy in their homes electrical energy too cheap to meter," pronounced Strauss. Malthusian worries over limited resources were mere bad memories from a benighted era of human existence: "our children will know of great periodic regional famines in the world only as matters of history." Strauss's proclamations were only one example of the technological enthusiasm that accompanied the atomic age. In 1958 the U.S. Atomic Energy Commission proposed Project Chariot in which it would construct an artificial harbor on Alaska's north slope through a series of nuclear explosions. Opposition from conservationists and Inupiat Eskimos shelved the idea, but it demonstrated the unbridled enthusiasm to find nonmilitary uses for nuclear devices. Even in scientific journals as prestigious as *Nature*, panglossian scientists could claim that "nuclear agro-industrial complexes" could support desert agriculture with "food factories" that grow crops on desalinated water. Fairfield Osborn had described such talk as "The grand and ultimate illusion . . . that man could provide a substitute for the elemental workings of nature." But to its boosters, nuclear power did just that. Physicist Alvin Weinberg argued that "with an inexhaustible source of energy, man could free himself from material want, essentially forever."

But by the late 1950s there was plenty of evidence to cast grave doubt on the boosters' pronouncements. The health and ecological consequences of nuclear fallout were chief among them. Should scientists take a public stand in debates over nuclear policies? The philosopher and peace activist Bertrand Russel called upon scientists to "appraise the perils that have arisen as a result of the development of weapons of mass destruction." Several key thinkers took up his cause. The Nobel Prize–winning scientist and peace activist Linus Pauling estimated that fallout from nuclear tests caused ten thousand people to die from leukemia. Pauling authored the Scientists' Bomb Test Appeal, quickly signed by over two thousand American scientists, that urged "an international agreement to stop the testing of nuclear bombs." Fallout from nuclear testing became a public issue. In 1955 only 17 percent of the public could correctly explain what fallout was. But by 1957, 52 percent described it as a "real danger."

The greatest demonstration of the dangers of nuclear fallout came from a Washington University professor of plant physiology who set about collecting children's deciduous teeth. Barry Commoner (1917–2012) earned a doctorate in cell biology from Harvard before serving as a lieutenant in the Naval Air Corps during World War II. He went on to become a professor at Washington University in St. Louis. His experience in the U.S. Navy helped develop his environmental views. Exploiting his scientific skills and training, the navy put Commoner in charge of a project to develop a devise that would allow bombers to spray dichlorodiphenyltrichloroethane (DDT) on beachheads to kill the insects, especially flies, that spread disease among soldiers. The military assumed that such a device would protect the health of frontline military. But Commoner's crew discovered that while the DDT sprayed from bombers eliminated the targeted hordes of flies, it inadvertently attracted many more because they swarmed to feed on the tons of dead fish that the DDT also killed. It was a classic lesson in ecology: humans can't tamper with one part of the ecosystem without affecting another.

Commoner combined such ecological insights with a populist, left-wing politics. He continually sought to engage the public about scientific subjects, most prominently the issue of nuclear fallout. In 1958 Commoner published an essay in *Science*, "The Fallout Problem," in which he noted that "the advance of science has thrust grave social issues upon us." Public health and environmental perspectives were desperately needed in the atomic debate. As Commoner put it in an interview many years later, the U.S. Atomic Energy Commission failed to notice that "rainfall washes suspended material out of the air, or that children drink milk and concentrate iodine in their growing thyroids." The U.S. Atomic Energy Commission failed not because of an elaborate cover-up, but because they "failed to perceive facts—even widely known ones—that were outside their limited field of vision." Commoner was pioneering the idea that scientists should be broad thinkers and above all be socially responsible citizens, sharing their knowledge and helping the public engage complicated scientific and technological issues. This stance—the informed scientist deploying knowledge for the greater public good—became a defining characteristic of environmentalism.

Figure 7.2 Baby Tooth Poster
Courtesy of the Committee for Environmental Information, The State Historical Society of Missouri

Figure 7.2a Using children's deciduous teeth, Barry Commoner found that strontium-90 infected children throughout the United States. The finding helped lead to the Limited Nuclear Test Ban Treaty of 1963.

In 1958 Commoner helped organize the St. Louis Committee for Nuclear Information and subsequently became its president. Commoner described the group's mandate as explaining "to the public—first in St. Louis and then nationally—how splitting a few pounds of atoms could turn something as mild as milk into a devastating global poison." (Ecologist Eugene Odum similarly noted that due to biological magnification it was possible to release an "innocuous amount of radioactivity and have her [nature] give it back to us in a lethal package.")

Of particular concern was fallout of the isotope strontium-90, a metal with a half-life of twenty-eight years. The human body metabolizes it like calcium, making it especially harmful to infants and toddlers. It can cause tumors, leukemia, and other blood abnormalities. But how much strontium-90 was actually entering human metabolisms? To find out, the St. Louis Committee for Nuclear Information, assisted by dentists and volunteer youth groups such as the Boy Scouts, Girl Scouts, and the YMCA and YWCA, collected many thousands of the baby teeth shed by children. Some children joined an Operation Tooth Club complete with a membership card and a button that read "I gave my tooth to science." Some 320,000 teeth were then tested for their concentrations of strontium-90. The results were devastating. They showed a one hundred-fold rise in radioactive strontium-90 levels in the baby teeth of children born from 1945 to 1965. Moreover, the amount of strontium-90 rose and fell in conjunction with the testing of atomic bombs. A concomitant study from the U.S. Public Health Service showed an alarming rise in the percentage of underweight live births and childhood cancers.

The results from the baby tooth survey energized the movement to ban atmospheric testing of nuclear weapons. It introduced the broad public to important scientific concepts such as the stratospheric air currents that carried strontium-90 around the globe and the ecological food chains through which it ended up in children's teeth. Public outcry produced a moratorium on testing in 1958 and the Limited Nuclear Test Ban Treaty of 1963, which prohibited its signees, the United States, Soviet Union, and Great Britain, from testing nuclear weapons in outer space, underwater, or in the atmosphere. President Kennedy signed the law less than three months before his assassination. It remains one of the great achievements of the environmental movement. Commoner later wrote in his environmental classic *The Closing Circle* that "the Nuclear Test Ban Treaty should be regarded . . . as the first victorious battle in the campaign to save the environment—and its human inhabitants—from the blind assaults of modern technology."

Commoner's work with DDT and nuclear fallout led him to espouse what we now call the "precautionary principle"—the idea that new chemicals and technologies should not be introduced into society before they are tested to see if they pose a public health risk. He continued to promote a scientifically informed public that could wisely adjudicate such issues.

Commoner argued that our economy, indeed our entire society, needed to be in step with his proposed "four laws of ecology": "everything is connected to everything else," "everything must go somewhere," "nature knows best," and "there is no such thing as a free lunch." The laws were deliberately informal, less a sophisticated ecological systems analysis than a way to popularize holistic understandings of ecology and society. They were an aide to help the public understand the environmental crisis. In 1970, *Time* magazine put Commoner on its cover and dubbed him the "Paul Revere of Ecology."

Other environmental activists heard different kinds of explosions in the nuclear age. For Stanford University biologist Paul Ehrlich (b. 1932), the ticking time bomb was not only atomic blasts, but the explosion in human numbers. In 1968 Ehrlich published one of the best-selling environmental books of all time: *The Population Bomb*. In that year the human population reached about 3.5 billion people. (It has more than doubled since.) Hundreds of millions of those people were severely malnourished; countries such as India suffered severe food crises. And the population, as Malthus had warned, was growing exponentially: at about 2 percent a year globally, and often over 3 percent in already impoverished countries. For Ehrlich, it was not just technology or an unbridled capitalism that drove ecological degradation (though he was more attentive to those factors than his critics allowed), but human numbers. The planet had finite resources but kept adding more and more humans that needed to consume them. The global baby boom—the atomic metaphor is no accident—threatened the future of humanity.

Paul Ehrlich grew up in suburban New Jersey spending most of his time collecting butterflies—they would remain a lifelong passion. Suburban life proved to be a great education for a young environmentalist. He witnessed the ripping up of meadows to make room for ever more tract housing and the near indiscriminate spraying of the pesticide

DDT. After the spray trucks rumbled through the neighborhoods, he found it increasingly difficult to find "food plants to feed caterpillars that weren't soused in DDT." Despite majoring in "liquor and women" as an undergraduate at the University of Pennsylvania, the budding scientist enrolled at the University of Kansas where he earned a master's and doctorate working with the renowned entomologist Charles Michener. At Kansas in the 1950s Ehrlich developed his activist bent, sitting in to desegregate local restaurants following their refusal to serve a visiting black Jamaican scientist. But scholarship, not activism, drove his early career. As a young population ecologist at Stanford University, Ehrlich authored, along with his colleague Peter Raven, one of the foundational papers of modern ecology. It was a study of coevolution—Ehrlich and Raven theorized the idea of different species reciprocally affecting each other's evolution—that posited insect herbivory as a driver of tropical plant speciation and hence biodiversity.

Figure 7.3 Paul Ehrlich combined his love of nature—especially butterflies and birds—with a grave concern about the collision of limited planetary resources with a rapidly growing human population. Here he interacts with a Florida Scrub Jay—a species known for its curiosity.
Courtesy of Paul Ehrlich

In the mid-1960s Ehrlich began giving talks around the San Francisco Bay area about the population-resource problem. The Sierra Club's David Brower convinced him to gather his thoughts into the book that became *The Population Bomb*. Ehrlich and his wife Anne wrote the book "in a few weeks of evenings" completing it in time, they (naively) hoped, to influence the 1968 presidential election. (The publisher insisted that Anne's co-authorship of the book remain uncredited; in their many subsequent books she is fully credited as co-author.) Ehrlich wished to saddle the manuscript with the textbook-like title "Population Resources and Environment"—an accurate description of its theme, but hardly a catchy phrase that would capture popular interest in the complex problems it examined.

The Population Bomb received little attention until the media personality Arthur Godfrey slipped a copy to the late-night television host Johnny Carson. Carson was wowed by the book and quickly invited its author onto his show. Paul Ehrlich was a great fit for television: gifted with a rich baritone voice to deliver his environmental Jeremiads, he was brilliant, handsome, bombastic, quick witted, and outrageous. Ehrlich appeared on "The Tonight Show Starring Johnny Carson" at least twenty times. *The Population Bomb* subsequently sold over two million copies and was translated into many languages. Its author became one of the stars of the burgeoning environmental movement.

Ehrlich began the book by exploding a little bomb of his own: "The battle to feed all of humanity is over," he wrote in the prologue. "In the 1970s hundreds of millions of people will starve to death in spite of any crash programs embarked upon now." Policy responses were merely a "stay of execution" unless they addressed the underlying fundamentals of limited resources and growing populations. Nor, according to Ehrlich, would technology save the day. *The Population Bomb* passionately countered the idea that the oceans could feed a rapidly growing humanity through harvesting more fish or farming its flora. Instead of a new technology-based abundance, Ehrlich offered a series of future scenarios—not predictions—to help envision possible outcomes of the population-resource crunch, delivered with the caveat that "we can be sure than none of them will come true as stated." Rather than technology saving humanity, Ehrlich argued that "We must rapidly bring the world population under control, reducing the growth rate to zero or making it negative. . . . Simultaneously we must, at least temporarily, greatly increase our food production."

Ehrlich's message resonated with a wide audience. In the spring of 1969 Stephanie Mills (b. 1948) delivered a devastating valedictory address to her class at Mills College entitled "The Future is a Cruel Hoax." Citing Ehrlich, Mills identified the source of her anxiety as overpopulation and the concomitant ecological destruction that sheer numbers ensure. Mills was "terribly saddened" by the fact that "the most humane thing for me to do is to have no children at all." Her critique quickly extended to a misguided economic system: "pushing to save the human race will turn no one an instant profit." It would be easier for her "to earn a living as a cocktail waitress" than as a "crusader . . . for human survival." The speech made headlines across the country; *The New York Times* called it "perhaps the most anguished . . . of the year's crop of valedictory speeches." Happily, Mills did manage to find a way to earn a living as a crusader, as she went on to an important career as an environmental activist, writer, and bioregional theorist.

The message of a limited and fragile Earth received another potent emotional boost from the U.S. space program. In December 1968, as their *Apollo 8* spacecraft entered lunar orbit, the astronauts aboard held a live broadcast in which they shared pictures of Earth taken from space. Most famous was *Earthrise*, a picture of the beautiful blue and white Earth surrounded by a never-ending blackness and contrasted against a lifeless expanse of moon in the foreground. Looking at *Earthrise* astronaut Jim Lovell mused that "the vast loneliness is awe-inspiring and it makes you realize just what you have back there on Earth." Those on land agreed; the small planet Earth needed love and protection. On Christmas Day 1968, *The New York Times* published a front-page essay by poet Archibald MacLeish who argued that *Earthrise* would transform how people understood their planet. "To see the earth as it truly is, small and blue and beautiful in that eternal silence where it floats," wrote MacLeish, "is to see ourselves as riders on the earth together." A letter writer to the *Times* emphasized that the image "reminds us that the rivers, the seas, the creatures, the air of this beautiful, life-giving planet exist nowhere else." *The Whole Earth Catalog* said of the image that it "began to bend human consciousness." Anthropologist Margaret Mead, speaking at an Earth Day rally, maintained that "the tenderness that lies in seeing the earth as small and lonely and blue is probably one of the most valuable things we have now."

The earth was small and limited, but the politics of protecting its ecosystems, especially from the explosion in human numbers, were convoluted, complex, and controversial. In 1968 Ehrlich and like-minded colleagues founded Zero Population Growth (now Population Connection). Ehrlich wrote that Zero Population Growth would "make clear to Americans the intimate connection between runaway population growth, our 'cowboy' economy, and the deterioration of our environment." To combat pollution—a significant subject in *The Population Bomb*—Ehrlich advocated for a ban of DDT and other biocides, strict control measures for toxins, and for a great investment in public transportation. The organization also saw ready access to abortion as an important family planning tool. It supported free childcare and generally urged women to enter the workforce, correctly assuming that socially empowered women had fewer children. The organization flirted with various policy ideas related to family planning, including developing new forms of birth control and the wide use of sterilizing agents.

Ehrlich had long been a civil rights advocate and had published scientific work on the biological meaninglessness of the concept of race. He was attentive to the differential social impacts of environmental degradation. In a press release criticizing President Richard Nixon's environmental policies, he wrote that it was the nonwhite poor "that must work and live in the smog and filth, they must labor in farm fields exposed to high risks of pesticide poisoning—they can't live upwind of the pollution with Nixon's millionaire cronies." Despite such social embedding of environmental risks, the racial politics of population control were vexed. Eugenicist elements were attracted to population and immigration control as a way to oppress or exclude nonwhite people. Ehrlich spent much of the 1970s battling eugenicist tendencies in the population movement, writing *The Race Bomb* (1978) among other works debunking racist ideology.

No less a figure than Martin Luther King Jr. agreed with Ehrlich on the population and resource issue. In 1966, upon receiving the Margaret Sanger Award from the Planned Parenthood Federation of America, he wrote a short essay that sounded a lot like Ehrlich's warnings. Imagining extraterrestrial visitors viewing American society, King noted that "Our visitors from outer space could be forgiven if they reported home that our planet is inhabited by a race of insane men whose future is bleak and uncertain." Why were earthlings "insane"? Because "we spend paltry sums for population planning, even though its spontaneous growth is an urgent threat to life on our planet." King further connected the population issue to resource depletion. "To relate population to world resources," he continued, "family planning, is possible, practical and necessary." American blacks, especially, were "atomized, neglected and discriminated against" thus they have a "special and urgent concern" with family planning. Overall, King understood lack of investment in population control, like the war in Vietnam, as a tragic and immoral misapplication of resources: "the modern plague of overpopulation is soluble by means we have discovered and with resources we possess." The tragedy was a society that refused to make socially beneficial investments.

Despite King's speech, many nonwhite people distrusted the idea of population control, finding it either a plot against their futures or a distraction from their immediate needs. At his best Ehrlich directly addressed such issues. In an Earth Day speech at Bowling Green State University, Ehrlich argued that the demand to save the natural world stemmed from the desire for a decent society: "We cannot expect members of minorities, or the poor or any other group which is not given a fair shake in our society to cooperate in an effort to save our civilization—unless we make it their civilization too." Thus "The battle to save our planet is not just a battle for population control and environmental sanity. It is also a battle against exploitation, against war, and against racism. That is, it is a battle for equity, peace and justice—without which the world would hardly be worth saving."

Ehrlich gleefully wrapped his scientific acumen into rhetorical barbs. Other researchers sought to let numbers do the talking. Just four years after *The Population Bomb* exploded onto the American scene, in 1972 a slim volume based upon computer modeling also examined the population-resource-pollution nexus. Entitled *The Limits to Growth*, it was the work of a group of Massachusetts Institute of Technology graduate students led by Dennis and Donella Meadows. The work was sponsored by the Club of Rome, an ad hoc group of avowedly apolitical businessmen, academics, and civil servants. The book modeled the planetary limits of five interrelated factors: population, food production, industrial production, consumption of nonrenewable resources, and pollution. Its models concluded that if 1970 levels of economic growth, resource use, and pollution continued unabated, modern civilization would face environmental and economic collapse sometime in the mid- to late twenty-first century. The book combined the then novel use of computer modeling with a view of environmental problems that was global and interconnected. *The Limits to Growth* thus managed to be simultaneously clear and dispassionate and countercultural and alarming. It sold twelve million copies and was translated into thirty-seven languages. It remains the top-selling environmental book ever published.

Economists generally hated the idea of biophysical limits, and many fiercely criticized Ehrlich and the *Limits* team. A group of economists writing in *The New York Times* described *The Limits to Growth* as "garbage in, garbage out." Conservative economist Henry C. Wallich used his *Newsweek* column to condemn *The Limits to Growth* as "a piece of irresponsible nonsense." Supporters zinged back. Economist Kenneth Boulding retorted that "anyone who believes exponential growth can go on forever in a finite world is either a madman or an economist." Why were most economists so critical of the idea of limits? Their reaction baffled Donella Meadows: "we could not understand the intensity of the reaction our book provoked." The fundamental issue was that economists typically assumed that growth was inevitably good and that economies can expand forever. For ecologists, biological limits are a simple given. They drive evolution. The economist John Kenneth Galbraith noted the difference. Biophysical limits to economic growth, he observed, are "the forbidden question" of economists. Rather than consider them, economists treat the subject with "a nearly total silence."

Still, many contemporary economists like to point out that the gloomiest predictions of Ehrlich and other doomsayers did not pan out. Though famine has claimed at least three hundred million lives since Ehrlich published *The Population Bomb*, the world did not experience disaster to the extent that Ehrlich and his colleagues thought it would. His "scenarios," the imagined glimpses of possible futures, were way off. So were the cornucopian critics correct? On some issues, Ehrlich was clearly on target. His skepticism of technology-created abundance and his worry about biocides have been amply borne out. His prescient concern over "the greenhouse effect" that was being induced by "using the atmosphere as a garbage dump" was also well ahead of its time.

Ecosystems are remarkably resilient, but it was the so-called green revolution, the development of high-yield cereal grains, that Ehrlich praised but clearly underestimated. Led by biologist Norman Borlaug (1914–2009), widely credited as the "Father of the Green Revolution," the combination of high-yield grains, fertilizers, irrigation, biocides, and better management saved many—perhaps a billion—people from starvation.

Borlaug, however, strongly rejected cornucopian interpretations of his work. First, the green revolution exerted terrible environmental costs in loss of biodiversity, reliance upon fossil fuels, and worker exposure to carcinogenic pesticides. In his 1970 Nobel Peace Prize acceptance speech, Borlaug went beyond such criticism to note that "we are dealing with two opposing forces, the scientific power of food production and the biologic power of human reproduction." Despite the spectacular achievements of the green revolution, the "rate of population increase exceeds the rate of increase in food production in some areas." For the world to forestall mass famine in the future, "the agencies that fight for increased food production and those that fight for population control [must] unite in a common effort." Borlaug argued that the green revolution did not overcome Malthusian limits, but merely postponed them.

Like Ehrlich, *The Limits to Growth* team offered scenarios of the future, and also some hard dates against which they assumed various resources vital to global economy would effectively run out. Their central contention was that no economy can grow forever. Most importantly, and a fact often lost in debate over the long-term viability of specific resources, was the *Limits* team's simple contention that "It is not known how much we can perturb the natural ecological balance of the earth . . . before vital processes are severely interrupted." How much waste and ecological disruption can the earth take before its ecosystem services no longer function for humans?

Americans received a shocking reminder of the limits of the natural world in the fall of 1973 when the Organization of Petroleum Exporting Countries chose to use "oil as a weapon." Weaponized oil came in the form of an embargo on oil shipments to the United States. Oil prices quickly doubled, then tripled, then quadrupled. Panic buying of gas ensued, and the long lines at gas stations snaked around corners and down blocks. As the senior oil analyst at the State Department put it, "this time the wolf is at the door."

President Nixon encouraged Americans to turn down their thermostats (to save fuel oil) and to carpool. Congress reduced the speed limit to fifty-five. A system of odd–even rationing allowed vehicles with license plates having an odd number as the last digit to purchase gas on odd-numbered days of the month, while others could buy on the even-numbered days. Many Americans did not take to conservation and efficiency; bumper stickers in Texas and Oklahoma read "Let the bastards freeze in the dark" or "Drive fast and freeze a Yankee." Congress responded in 1975 with the Energy Policy and Conservation Act that set efficiency requirements for appliances with the Energy Conservation Program for Consumer Products Other Than Automobiles and for automobiles with the Corporate Average Fuel Economy standards. It also established the Strategic Petroleum Reserve.

Despite those important policy advances, the Nixon and Ford administrations mostly floundered the energy crisis. Ever greater energy production in the form of increased drilling and subsidizing nuclear energy were the primary policy responses. Nixon's initiative was titled "Project Independence," which was mostly a rollback of environmental regulations. Jimmy Carter (b. 1924), elected in 1976, urged the United States to take the path of energy conservation and investment in renewable energy sources. An engineer by training, Carter was not a great speaker—Senator Eugene McCarthy dubbed him an "oratorical mortician"—but he was forthright and attempted to speak honestly about the moral economy and the earth's natural limits.

In April 1977, Carter delivered a speech on energy that acknowledged the difficult facts of dependence on foreign oil and that conservation must become "our first goal." Noting the substantive social change that new energy regimes would require, Carter, using the words of philosopher William James, likened them to "the moral equivalent of war." Nor did he sugarcoat the impact: "a policy which does not ask for changes or sacrifices," leveled Carter, "would not be an effective policy." But Carter's proposals bogged down in a hostile Congress, leading many Americans to question his leadership. By 1977 a CBS poll found that only 43 percent of Americans thought there was a "real" energy crisis; more thought it was fiction created by oil companies to boost profits. The majority, in other words, refused to grapple with the notion of natural limits.

Carter tried again with a speech in July 1979. He spoke affectingly of a "crisis of confidence" begat in part by discovering that "owning things and consuming things does not satisfy our longing for meaning." The policy part of the speech included trade quotas with a goal of capping oil imports at 1977 levels, an energy security corporation that would invest in new energy sources, an energy mobilization board, and, above all, a "bold conservation program." The public responded well to the speech—calls to the White House were three-to-one favorable.

One man wrote to the president that "you are the first politician that has said the words that I have been thinking for years. Last month I bought a moped. . . . I have cut my gas consumption by 75 [percent]." But then two things happened that prevented Carter from capitalizing on the goodwill. Instead of rallying around his success, Carter feuded with his cabinet, squandering the political capital the speech generated. Second, the pundit class got a hold of the speech and treated it like a chew toy. Carter was widely denounced for lecturing Americans about their wasteful ways. The speech became known as the "malaise" speech, even though Carter never uttered the offending word. Republican presidential candidate Ronald Reagan scorned such talk and promised the American people an orgy of consumption instead of the moral benefits of sacrifice. There was no room in his party for environmental killjoys. Today Carter's speech is widely thought of as a political disaster.

Even as Americans rejected any tampering down of an accumulationist ethos, the unanticipated consequences of consumption were becoming more and more clear. In 1974 researchers Sherwood Rowland and Mario Molina discovered that chlorofluorocarbons (CFCs), a chemical widely used as a coolant and as a spray propellant, destroyed the stratospheric ozone layer. The scientists found that ultraviolet light breaks down CFCs as winds sweep them up into the ozone layer. The freed chlorine atoms then gobble up ozone molecules, depleting the ozone layer. The extra ultraviolet radiation that reached the Earth's surface through the thinned-out ozone caused cataracts and cancers, among many other problems.

The science was complicated, but in day-to-day terms it meant that the simple act of applying hairspray turned out to have profound, even catastrophic, environmental consequences. Industry, led by DuPont which marketed CFCs under the trademark Freon, fiercely attacked the science behind ozone depletion. Anticipating the strategies used by climate disruption denialists, DuPont argued that the science was unsure, theoretical, and that more research, not regulation, was the proper response. Conservative newspaper commentators followed industry's lead, vigorously attacking the "aerosol scare" and indicting environmentalists for supposedly assuming that aerosols were guilty until proven innocent.

But Americans voted the issue with their dollars. Ozone-depleting CFCs became anathema to aerosol consumers. Industry quickly replaced them with benign alternatives. When the United States banned the use of CFCs in aerosol cans in 1978, only a few products were actually affected, because most had switched to other propellants. Meanwhile, skepticism of the entire idea of ozone depletion was rife in conservative circles. But in the mid-1980s a severe annual depletion of ozone—the "ozone hole"—began to appear above Antarctica. The hole was so large that the British scientist who first measured it, taken aback at its size, assumed that his instruments were faulty and promptly sent them home to be repaired. But thanks in part to the discovery of the enormous Antarctic ozone hole, in 1987 fifty-seven industrial nations signed the Montreal Protocol, which mandated a global phase-out of CFCs and other ozone-depleting chemicals. Rowland and Molina, who had been hounded by the chemical industry for years, were entirely vindicated and in 1995 were awarded the Nobel Prize for their discovery.

It wasn't just hairspray that unexpectedly led to the discovery of environmental problems. It also happened when scientists investigated the causes of the extinction of the dinosaurs. When a large meteor struck the earth sixty-five million years ago at the end of the Cretaceous period, the resulting debris spread around the globe and changed the climate almost instantly. Day turned to night; temperatures plunged and plants could not reproduce. The dinosaurs perished. Inspired by this finding, a group of astrophysicists led by Carl Sagan (1934–1996), a great popularizer of science known for his 1980 television series *Cosmos*, began to model what the world would look like following a nuclear exchange. Would nuclear explosions cause damage similar to a large asteroid strike?

Part of the issue was the sheer power of nuclear weapons. The bombs that decimated Hiroshima and Nagasaki pale in comparison to the power of modern nuclear weapons. In their book *The Nuclear Seduction*, William A. Schwartz and Charles Derber note that, "A one-megaton nuclear bomb equals half of the total destructive power of all bombs used by the Western Allies in Europe during all of World War II. It would take a train [three hundred] miles long to transport the equivalent dynamite." Beyond the nearly unimaginable destructive power of such an explosion, what long-term effects would even a limited nuclear exchange have on the planetary ecosystem? In 1983 both Sagan and Paul Ehrlich, among other renowned scientists, published on the issue. What they found was harrowing. Nuclear fallout would not just poison people, but overwhelm ecosystems and prevent them from functioning. Smoke would shroud the world in a permanent twilight. Photosynthesis would collapse. Freezing temperatures would destroy crops. Society would break down, with the extinction of humankind possible. It was the nuclear winter.

Sagan introduced the idea of the nuclear winter to the public in the pages of *Parade Magazine*. Ehrlich and Sagan headlined a 1983 scientific conference, "The Long-Term Worldwide Biological Consequences of Nuclear War," held in Washington, District of Columbia. The results of the conference were published as *The Cold and the Dark: The World after Nuclear War*. Both the Pentagon and the National Academy of Sciences endorsed the idea of nuclear winter, and a popular movement against the nuclear arms race, the Nuclear Weapons Freeze Campaign, adopted the nuclear winter as an important reason for disarmament.

The science of nuclear winter and the popular movement for a freeze had profound effects on policy. President Ronald Reagan and Soviet Premier Mikhail Gorbachev cited nuclear winter theory as a reason to scale back the arms race. In 1987 the United States and the Soviet Union agreed to the Intermediate-Range Nuclear Forces Treaty, and the process continued with the Strategic Arms Reduction Treaty of 1991. The massively complicated Strategic Arms Reduction Treaty required the removal of roughly 80 percent of all the strategic nuclear weapons then in existence.

Since the mid-1980s, nuclear winter theory has undergone substantive revisions. Recent analyses that are more finely grained have shown new outcomes, still perilous, but not as devastating as initially feared. The temperature drops following a limited nuclear exchange, for example, would not be as extreme as early models suggested. A small-scale nuclear war would create a nuclear autumn, but not a deep winter. Even so, the results would be terrifying. A sky filled with soot would push the beginning of spring back ten days, and begin winter two weeks early. The worldwide wheat crop would fail, and most birds would likely go extinct. Nuclear autumn would end much of the life on the planet.

The nuclear autumn is a metaphor not just for atomic war but for a lack of biological growth—for a sterile rather than a vibrant and fecund earth. But economics seemed to turn the metaphor on its head. Growth is the only good in capitalistic economics. But the limits of nature force profound questions upon that formulation. Can economies be sustainable and still grow in the sense of consuming ever more resources? Or is there such a thing as "green growth" in which economies create wealth without consuming ever greater amounts of the natural world? In the 1970s, a renegade few economists began debating these ideas seriously.

The "Dean" of those ecological economists was Herman Daly (b. 1938). Daly taught as an academic economist at Yale and Louisiana State University before working at the World Bank as a senior economist in the Environment Department. While in that post he helped to develop policy guidelines related to sustainable development. In the early 1970s Daley theorized the idea of a steady state economy. The phrase "steady state economy" harkened back to the great British philosopher and economist John Stuart Mill, who wrote in his 1848 *Principles of Political Economy* that "the increase of wealth is not boundless. The end of growth leads to a stationary state." Mill's stationary state implied "no stationary state of human improvement." Instead, what would grow is "mental culture and moral and social progress . . . [and] the art of living," all enabled when human ingenuity is no longer "engrossed by the art of getting on." Daly defined the steady state economy as "an economy with constant stocks of people and artifacts, maintained at some desired, sufficient levels by low rates of maintenance throughput, that is, by the lowest feasible flows of matter and energy from the first stage of production to the last stage of consumption." Population and consumption of raw materials would remain at relatively consistent levels, rather than ever increasing the commodification of nature.

Advocates of the steady state economy emphasize that it is not a stagnant economy, but a dynamic equilibrium in which resource use is stable, but the economy is vibrant, adapting to new technologies and social need. More broadly, ecological economics argues that a diversification of economic goals would allow for new measures of the social-economic good. Herman Daly developed one such measure, the Index of Sustainable Economic Welfare, which does not just measure the aggregate value of all goods consumed, but income distribution and the costs of pollution and other forms of environmental degradation.

Daly's legacy is clear. Even within mainstream economics, more and more researchers are trying to understand how to abate negative environmental externalities, in which the environmental costs of an economic action are imposed on a third party. Polluters, for example, can often pollute and instead of paying the costs of their pollution those costs are imposed on the larger society in the form of health care, loss of beauty, and the tax monies used to "clean up" the environment. One common economic refrain is to "internalize the externalities"—that is, to make polluters pay for their pollution, thus creating incentives to not pollute in the first place. How to force such considerations are a matter of ongoing policy debate.

Innovative economic thinking is needed because according to the world scientific community, the global ecological situation grows ever more dire. Where once figures like Paul Ehrlich or Dennis and Donella Meadows lacked institutional backing in their warnings about the future, the scientific community as a whole has become increasingly adamant in its demand for political action to combat environmental deterioration. A more unified scientific voice, speaking through institutional rather than personal forums, began with *The Global 2000 Report to the US President*. *Global 2000* was commissioned by Jimmy Carter in 1977 and published in 1980 by the Council on Environmental Quality. Fourteen government agencies and the World Bank collaborated to write the report. It concluded that, "the world in [the year] 2000 will be more crowded, and more vulnerable to disruption than the world we live in now. Serious stresses involving population, resources, and environment are clearly visible ahead. Despite greater material output, the worlds people will be poorer in many ways than they are today." The report represented a first in environmental policy making: it sought to implement long-term environmental planning beyond the vagaries of which political party was in power.

President Ronald Reagan promptly ignored the report, an attitude supported by cornucopian economists such as Julian Simon (1932–1998). Simon told rich and powerful capitalists what they wanted to hear, which was that in practical terms resources were unlimited. In 1981 he argued that "There is no reason to believe that at any given moment in the future the available quantity of any natural resource or service . . . will be much smaller than it is now, or non-existent." Fifteen years later he followed up that pronouncement with the absurd claim that "We now have in our hands—really, in our libraries—the technology to feed, clothe, and supply energy to an ever-growing population for the next seven billion years." Such claims reflected the old divide between cornucopian economics and the ecological scientists. Though nuclear power itself was no longer offered as the engine of never-ending growth, Simon and other cornucopian economists assumed that human resourcefulness would always somehow overcome the limits of the natural world.

Further statements by the scientific community dismissed cornucopian claims and were much stronger in language and adamancy than *The Global 2000 Report*. Of particular note is the November 1992 appeal issued by seventeen hundred leading scientists, including the majority of Nobel laureates in the sciences, entitled *World Scientists' Warning to Humanity*. The document begins by asserting that "human beings and the natural world are on a collision course." It emphasized that "the earth is finite. Its ability to absorb wastes and destructive effluent is finite. Its ability to provide food and energy is finite. Its ability to provide for growing numbers of people is finite." Given that reality, "current economic practices which damage the environment . . . cannot be continued without the risk that vital global systems will be damaged beyond repair." The statement did not offer specific policy proposals, but did emphasize that "We must, for example, move away from fossil fuels to more benign, inexhaustible energy sources to cut greenhouse gas emissions and the pollution of our air and water. . . . [and] We must stabilize population." Nor should the impossibility of knowing the precise future impede action: "Uncertainty over the extent of these effects cannot excuse complacency or delay in facing the threat."

The *World Scientists' Warning to Humanity* paired with an unprecedented joint statement from the Royal Society of London and the U.S. National Academy of Sciences. Their statement, entitled "Population Growth, Resource Consumption, and a Sustainable World," was also issued in 1992 to coincide with the United Nations Conference on Environment and Development—the so-called Earth Summit held that June in Rio de Janeiro, Brazil. Deploying more cautious language than the *Warning*, it nevertheless sounded a similar alarm. "The future of our planet is in the balance. . . . If current predictions of population growth prove accurate and patterns of human activity on the planet remain unchanged . . . [humanity] . . . may not be able to prevent either irreversible degradation of the environment or continued poverty for much of the world." The statement concluded by emphasizing that "science and technology alone are not enough. Global policies are urgently needed to promote more rapid economic development throughout the world, more environmentally benign patterns of human activity, and a more rapid stabilization of world population." Where once Ehrlich and the *Limits* team could be dismissed as outliers, the scientific community increasingly sounded similar alarms in a largely unified voice.

The United Nations took up the call for consensus reports on the state of the environment. In 2000, the United Nations Secretary-General Kofi Annan called for an assessment of ecosystem change and its impact on human well-being. The result was 2005 Millennium Ecosystem Assessment (MA)—the most comprehensive sustainability assessment ever undertaken. The MA report minced no words, proclaiming that, "At the heart of this assessment is a stark warning. Human activity is putting such a strain on the natural functions of the Earth that the ability of the planet's ecosystems to sustain future generations can no longer be taken for granted." Over the last fifty years, humans had radically changed the earth, resulting "in a substantial and largely irreversible loss in the diversity of life." The MA noted positive gains for many people during that time, but cautioned against the "growing costs in the form of the degradation of many ecosystem services, increased risks of nonlinear changes, and the exacerbation of poverty for some groups of people." Avoiding the worst required significant change, argued the MA, but "the changes in policy and practice required are substantial and not currently underway."

The MA was a long way from the UNSCCUR and the ITCPN. Where once warnings about global environmental limits, from Fairfield Osborn to Paul Ehrlich to *The Limits to Growth*, were considered extreme, many scholars now believe humanity, in its transformations of the earth, has created a new geological epoch, the Anthropocene. The idea of human power so great as to create a new geological era is an intoxicating notion—for good and ill. But what the environmental community has insisted upon is that human power, however great, does not transcend nature. The basic fact of human existence is that people live within the limits of the natural world.

CHAPTER 8

ABUNDANCE IN THE AGE OF ECOLOGY

If the Bill of Rights contains no guarantee that a
citizen shall be secure against lethal poisons
distributed either by private individuals or by public
officials, it is surely only because our forefathers,
despite their considerable wisdom and foresight,
could conceive of no such problem.

–RACHEL CARSON, *Silent Spring*, 1962

THE ROAD to environmentalism begins with the
roads themselves. The United States has built well
over four million miles of them, many following
World War II when the country enjoyed robust economic
growth and plowed untold resources into the automobile
suburb. In 1950, 57 percent of Americans lived in central
cities; by 1990 that number declined to 37 percent. Millions
of Americans moved from northeastern and Midwestern

cities into low-density, energy-intensive, automobile-dependent suburbs in the South and West. Daily life became fully dependent on the automobile: going to work, school, church, shopping, or visiting friends meant getting into a car and driving. Suburban life gobbled up farmland and forest, oil and coal. The suburbs themselves were built in assembly line fashion, standardized and notorious for conformity: "Little boxes made of ticky tacky," according to songwriter Malvina Reynolds.

Suburban Americans drove from their little boxes to shopping centers. Shopping came to mean much more than fulfilling material needs and enjoying abundance; it became a way to fashion identity and even spiritual fulfillment. The economy produces far more goods than people reasonably need. Therefore wants, even needs, must be created. The solution was to create a society not just of commercial plenty, but of material wastefulness.

Theorists of commercial life were clearly aware of these problems. As historian William Leach observes in *Land of Desire*: "From the 1890s on, American corporate business, in league with key institutions, began the transformation of American society into a society preoccupied with consumption . . . with luxury, spending, and acquisition, with more goods this year than last, more next year than this." Retail analyst Victor Liebow articulated the key idea in 1955:

> Our enormously productive economy . . . demands that we make consumption our way of life, that we convert the buying and the selling of goods into rituals, that we seek our spiritual satisfaction, our ego satisfaction in commodities. . . . We need things consumed, burned up, worn out, replaced, and discarded at an ever increasing rate.

Relentlessly advertising consumption as the American Way of Life was one way to persuade Americans to constantly shop. "Television actually sells the generalized idea of consumption," continued Liebow. Advertising was not intended to inform, but to "create and maintain the multiplicity and intensity of wants." Environmentalists decried such wastefulness. David Brower, reminding his audiences that commercial hunters killed bison for their tongues alone, decried America as having a "buffalo-tongue economy." For Brower, waste overwhelmed the miracles of production.

Most consumers were unaware of the environmental costs of their consumption. A key factor was the commodity form itself: just as consumers don't see the conditions of the workers who make the goods they consume, they rarely see the environmental costs of production and consumption. Things are made elsewhere. Trash is carted off, away from suburban homes, to a landfill. Out of sight is out of mind.

Highways themselves prompted some early protests. In 1954 the government proposed to replace the 185-mile-long Chesapeake and Ohio Canal with a highway. Among those horrified by the idea was Supreme Court Justice William O. Douglas (1898–1980). When he read of plans for the road in the *Washington Post*, he dashed off a letter to the paper in which he defended the canal as "one of the most fascinating and picturesque in the Nation. . . . It is a refuge, a place of retreat, a long stretch of quiet and peace . . . a place not yet marred by the roar of wheels and the sound of horns." Douglas challenged the editors of the *Post* to walk the entire path with him. They accepted his offer, and that March a group of fifty-eight hikers, including the president of the Wilderness Society Olas Murie, set out to explore what might be lost to the automobile. The hike attracted a great deal of media attention. *Time* magazine ran a story. So did the Associated Press, and CBS, NBC, and ABC news. Movie theaters showed a newsreel of the hike. The *Post* changed its editorial position. The publicity surge helped defeat plans for the highway. After years of restoration, in 1971 the canal became a national park. Hiking a threatened area became a form of protest. Four years later, Douglas and wilderness advocate Polly Dyer organized a successful walk along the Pacific coast to protest a proposed coastal road in Olympic National Park.

Protecting special places like the canal or Olympic National Park was one way to tame commercialism. But the most important environmental critic of "the gods of profit and production" and a society "dominated by industry, in which the right to make a dollar at any cost is seldom challenged" was a supposedly gentle nature writer known for her love of the ocean. That writer was Rachel Carson (1907–1964). Personally shy, even demure, Carson's 1962 book *Silent Spring* is a muckraking environmental classic that showed how "chemicals are the sinister and little recognized partners of radiation in changing the very nature of the world."

Rachel Carson grew up in Springdale, Pennsylvania, just north of Pittsburgh. Her mother was greatly influenced by the nature study

Figure 8.1 Rachel Carson's Silent Spring galvanized a growing environmental movement. A committed naturalist, in this picture Carson views raptors at Rosalie Edge's Hawk Mountain sanctuary.
Courtesy of the Linda Lear Center for Special Collections and Archives, Shain Library, Connecticut College

movement. The two would often head outdoors, Anna Comstock's *Handbook of Nature Study* in tow, to explore the surrounding hillsides. Carson attended the Pennsylvania College for Women (now Chatham University), graduating in 1929. A lover of oceans, she studied at the Woods Hole Marine Biological Laboratory and received her master's in zoology from Johns Hopkins University in 1932. Carson was at work on her doctoral degree when, pressed by her families' economic difficulty, she took a job writing scripts for the U.S. Bureau of Fisheries. In 1936 she rose to become editor-in-chief of all publications for the U.S. Fish and Wildlife Service. When not writing for the government she published books about the ocean: *Under the Sea-Wind* in 1941 and in 1952 the wildly successful *The Sea Around Us*, which topped *The New York Times* bestseller list and won the National Book Award. She authored another bestseller, *The Edge of the Sea*, in 1955.

Her success as a writer allowed her to leave her job with the Fish and Wildlife Service and work independently. Increasingly alarmed by nuclear fallout and the profligate use of synthetic pesticides, Carson switched her focus from celebrating the natural world to warning the public about its abuse. In 1945 she tried to interest *Reader's Digest* in an article on the ill effects of the pesticide dichlorodiphenyltrichloroethane (DDT), but the publication would not pursue her idea. In 1958 her friend Olga Owens Huckins wrote to her about no longer being able to hear songbirds from her kitchen because pesticides had drastically reduced their numbers. The letter resonated with ideas and metaphors long fermenting in Carson's consciousness. As she later wrote in *Silent Spring*, "if this 'rain of [pesticide] death' has produced so disastrous an effect on birds, what of other lives, including our own?" No longer would the polluting costs of production be masked. Carson, a writer and scientist, was compelled by circumstances to become a crusader and social critic.

Silent Spring was directed squarely against the chemical industry's overproduction of deadly pesticides. Though often highly technical in nature, Carson delivered the best scientific information of the time with writerly aplomb. It was a devastating critique. She began the work with "A Fable for Tomorrow," the tale of "a town . . . where all life seemed in harmony with its surroundings," but which unthinkingly introduced deadly chemicals (they were "like snow upon the roofs and lawns, the fields and streams") into its midst. The town becomes eerily silent; no birds call. Apple trees bloom but have no pollinators. Vegetation dies. The streams have no fish. The people are plagued with strange illnesses.

For Carson "a grim specter" of chemical pollution was haunting modern industrial, acquisitive society, threatening to silence the spring. Birds were not the only ones to suffer. "For the first time in the history of the world," warned Carson, "every human being is now subjected to contact with dangerous chemicals from the moment of conception until death." The same dangerous chemicals are found in "fish in remote mountain lakes, in earthworms burrowing in soil, in the eggs of birds—and in man himself. . . . They occur in the mother's milk, and probably in the tissues of the unborn child."

She compared the deaths of the Japanese fishermen aboard the *Fukuryū Maru* with a Swedish farmer who died from pesticide poisoning. Radiation connected to chemical pollutants because "the basic issue is the contamination of the environment." It was a recurring theme in *Silent Spring*: "We are rightly appalled by the genetic effects of radiation," wrote Carson. "How then, can we be indifferent to the same effect in chemicals that we disseminate widely in our environment?" Carson explained food chains and how the continual adaptation of insects to pesticides meant that "the chemical war is never won, and all life is caught in its violent crossfire." Even more fundamentally, *Silent Spring* charged that radiation and the overuse of chemical biocides sprung from the same source: the modern ideology of human domination of the natural world. For Carson, the idea of controlling nature was an "arrogance," a relic of "the Neanderthal age of biology." The real question was whether "civilization can wage [such] relentless war on life without destroying itself and without losing the right to be called civilized."

War was an appropriate metaphor; the quantity of biocides sprayed on agricultural lands was stunning. In 1947 the United States produced more than 125 million pounds of such chemicals. By 1960, farmers applied 637 million pounds of pesticides to their crops. Roughly 60 percent of these synthetic compounds, some 375 million pounds, were applied on food. Trucks routinely sprayed DDT in suburban neighborhoods. The commercially powerful pesticide industry was also politically deadly, with many powerful friends in government and media.

Silent Spring immediately found its audience. First serialized in *The New Yorker*, it was a book-of-the-month club selection and a smash bestseller. The Sierra Club officially endorsed Carson's work. "Chemists say they know what they are doing," wrote David Brower. "We are sure they do—up to a point. It is at this point that Miss Carson's alarming analysis begins." *The New York Times* dubbed *Silent Spring* "a [twentieth]-century 'Uncle Tom's Cabin.'"

Part of the reason *Silent Spring* struck such a nerve was that Americans were becoming more aware of the potential hazards of chemicals. In 1959 the government warned that the cranberry crop was tainted by the herbicide aminotriazole. (Research suggested the chemical suppressed thyroid function and encouraged potentially cancerous tumors to form.) The pharmaceutical thalidomide, prescribed as a nausea suppressant to pregnant women, turned out to induce phocomelia in developing fetuses—the malformation of limbs. Thousands of babies were born with striking disfigurements. The permeability of the human body to environmental hazards was also emphasized by organizations working on the nuclear fallout issue—not just Barry Commoner's Committee for Nuclear Information, but the National Committee for a Sane Nuclear Policy and Women Strike for Peace.

Roy Attaway, an outdoor columnist for the *Charleston News-Courier*, summed up many people's reaction when he wrote that "It is not pleasant to realize that your child will be born with small doses of lethal poisons stored in its tissues. It is not pleasant to realize that you and I and every citizen of the United States have lethal poisons stored in our tissues. It is particularly unpleasant to realize that we have no control over the extenuating circumstances." As *Silent Spring* climbed the bestseller charts, Carson appeared on "CBS Reports," an hour-long news program hosted by Eric Sevareid. Her cheerful and thoughtful appearance displaced any reservations that she was shrill or a zealot. Not known to the viewing audience was that she was dying of breast cancer. Carson was so weak that during breaks in the filming she could not hold up her head. Sevareid worried she would not live to see the program air.

Once people began looking, the ill effects of biocide poisoning seemed to be everywhere. In 1963 the most visible effects were along the lower Mississippi River watershed where poisoning from the biocides chlordane, toxaphene, heptachlor, dieldrin, and endrin caused massive wildlife kills. Dying fish rose to the surface of the Mississippi, bleeding from their mouths and fins. The bodies of turtles drifted down streams. Dead catfish weighing as much as seventy-five pounds floated to the surface, as did a dead gar that weighed 150 pounds. Dead crabs lay along the banks. Thousands of crows, cranes, and robins perished. When scientists placed Mississippi mud into aquariums full of healthy fish, the fish died. The *Washington Post* editorialized that the fish kills vindicated Rachel Carson. Government officials began seriously debating whether to ban persistent pesticides.

Defenders of the status quo struck back with a scared and wounded ferocity. The chemical industry commenced an extensive public relations campaign that included circulating "The Desolate Year," a pamphlet and "fact sheet" mocking "A Fable for Tomorrow." Much of the reaction to *Silent Spring* was overtly misogynist. One agriculturalist told a senate committee that "You're never going to satisfy organic farmers or emotional women in garden clubs." A review in *Time* accused Carson of using "emotion-fanning words," to present a case that was "unfair, one-sided, and hysterically overemphatic," because it was based on her "mystical attachment to the balance of nature." In a letter to Dwight Eisenhower, former Secretary of Agriculture Ezra Taft Benson wondered why a "spinster was so worried about genetics"; he balefully concluded that Carson was "probably a communist."

The smear campaign continues to this day, blaming Carson for malaria deaths in the developing world. The charge is that the biocide DDT—banned for commercial use, but not manufacture, in the United States since 1972—should be liberally applied in developing countries to combat the spread of malaria. But many countries fail to do so, these critics of Carson maintain, because of *Silent Spring* and its legacy. The accusation is grossly inaccurate and wildly unfair for many reasons. Most obviously, Carson—a private citizen who died in 1964—could not and did not ban DDT in foreign countries. Indeed, she supported the prudent use of pesticides. Most importantly, overreliance upon organochlorines has led to mosquitos developing immunities to pesticides. Malaria often spikes a few years into a campaign to eradicate mosquitos with DDT. Hence malaria has spread in countries reliant upon chemical mosquito control—a problem Carson foresaw and warned about. People of good will should understand that forcing developing countries into a Faustian bargain between malaria and carcinogenic biocides does not serve any humane interest.

Carson understood that she was subject to an "enormous stream of propaganda." *The New York Times* reported that "The [three hundred million dollar] pesticides industry has been highly irritated by a quiet woman author whose previous works on science have been praised for the beauty and precision of the writing." She criticized not just the private sector but the role of government in subsidizing harmful agriculture. Corporate lobbying, wrote Carson, influenced government and could also purchase a "scientific front" from research universities. "We allow the chemical death rain to fall as though there were no alternative," charged Carson. "Whereas in fact there are many, and our ingenuity could soon discover many more if given opportunity." She thus understood the environmental crisis as a crisis of democracy: "What happens," asked Carson, "when the public interest is pitted against large commercial interests?" Too often the public was "fed little tranquilizing pills of half truth. We urgently need an end to these false assurances, to the sugar coating of unpalatable facts."

Government and other scientists jumped into the debate over *Silent Spring*; both vindicated Carson. President John F. Kennedy charged his Science Advisory Committee with examining the issue. The committee's report, issued in 1963, called for much more extensive monitoring of pesticide residues, further research, and more open documentation of insect control programs. Most importantly, it concluded that "The elimination of the use of persistent toxic pesticides should be the goal." Carson rightly claimed that it "vindicated" her work.

Leading agricultural ecologists also supported Carson. The most important was University of California at Davis Professor Robert L. Rudd, whose 1964 book *Pesticides and the Living Landscape* fully supported the conclusions of *Silent Spring*. Like Carson, Rudd was concerned with pesticide effects on human health. He noted that pesticide poisoning accounted for about 150 deaths annually. As with Alice Hamilton, occupational exposure concerned him greatly. He was especially worried about "vulnerable . . . Mexican *braceros*" who had little training in handling dangerous chemicals. Despite the hugely favorable professional reaction to his work, Rudd paid a severe price for what he called his "challenge to a basic, well-entrenched system." His academic promotion was delayed, and he was dismissed without cause from his post at The University of California Agricultural Experiment Station.

Silent Spring alerted Americans not just to the problem of biocides, but to the costs of suburbanization. Suburban construction ate up a million acres a year in the 1950s. Septic tanks polluted local groundwater. (Some experts estimated that septic tank failure accounted for 40 percent of water-borne illnesses between 1945 and 1980.) Those residents of the suburbs hoping for a bit of country life were appalled when more bulldozers arrived to carve out still more housing developments. Grassroots organizations such as People for Open Space and the Open Space Action Committee sprung up around the country. In 1966 the *Saturday Evening Post* reported that "In every city and in thousands of towns and obscure neighborhoods, there are housewives and homeowners banding together to fight, block by block, sometimes tree by tree, to save a small hill, a tiny brook, a stand of maples." As ecology entered more and more into the public consciousness, such groups shifted their critiques from recreational and aesthetic justifications for open space to preserving the ecological balance of their communities.

One of the most thoughtful critics of suburbanization was also Rachel Carson's greatest champion within the Kennedy and Johnson administrations: Secretary of the Interior Stewart Udall (1920–2010). In 1963 Udall published a classic of environmental literature: *The Quiet Crisis.* He made the costs of suburban development clear: "In a great surge toward 'progress,' our congestion increasingly has befouled water and air and growth has created new problems on every hand . . . as our cities have sprawled outward, new forms of abundance and new forms of blight have oftentimes marched hand in hand." Buttressing unthinking growth was the belief that technology could "fix everything tomorrow." He derided such notions the "Myth of Scientific Supremacy."

Like Harold Ickes, Udall came to the Interior Department as a longtime civil rights activist. Among his civil rights accomplishments, Udall, deploying his jurisdictional authority over the National Football League's Washington Redskins's new stadium, forced the team to repeal its ban on black players in 1962. Udall thus understood environmental and social concerns as part of the same fabric. "Plans to protect air and water, wilderness and wildlife are in fact plans to protect man," wrote Udall.

Udall teamed with Lady Bird Johnson (née Taylor, 1912–2007)—he recalled that "She treasured me, and we were wonderful friends"—to build an impressive legacy of environmental achievement in the Johnson administration. Among the major legislative victories were the Wilderness Act of 1964, the 1965 Land and Water Conservation Fund, and the Wild and Scenic Rivers Program of 1968. All passed with strong bipartisan support. The Land and Water Conservation Fund was a wildly successful program. It funneled fees from offshore oil and gas drilling leases to secure national park lands, beaches, bike paths, and historic homes for public use. Often, Land and Water Conservation Fund monies were used as matching grants for local people working to preserve nearby treasures. Congress, however, never fully funded it—a large portion of its revenues were appropriated to other purposes—and in 2015 the Republican Congress defunded it entirely. But in the 1960s when public lands were valued by both parties, Udall presided over 3.85 million acres of new acquisitions, including four national parks, six national monuments, nine national recreation areas, twenty historic sites, fifty wildlife refuges, and eight national seashores.

Even more than Udall, Lady Bird Johnson was the public face of Great Society environmentalism. Beautification was her issue, but it was not a simple one. "Getting on the subject of beautification is like picking up a tangled skein of wool," she wrote in her diary. Like John Muir, she understood that "All the threads are interwoven" because beauty connected to "pollution and mental health," the "crime rate," "transit," and "the war on poverty." She helped win passage of the Beautification Act of 1965 (which limited billboards and junkyards along highways) and created the First Lady's Committee for a More Beautiful Capital.

Capital beautification was much more than the planting tens of thousands of daffodil bulbs and many hundred azalea and dogwood trees. It was serious neighborhood reform. Johnson led a campaign to help Washington's poor, black Shaw neighborhood with trash removal and rat control. That beautification work developed into Project Pride, which enlisted students from Howard University and local high schools to clean up neighborhoods. Mrs. Johnson funded the project with a seven thousand dollar grant from the Society for a More Beautiful Capital. "Where flowers bloom, so does hope," proclaimed Johnson.

Lady Bird Johnson sought to tame commercialism and suburban sprawl with beautification. Other activists sought to reform commercial practices as a way to democratize corporate power. Among the most successful was a child of Lebanese immigrants who hitchhiked from his home in Connecticut to Washington, District of Columbia, to embark upon his muckraking career as a "public citizen." Ralph Nader (b. 1934) leapt onto the public scene with his criticisms of the automobile industry in his 1965 book, *Unsafe at Any Speed: The Designed-In Dangers of the American Automobile.* The book helped launch Nader into a long and impressive career as a consumer watchdog and advocate. In 1971 he founded the consumer advocacy group Public Citizen. Nader authored many books, including *The Menace of Atomic Energy* (1977) and *Who's Poisoning America* (1981).

General Motors responded to *Unsafe at Any Speed* with a propaganda campaign and by spying on Nader, hoping to find material with which to smear the activist. Nader found out about being tailed, sued General Motors and won a settlement of $425,000; he used the money to seed public interest organizations. *Unsafe at Any Speed* prompted the passage of the National Traffic and Motor Vehicle Safety Act of 1966, seatbelt laws in forty-nine states (all but New Hampshire), and a number of other road and car safety initiatives.

Though best remembered for its criticisms of the Chevrolet Corvair, *Unsafe at Any Speed* also tackled the pollution problems caused by automobiles. He entitled a chapter "the power to pollute" which focused on the highways and smog of Los Angeles. "The question is not whether we can build a car that won't pollute the air," argued Nader in 1967, "the question is whether we can overcome the resistance of the auto industry and the oil industry to get it built." The way to overcome that resistance was through mass citizen action. Ralph Nader mobilized college students to form Public Interest Research Groups—dubbed "Nader's Raiders" by the press. He went on to champion and help pass key environmental reforms including the Safe Drinking Water Act and the clean air and clean water acts.

Another way to criticize suburbanization and hyperconsumerism was to work to revitalize urban spaces—and to think through the ideologies of nature embedded in the suburban ideal. More than any other thinker, Jane Jacobs (1916–2006) in her landmark 1961 book *The Death and Life of Great American Cities*, articulated what she described as a "schizophrenic" attitude toward nature in the suburbs. According to Jacobs, the suburbs did not connect people with the natural world but rather an "insipid, standardized, suburbanized shadow of nature." What actually happened with suburban development is that "each day, several thousand more acres of our countryside are eaten by the bulldozers, covered by pavement, [and] dotted with suburbanites who have killed the thing they thought they came to find." Suburban sprawl sacrificed agriculture lands for "highways or supermarket parking lots." Woodlands are "uprooted," the "rivers polluted," and the "air itself filled with . . . gasoline exhausts." Jacobs predicted that the suburbs would be "despised by their own inhabitants tomorrow." The long history of criticism of the suburbs and recent trends of Americans migrating back into urban cores suggest she may have been correct.

As happened in the Progressive Era, the vibrant environmentalism of the 1960s engaged working-class people and examined the workplace as a site for environmental reform. Labor was not new to issues of environmental quality. In 1948, a smog in the mill town of Donora, Pennsylvania, just twenty-four miles southeast of Pittsburgh, alerted many labor activists of the need to consider pollution as a labor issue. That October a temperature inversion kept a thick yellow smog over the city that under normal weather would have dissipated into the atmosphere. Donora's smog was a poisonous mix of carbon monoxide, sulfur dioxide, and metal dust. Doctors quickly ordered the elderly and those who were having trouble breathing to leave town. Witnesses reported the smog was so thick they could taste it. It killed twenty people and sickened at least six thousand more, stunning totals for a town of only fourteen thousand people. Had the fog lasted longer, thousands more might have died. The United Steelworkers aggressively investigated the incident. In an age when labor unions sought to expand their influence communitywide, the killer smog emphasized the connections between workplace safety, public health, and environmental well-being.

Among those in the labor movement most deeply concerned with environmental quality was one of the most important labor leaders of the mid-twentieth century: Walter Reuther (1907–1970) of the United Auto Workers (UAW). Known as the "most dangerous man in Detroit" for his ability to take on the auto industry, Reuther combined a real love of nature—he was an avid fisherman—with an expansive vision of fundamental social reform. In an era when labor was winning significant gains in terms of leisure time, Reuther wondered "what good" is "higher pay" and a "shorter work week" or a "longer vacation" if "the lakes you want to take your family to are polluted and you can't fish in them, or swim in them, or, if the air is poisoned, and our cities are becoming big asphalt jungles?" In 1965 the UAW organized a "United Action for Clean Water" conference. Reuther, sharing key ideas with Lady Bird Johnson, wanted the conference to launch "a popular crusade . . . for clean water [and] for cleaning up the atmosphere, the highways, the junkyards and the slums."

As the 1960s progressed and the depths of environmental problems became more clear, Reuther's environmentalism became even more broadly engaged—and enraged. Environmental problems, argued Reuther, arose from "a crisis in our value system." That moral struggle encompassed the entire human future. Sounding a great deal like Paul Ehrlich, Reuther argued in 1968 that "If we continue to destroy our living environment by polluting our streams and poisoning our air . . . we put the survival of the human species in jeopardy. . . . We may be the first civilization in the history of man that will have suffocated and been strangled in the waste of its material affluence—compounded by social indifference and social neglect." Such a crisis demanded a response from labor. In January 1970, Reuther announced that "I think the environmental crisis has reached such catastrophic proportions that . . . the labor movement is now obligated to raise this question at the bargaining table." The UAW even went so far as to call for the replacement of the internal combustion engine.

Just as Reuther was bringing an environmentalist critique to auto workers, Cesar Chavez (1927–1993) was organizing agricultural laborers around the issue of worker exposure to biocides. Chavez furthered Rachel Carson's brilliant critique, bringing her broadly construed warnings about biocide health effects on "mankind" to the specific lives of the mostly migrant, mostly Mexican-American farmworkers in his union. The issue caught fire in 1968 when a sixteen-year-old farmworker died from poisoning after spraying strawberries with pesticides that were illegally obtained, mislabeled, and applied without safety equipment or training. "We will be damned—and we should be—if we will permit human beings to sustain permanent damage to their health from economic poisons," thundered Chavez.

The incident quickly connected environmental and worker health for the members of the union Chavez found with Dolores Huerta (b. 1930), the National Farm Workers Association (later to become United Farm Workers). Environmental abuses were a central part of the union's concerns. "If we ignored pesticide poisoning," said Chavez, "then all the other injustices our people face would be compounded by an even more deadly tyranny." Farmworker health was clearly a significant issue. In 1966, California's Bureau of Occupational Health acknowledged "1,347 cases . . . of occupational diseases" that derived from "exposure to certain pesticides and insecticides." A total of 136 exposures resulted in death. Chavez publicized a private study of farmworker children that discovered serious problems with pesticide poisoning, specifically high levels of DDT. Biocides, warned Chavez, could "choke out the life of our people and also the life system that supports us all."

In 1969 laboratory analysists found significant residues of DDT, aldrin, and parathion on grapes. Huerta and Chavez led a boycott of table grapes that brought the plight of farmworkers to national attention. Millions of consumers stopped buying grapes. Huerta recalled that "César and I witnessed firsthand the silent, tragic poisoning, by tons upon tons of pesticides and fertilizers, of not only those who toiled in the fields but also their families waiting at home." The injustice was a human right issue and a violation of "*amor por el terruño*—love for the land." The farmworker strike and consumer boycott attracted a great deal of publicity; eventually farmworkers won the right to union representation, and in 1975 California passed the California Agricultural Workers Labor Relations Act, the only law in the country that protects farmworker's ability to organize.

As severe as the human health costs of biocide poisoning are, they were not the most widely dispersed environmental toxins that poisoned America's children. That distinction belongs to lead. Leaded paint colored the nation's homes, hospitals, schools, and children's toys. In the 1920s, tetraethyl lead was introduced as an additive for gasoline. Over the course of the twentieth century, tens of millions of Americans were poisoned by it. Industry diverted attention away from lead additives in everyday products to the Americans most affected by it. In 1957, Manfred Bowditch of the Lead Industries Association argued that "Most of the cases [of lead poisoning] are in Negro and Puerto Rican families, and how does one tackle that job?"

Social change activists seized on lead poisoning as a poverty and civil rights issue—what today is called environmental justice—in the 1960s and 1970s. In New York City, The Young Lords, a human rights and Puerto Rican nationalist group, conducted lead poisoning tests and staged sit ins demanding action on lead poisoning from the city's Department of Health. The Black Panther Party engaged in similar actions in Boston and Oakland. In St. Louis, efforts against lead were headed by renowned civil rights activist Ivory Perry. Perry worked with Barry Commoner, among many others, in a years-long crusade to help impoverished people receive testing and treatment for lead poisoning and to reform substandard, lead-infected housing.

Physicians, alerted to the lead issue from their clinical practices as well by the publicity of environmental rights campaigners, began to join the fray. Philadelphia's Herbert Needleman, borrowing a tactic from Barry Commoner and the Committee for Nuclear Information, collected children's deciduous teeth—he called it The Philadelphia Tooth Fairy Project—to test for lead poisoning. He found that otherwise healthy children suffered from lower IQ scores, poorer language function, and poorer attention due to even trace amounts of lead poisoning. Children were not affected equally: "Urban children had nearly five times the concentration observed in their suburban counterparts." Needleman also conducted basic research demonstrating the ill health effects of lead absorbed from automobile exhaust. Industry responded by attacking Needleman, hiring experts to undermine his research. Independent researchers eventually vindicated Needleman's findings.

By the late 1960s concern for the environment seemed to be everywhere. In 1967 the Reverend Martin Luther King spoke of people in cities "gasping polluted air and enduring contaminated water," an environmental recognition that "all life is inter-related. We are all caught in an inescapable network of mutuality." Popular music reflected the growing concern. Neil Young sang about "Mother Nature on the run/ In the nineteen seventies." Joni Mitchell lamented that "They paved paradise/ And put up a parking lot." More than any other singer, Marvin Gaye captured the feeling with "Mercy Mercy Me (The Ecology): "Where did all the blue skies go?/ Poison is the wind that blows from the north and south and east," sang Gaye. "Radiation underground and in the sky/ Animals and birds who live nearby are dying/ What about this overcrowded land/ How much more abuse from man can she stand?"

It was a good question, one that was brought home by two highly visible environmental tragedies that struck two years before Gaye's song became a hit. On January 28, 1969, the blowout of an oil well platform off the coast of Santa Barbara, California, was a calamity fit for television, complete with oil-coated wildlife and a crude black tide that befouled a stunning coastline. *The New York Times* called the disaster the "ecological shot heard 'round the world.'" The nation saw firsthand some of the environmental costs of automobile culture. One year after the blowout, environmental historian Roderick Nash read a proclamation he authored, the "Santa Barbara Declaration of Environmental Rights," live on network television.

Across the country in Cleveland, an even more gut-wrenching event captured the public's attention. That June, the seemingly impossible happened: a major river caught on fire. It had actually happened many times. The Cuyahoga River, polluted by industrial effluent, was prone to such incidents. A local joke held that those who fell into the Cuyahoga did not drown; they decayed. The 1969 fire was small and easily contained (a 1959 river fire lasted for eight days!) and initially attracted little attention. But that August *Time* magazine published an arresting photo of the fire. In an era of environmental concern, what image of environmental insanity could be more emotionally wrenching than a river so polluted it caught on fire?

In 1969 Cleveland enjoyed the leadership of Carl Stokes (1927–1996), the first black mayor of a major American city. Stokes worked to revitalize Cleveland as a livable city by, among many other initiatives, combating air and water pollution. He quickly learned the limits of his office. The day after the fire, he publicized the event, leading journalists on what historians David and Richard Stradling describe as a "pollution tour." "There may be some wry humor in the phrase 'the river is a fire hazard,'" Stokes told the assembled crowd, "but it's a terrible reflection on the city surrounding it when it does indeed become one."

The pollution tour was really a tour in politics. Stokes showed journalists sewage pouring from a pipe that broke just before it reached a treatment plant. To emphasize the point further he took them to the border between Cleveland and Cuyahoga Heights where a pipe from the suburb emptied into the river. Who would join the costs of infrastructure repair? Stokes also told journalists how Cleveland's many factories polluted the river because the State of Ohio continued to issue them pollution permits; what jurisdiction did the city have over such matters?

Americans responded to the environmental crisis with organization and protest. Membership in the established environmental groups skyrocketed. In 1962 the Audubon Society boasted forty-one thousand members; by 1970 that number nearly doubled to 81,500. The Sierra Club jumped from twenty thousand members in 1959 to 113,000 in 1970; the Wilderness Society from twenty-seven thousand in 1964 to fifty-four thousand in 1970. Thousands of new, local groups sprang up all around the country. In 1970 the economist Robert Heilbroner noted that "Ecology has become the Thing." *Fortune* magazine wondered at the "immense transformation [that] has occurred in public concern about the environment." *Audubon* magazine boasted that "now, suddenly, everybody is a conservationist."

American conservationists—and it did seem to be nearly "everybody"—faced up to the environmental challenge with a massive protest created by an establishment senator who borrowed the key tactic from the anti-war movement. Wisconsin Senator Gaylord Nelson, a longtime environmental and social justice advocate, watched as teach-ins against the Vietnam War became an effective tactic. He wondered if the environmental movement could harness the vibrant energy of student protest. "If we could tap into the environmental concerns of the public and infuse the student anti-war energy into the environmental cause," recalled Nelson, "we could generate a demonstration that would force this issue onto the national political agenda."

Senator Nelson announced the idea for a "national teach-in on the environment" to the national media. It was an immediate hit. Nelson later recalled that "the wire services carried the story from coast to coast. The response was electric. It took off like gangbusters . . . inquiries poured in from all across the country." Nelson established an independent nonprofit office in Washington, District of Columbia, Environmental Teach-In, Inc., to plan the event. He recruited Harvard law student Denis Hayes to be the national coordinator. Seed money came from Walter Ruether's UAW. The organizing staff came from social justice work. Hayes was an anti-war activist; Arturo Sandoval a Chicano activist from New Mexico. Barbara Reid was a veteran of Robert Kennedy's 1968 presidential campaign; Sam Love a civil rights organizer from Mississippi. Environmental Teach-In, Inc., published a full page advertisement in *The New York Times* that assigned the National Teach-In a new name: Earth Day.

The organizers made two key decisions. First, Earth Day would not be centrally directed by Nelson or the organizing committee. Local organizers determined their curriculum and protest. The event was truly, even radically, democratic. Second, the event was both educational and political. It taught and inspired; this is what historian Adam Rome has appropriately termed the "genius" of Earth Day. The genius was on full display on April 22, 1970. The call to action inspired thousands of events across the country. Over twenty million Americans—one in ten—participated in Earth Day events. Two thousand colleges, ten thousand elementary and high schools, and over one thousand communities held Earth Day events. It is, by an overwhelming margin, the largest day of protest in American history.

Earth Day events—they often were spread across an entire week, sometimes longer—were as varied as the communities that staged them. Walter Reuther gave a speech in which he blasted the auto industry for failing "to meet its public responsibility. . . . It is asinine . . . to have hundreds of thousands of people all going to the same place at the same time for the same purpose and all of them dragging two tons of gadgets with them." As an alternative, he proposed a massive investment in public transportation. Reuther was hardly the only speaker to take on the automobile. In New York City Earth Day activities closed Fifth Avenue as a challenge to car culture. *The New York Times* reported that once freed from automobiles, Fifth Avenue revealed "a festive air." When Earth Day ended, "even the police seemed reluctant to let the fume-belching cars and buses return." Speakers at the New York City Earth Day ranged from actor Dustin Hoffman to anthropologist Margaret Meade. Music included performances by Leonard Bernstein, Pete Seeger, and the "Voice of the Civil Rights Movement," the singer Odetta, who sang "We Shall Overcome."

In Cleveland, more than one thousand Cleveland State University students and faculty staged a "death march" from the campus to the banks of the Cuyahoga River. The headline in the next day's *Cleveland Press* read, "Hippies and Housewives Unite to Protest What Man is Doing to Earth." In Miami, a group known as the Eco Commandoes dumped bright yellow dye in sewage plants to show residents what happened to their waste. Earth Day itself included a Dead Orange Parade—mocking college football's Orange Bowl parade—interspersed with women and children carrying banners. One read, "You Pollute We Pay." Local librarians wore gas masks to protest air pollution.

In St. Louis, Freddie Mae Brown, a social worker and founder of the St. Louis Metropolitan Black Survival Committee, staged a "guerilla street theatre" production of a play entitled "Black Survival: A Collage of Skits." The play emphasized the problems of urban pollution. "What would you do," asks the narrator at the end of the play, "if a loved one of yours became too weak to breathe the air?"

In Albuquerque, New Mexico, Arturo Sandoval, the western coordinator for Environmental Action, led a march that emphasized the environmental injustices of the barrio. Afterward, he gave a speech arguing that Chicano culture could save society. Most Americans were "afraid of their humanity because systematically they have been taught to become inhuman. . . . They have been taught that money is God." Instead, Americans should embrace the concept of *la raza*, which "goes beyond skin color" to "an understanding of their humanity." Such an attitude would help "humanize technology" and would inform the creation of "human, life-supporting kinds of environments."

In Salina, Kansas, a group of women formed Salina Consumers for a Better Environment. "We must be concerned," one argued, "not that our children have every material convenience, but that they have air to breathe." They held a workshop at the local YMCA on reducing pollution and waste. That evening, a local professor, Wes Jackson, gave a speech in which he argued for a change in consciousness in which people realized that the "planet is to be lived on, not exploited; that it is to be transferred to the next generation, not destroyed."

Earth Day activists thought globally and acted locally, but also realized, as Mayor Stokes showed with his pollution tour, that environmental problems demanded a federal response. That response arrived in a stunning array of legislation that remain the basis of American environmental law. The popular outcry was so powerful that for about a year and a half it turned president Richard Nixon into an environmentalist. On January 1, 1970, Nixon signed a law sometimes referred to as the "environmental magna carta," The National Environmental Policy Act (NEPA). Developed by Senator Henry "Scoop" Jackson, NEPA requires federal agencies to assess the environmental effects (with an Environmental Impact Statement) of any proposed federal action. Environmental quality was now a standard of measurement in American life. Legally, NEPA marked the beginning of the environmental era in U.S. governance.

NEPA also established the Council on Environmental Quality—an advisory board to the president on environmental affairs. Throughout the 1970s the Council on Environmental Quality sponsored studies of environmental problems, thereby forcing them onto the national agenda. The weakness of the Council on Environmental Quality lies in its advisory capacity. Presidents hostile to the environment simply allow it to lay dormant. But NEPA signaled a profound shift in American priorities. Shortly after signing NEPA, President Nixon halted construction of the Cross-Florida Barge Canal. The project, opposed by Florida environmentalists led by Marjorie Harris Carr, was the kind of New Deal–style infrastructure spending that was once uncontroversial. But environmental quality was a new value. The canal would severely impair the Ocklawaha River. Today the canal path is walkable as the Marjorie Harris Carr Cross Florida Greenway.

In December 1970 Nixon established the Environmental Protection Agency (EPA). The agency was a reorganization of the federal bureaucracy, uniting under one roof the patchwork public health and regulatory bureaus that impacted environmental quality. For the first time, the federal government dedicated an agency with an independent budget

Figure 8.2 Earth Day activities in Denver, Colorado. Like many Earth Day protests, these were led by students. Here, Arvada High School students take to the streets to protest.
Courtesy of The Denver Public Library, Western History Collection

to environmental issues. By 1972 the EPA's budget was $2.5 billion; it employed more than seven thousand people. With the creation of the EPA, the federal government assumed responsibility for environmental quality in a way never before seen.

The EPA was forced to quickly define its mission because of consequential new laws. The Clean Air Act of 1970 charged the EPA with setting air quality standards based upon the best available science. It required new "point source" polluters (pollution emanating from a single source—think a smoke stack) to obtain federal permits that required technologies that reduced the dispersal of pollutants. The law grandfathered the wastes generated by existing sources of pollution—a major flaw. But the success in achieving cleaner air has been nothing short of remarkable. Between 1970 and 1990, smoke pollution decreased nearly 80 percent, lead emissions 98 percent. The law prevented more than two hundred thousand premature deaths, eighteen million cases of respiratory illness in children, as well as 670,000 cases of chronic bronchitis and over 840,000 asthma attacks. It is one of the greatest civil rights achievements in American history.

Figure 8.2a East High School students clean up by collecting garbage. Courtesy of The Denver Public Library, Western History Collection

More foundational laws quickly followed. The Occupational Safety and Health Act (1970) required employers to provide workers with a safe workplace—including not subjecting them to toxic pollutants. The Water Pollution Control Act Amendments (colloquially the "Clean Water Act") of 1972 set national standards that all surface waters should be "fishable and swimmable" by 1983. Nixon vetoed the measure, but Congress easily overrode his executive action. The law provided huge subsidies to municipalities to repair and upgrade waste treatment facilities. The federal government was finally helping mayors in the way that Carl Stokes wanted. The law dramatically improved water quality. Before the Clean Water Act, fewer than a third of the waters in the America passed the "fishable and swimmable" test; now about two-thirds do. According to a 2012 EPA report, 90.7 percent of U.S. community water systems met "all applicable health-based standards" in 2011.

The emphasis on human health did not leave wildlife behind. In 1973 Congress passed the Endangered Species Act (ESA). The ESA, passed with strong bipartisan support, prevented anyone from "taking" an endangered species. The act charged the Fish and Wildlife Service with listing both "threatened" and "endangered" species, and preventing the destruction of "critical habitat" for their survival. The law thus enshrined biodiversity as a value. Many charismatic species, including bald eagles, peregrine falcons, whooping cranes, the American alligator, and grizzly bears owe their continued existence to the ESA. The ESA protects more than sixteen hundred plant and animal species in the United States, many of which are successfully recovering. In the 1990s the ESA became the target of property rights advocates. The law officially expired in 1992, and Congress only extends it on a year to year basis; permanent reauthorization has failed and the law has become another piece of malleable legislation.

During the 1970s, Congress passed several other key environmental laws. Ocean health received a great boost in 1972 when the Marine Mammals Protection Act and the Coastal Zone Management Act went into force. The Safe Drinking Water Act passed in 1974, the Toxic Substances Control Act in 1976. In 1977 Congress strengthened and extended both the Clean Air Act and the Clean Water Act. As John Adams of the Natural Resources Defense Council noted, "In 1970 there were . . . no real environmental laws. . . . Now we have forty or fifty federal statutes."

The environmentalism that flourished with Earth Day was as varied as environmental problems themselves. First published in 1968, the *Whole Earth Catalog* voiced a new kind of environmental advocacy that embraced science and technology as keys to personal freedom and environmental quality. The impresario behind the catalogue, Stewart Brand (b. 1938), was as bold in his embrace as technology as he could possibly be: "we are as Gods," wrote Brand, we "might as well get good at it." Behind such hubris was a recognition that humans are profoundly altering the natural world; if humans are managers of nature, they should at least be wise ones. Brand was a kind of hippie libertarian, an optimist shaped, as historian Andrew Kirk writes, by "a love of good tools, thoughtful technology, scientific inquiry and a Western libertarian skepticism of the government's ability to take the lead in these areas." Brand's genius was to marry environmentally appropriate technology with the ideals of personal liberation and distrust of centralized power that marked the 1960s.

In the wake of the 1973 energy crisis, Brand's vision of technology, in modified form, was taken up by Amory B. Lovins (b. 1947). A child prodigy who joined the Oxford University faculty at age twenty-one, Lovins became an effective champion of conservation and renewable energy sources. He specialized in energy, both its physics and how it is managed socially, as a staff member of Friends of the Earth. In 1982 he left Friends of the Earth to found, with his wife Hunter, the Rocky Mountain Institute, a think-tank working on renewable energy and sustainable development.

In a widely discussed 1976 article in *Foreign Affairs*, Lovins called for the "soft energy path" of conservation, energy efficiency, and renewable technologies against the "hard path" of "centralized high technologies" such as nuclear power. The environmental advantages were many, and soft energy could be easily taken up by regular citizens—Lovins was a great champion of simple but effective solutions such as passive solar design—and by residents of the developing world. Like Stuart Brand, Lovins was entrepreneurial, enamored with technology and favored decentralized power. "Today . . . 'industrial capitalism' . . . is inadvertently liquidating its two most important sources of capital, the natural world and properly functioning societies," argued Lovins. "No sensible capitalist would do that."

Other forms of environmentally decentralized living focused on the production of food, not energy. The 1960s and 1970s featured various attempts to move "back to the land" but none so profound as the return of the writer Wendell Berry (b. 1934) to his Kentucky farm. Skeptical of hypercapitalism, mobility, and hard path technology, Berry began farming his small homestead in 1965. From there he launched a career criticizing industrial agriculture and the peripatetic, consumptive American society that lacked meaning and commitment to place. "Agriculture using nature," wrote Berry, would "consult the genius of the place." This was in sharp contrast to "the modern home . . . [which] takes in the world's goods and converts them into garbage, sewage, and noxious fumes—for none of which have we found a use."

Berry's didactic poem "Manifesto: The Mad Farmer Liberation Front" bewailed a society taught to "Love the quick profit, the annual raise/ vacation with pay." The cost was to "Be afraid/ to know your neighbors and to die." Meanwhile society will impose its purely commercial values: "When they want you to buy something/ they will call you. When they want you/ to die for profit they will let you know." Berry's most famous book, 1977's *The Unsettling of America: Culture and Agriculture*, passionately argued against industrial agriculture and in favor of small-scale, local farming. His work strongly influenced the environmental and local food movements.

The 1970s' peace movement and critique of commercialism also birthed one of environmentalism's most radical and effective organizations. Like much of the environmental movement, protest of nuclear testing drove the creation of Greenpeace. Two Quaker couples (Irving and Dorothy Stowe and Jim and Marie Bohlen) moved to Vancouver in dismay of what they considered an overbearing American militarism. There they joined with local activists, especially a countercultural journalist named Bob Hunter (1941–2005), to form the loose-knit organization. The activists were united, in the words of historian Frank Zelko, by "a deep suspicion of notions of progress, growth, and security that mainstream society took for granted." To combat social and ecological destruction, they "created a new and potent method for confronting powerful institutions engaged in environmentally irresponsible activities."

The method, direct confrontation, came from the anti-war movement. In 1970 Greenpeace—then a loose collection of countercultural activists and Sierra Club members in British Columbia—protested American underground nuclear testing in the Aleutian Islands with the "Don't Make a Wave" campaign. Writing for the *Vancouver Sun*, Bob

Hunter described the testing in the geologically unstable region as "a game of Russian roulette with a nuclear pistol pressed against the head of the world." They outfitted an old fishing boat, the *Phyllis Cormack*—rechristened the *Greenpeace*—to confront the nuclear testers. They financed their work with the proceeds of a hastily arranged concert headlined by Joni Mitchell, an on-the-cusp-of-stardom James Taylor, and leftist folk singer Phil Ochs. The mission failed to stop the testing, but drew attention to the issue and forged a strong bond between the peace and environmental communities. It also reified the idea of direct action. Greenpeace members repeatedly used their bodies when confronting nuclear testing, and after 1973, whaling vessels.

Bob Hunter led the organization into the anti-whaling direction, causing some of the older, anti-nuclear campaigners to drop out. Greenpeace campaigned for whales because they were endangered and because working for their health embodied the new kinds of ecological relationships Greenpeace thought humanity needed to prevent its self-destruction. In an atomized and disenchanted world, working to save whales was a way to forge meaning for the lifeworld. In this way Greenpeace—and many other environmental campaigners—married a countercultural ethos with ecological science. Saving nature gave people meaning.

Whales were also charismatic megafauna—big, alluring animals whose fate played well to the media. Hunter was a close reader of media theorist Marshall McLuhan and became a proponent of what he called "mind bombing"—providing media with emotionally arresting images meant to galvanize viewers. Direct confrontation thus included sailing precisely between a harpoon and a whale, or underneath a barrel of toxic waste about to be illegally dumped into the ocean. Mass media dissemination of such images, argued Hunter, would target viewer consciousness and change hearts and behaviors in a way the political process never could.

In the late 1970s Americans learned that toxic waste had been dumped all over the country, including in lands developed as suburban housing. Such was the case of Love Canal, a neighborhood in Niagara Falls, New York. The canal was partially built in the 1890s by William T. Love, a dreamy real estate entrepreneur who envisioned building a "model manufacturing city" of "great architectural beauty." It would be powered by hydroelectric energy supplied by nearby Niagara Falls—a sharp contrast to coal-powered industrialism. Love's city was to enjoy clean drinking water, efficient services, and even mail delivered by "pneumatic conveyers." But after digging part of his canal, he ran out of money and moved west. Locals used the canal as a swimming hole until Hooker Electrochemical (now Occidental Chemical) bought it and filled it with twenty-two thousand tons of toxic waste. Most of the waste came from Hooker's work provisioning the World War II military.

Hooker sold the land to the city of Niagara Falls school board for a dollar in 1953. The deed of sale clearly described the piles of deadly chemicals; the city assumed all liability. When the land was sold to a housing developer, Hooker spokesman A.W. Chambers explained to the *Niagara Falls Gazette* that "there are dangerous chemicals buried there in drums, in loose form, in solids and liquids." Nevertheless, the city permitted construction of hundreds of houses on the property. An elementary school was built near the center of the landfill. The new developments promised all the amenities of suburban living. By 1978 the neighborhood boasted about eight hundred single family homes and 240 low-income apartment buildings.

Residents of the new, working-class suburb lived in a neighborhood of wonders. When kids threw rocks onto the ground, they sometimes exploded. Occasionally a manhole cover would spontaneously combust. Other signs were even more troubling. Baseball players diving to snag a line drive might come up with chemical burns. Kids dubbed a local creek "Beverly Hillbillies"—after the television show—because they could stick a piece of wood in the water and it would come up slimy and black like oil. Little vegetation grew. Dogs lost their hair. By the late 1970s investigative newspaper coverage and grassroots door-to-door health surveys revealed an abundance of terrifying illnesses among residents— epilepsy, asthma, migraines, and nephrosis—as well as unusually high rates of birth defects and miscarriages. Love Canal seemed a lot like the town described by Rachel Carson in "A Fable for Tomorrow."

Pushed by local residents, in 1978 the New York State Department of Health began collecting air and soil tests and conducted a health study of the 239 homes that immediately encircled the canal. The Health Department found an increase in reproductive problems among women and high levels of chemical contaminants in the soil and air. That August, residents formed the Love Canal Homeowners Association (LCHA) to combat the environmental contamination of their community. The LCHA was led by Lois Gibbs (b.1951), a determined, quick-witted, and telegenic housewife. The LCHA framed the problems at Love Canal as a public health crisis partly to generate coverage from media in love with the narrative of housewives agitating to protect their children.

In August 1978, the state recommended the closing of the school, evacuated the 239 households closest to the dump (by purchasing them), and surrounded the contaminated area with a fence. Gibbs later called it "a gated community for chemicals." But what of those residents outside the fence? The LCHA pushed to have the entire neighborhood relocated. Dr. Beverly Paigen of the nearby Roswell Memorial Institute conducted a survey of the existing families that found increases in miscarriages, still births, crib deaths, nervous breakdowns, hyperactivity, epilepsy, and urinary tract disorders. Between 1974 and 1978, 56 percent of the children in Love Canal were born with a birth defect. A 1979/1980 study found that of twenty-two pregnancies among Love Canal residents, only four resulted in a normal birth.

Even when government took action on behalf of the community, it tended to dismiss the predominantly black renters in favor of predominately white homeowners. Community activist Elene Thornton led the Concerned Love Canal Renters Association. At odds with homeowners, they turned to the local National Association for the Advancement of Colored People and a church organization, the Ecumenical Task Force, for help. The media largely ignored Concerned Love Canal Renters Association. But they paid a lot of attention to the white Love Canal residents demanding justice. A three-year-old boy wore a T-shirt announcing that he was a "Love Canal Guinea Pig. Used by New York State and federal government." On Mother's Day, Love Canal residents staged a "Die In." Frustrated with inaction, activists burned an effigy of President Carter. More than a hint of violence was in the air. Gibbs and her neighbors eventually held two officials from the EPA captive in a ploy to get the president's attention. It worked. In 1980 President Carter ordered the evacuation of the entire community and the government purchased the remaining homes at market value.

Love Canal introduced Americans to the phrase "hazardous waste." The government responded in 1980 with an important law, the Comprehensive Environmental Response, Compensation, and Liability Act (CERCLA), also known as the Superfund. It authorized the EPA to identify and assess contaminated sites and established a federal multibillion-dollar trust fund—the Superfund—to help in emergencies

Figure 8.3 Love Canal focused the country's attention on the problem of hazardous waste. The incident lead to the passage of the "superfund" to clean up toxic waste sites, and the underappreciated establishment of environmental liability as a matter of real estate law

and to pay for clean up when a polluter could not be identified. Within a decade the EPA identified well over a thousand sites. The Superfund created a powerful incentive not to pollute and revolutionized real estate law by instituting the principle of environmental liability. Unfortunately, the Superfund has also been severely hampered by legal squabbling over the sites, mostly former users suing each other to share clean-up costs. Also at issue is the problem of a "cleaned-up" environment—who establishes such a standard? What measures ensure a safe environment?

The Love Canal neighborhood was refurbished and renamed Black Creek Village; new homes were sold in the 1990s. In recent years residents of the new community have sued, citing health complaints strikingly similar to the original ailments from the 1970s. Lois Gibbs left the area and went on to make a career in environmental health work. She currently serves as executive director of an organization she formed, the Center for Health, Environment and Justice, formerly the Citizens' Clearinghouse for Hazardous Waste. Despite its many problems, the Superfund initiated sweeping transformations of how toxic waste is disposed. Indeed, the safe disposal of toxic wastes mandated by CERCLA is a great but often overlooked achievement of environmental policy. CERCLA has helped remediate many of the nation's worst toxic waste disposal sites, greatly enhancing quality of life. The public is far less exposed to such hidden hazards as it once was. But despite these important achievements, CERCLA is also the last major environmental law that has been passed in the United States.

CHAPTER 9

SCIENCE DENIAL IN THE AGE OF GLOBAL DISRUPTION

Dear future generations, please accept our apologies.
We were roaring drunk on petroleum.
–KURT VONNEGUT, 2006

O N THE morning of July 8, 1943, a dense fog disoriented Los Angeles commuters. The air smelled acrid and bitter. Eyes and throats burned, so much so that rumors spread that the fog was from a Japanese chemical attack. A judge threatened to close his courthouse because no one inside could breathe. That fog lifted, but thick, yellow-brown air became a regular part of the Los Angeles skyline. Locals started describing the air as "smog"—a portmanteau of "smoke" and "fog." It was a vexing problem in a city whose Hollywood film industry relied upon clear skies. Six years later, a professor at the California Institute of Technology, Arie Haagen-Smit, figured out exactly what the "smog" was: ground-level ozone. Ozone is created when volatile organic compounds—such as the partially burned exhaust from automobiles and the hydrocarbons released by oil refineries—interact with sunlight. The ozone problem, explained the professor, came from "the petroleum industry" and the "automobiles driving around Los Angeles." Car pollution threatened the world's greatest car culture.

If internal combustion engines threatened public health, then the entire petroleum industry was at risk. By the 1960s, evidence mounted that the waste products from burning petroleum caused vastly more severe problems than Los Angeles smog: they were changing the very atmosphere of planet Earth. In 1965 President Lyndon Baines Johnson delivered a special message to Congress in which he decried the "poisons and chemicals which are the by-products of technology and industry." More fundamentally, the president informed Congress that "Air pollution is no longer confined to isolated places. This generation has altered the composition of the atmosphere on a global scale through radioactive materials and a steady increase in carbon dioxide from the burning of fossil fuels." In 1968 studies showed that increased carbon dioxide could heat the planet so greatly it could cause a catastrophic collapse of the Antarctic ice sheets. Los Angeles smog could be abated through regulation, but polluting the global atmosphere demanded fundamental changes to the entire society.

The American Petroleum Institute and major oil companies watched the emerging science closely. In 1968 two Stanford Research Institute scientists, Elmer Robinson and R.C. Robbins, produced a report for the American Petroleum Institute that summarized the existing science of carbon pollution and global climate change. The report warned that rising carbon dioxide would increase surface temperature on planet Earth, which would result in melting ice caps, rising seas, and other critical ecological damages. Industry could have adapted to such news by investing in different forms of energy production. Instead it mounted a propaganda campaign that denied the efficacy of climate science. Rather than attack science directly, the oil industry adopted and helped shape a public relations strategy used by the tobacco industry: assert that the relevant science is unsettled, contradictory, ambiguous, and thus a reasonable response entailed more research, not legislative action. Industry employed ideologically motivated scientists—often renowned but rarely experts in the relevant fields—to help them bring their case to the public. The strategy proved to be devastatingly effective.

The push to undermine climate science contributed to a fierce political backlash against environmentalism and other progressive causes. The key political figure in this backlash is Ronald Reagan (1911–2004) who assumed the presidency in 1980. He was known for environmental malapropisms: he once asserted that "trees cause more pollution than automobiles do." Nor did he like nature. Asked about a stand of old-growth redwoods he allowed that "I saw them; there is nothing beautiful about them." Despite such pronouncements, as governor of California Reagan achieved a reasonably strong environmental record. But as in the case of Richard Nixon, that record was not due to conviction but to the political necessity of ameliorating a strongly pro-environment public. After he assumed the presidency in 1980, Reagan turned away from environmental moderation and set about to "free" business interests from regulations, especially environmental law. When criticized for his approach, he responded that environmentalists will not "be happy until the White House looks like a bird's nest."

The New Right politics that propelled Reagan into office resulted from a coalition of two disparate constituencies—the populist Christian right and corporate plutocrats—that for different reasons opposed environmental protection. Fundamentalist Christians disavow science for theological reasons and especially disdain evolution by natural selection, the basis of the biological sciences. Conservative Christians also espouse a radical individualism. As historian Mark Stoll writes, "Theologically, evangelicalism has accentuated the role of individuals. . . . [In] the [nineteenth] century . . . this meant defending slavery; today, it means championing social and economic individualism and weak government." A religion committed to extreme individualism cannot abide social solutions to collective issues such as environmental quality. Recently, some right-wing Christians have gone so far as to dub environmentalism the "Green Dragon" and urged its followers to "slay" the dangerous green beast.

Second, many multinational corporations, especially those in the oil industry, have a pronounced antipathy toward environmental regulation. They have used their massive financial power to support anti-environmental politicians and to fund "think-tanks" that produce anti-environmental propaganda. Chemical and pesticide manufacturers, the oil and coal industries, timber and real estate developers are truly challenged by environmental policies. Rather than respond by not polluting they have attacked the very idea of environmental protection. Always powerful, these huge industries found that conservative Christians also called for weak government, radical individualism, and a commitment to unfettered corporate capitalism. Together, this coalition has dominated American politics for decades.

This new political coalition first came to the fore in debates over the use of public lands. The so-called Sagebrush Rebellion, and more broadly, the "wise use movement" of the late 1970s and early 1980s helped drive Reagan into office. Corporate-libertarian in economic philosophy and accustomed to ranching, mining, logging, and driving off-road vehicles on public lands, Sagebrush Rebels adopted the language of "states' rights" and surged into national consciousness with the election of Reagan. Supported by an array of conservative funders and institutions such as Joseph Coors and the Mountain States Legal Foundation, Sagebrush Rebels found their public face when President Reagan appointed James Watt (b. 1938) to be secretary of the interior.

Watt embodied the politics of the New Right: he was a fundamentalist Christian who proudly declared his "bias for private enterprise" and disdain for liberals and environmentalism. Tall, bald, and bespectacled, the owlish Secretary Watt dismissed settled law, regularly substituting administrative fiat for statutory legality. He was determined to open all public lands for resource exploitation at a scale that makes the battle over Hetch Hetchy seem trivial in comparison. He fought to allow oil drilling off the California coast—infuriating residents of Santa Barbara—and worked to open wilderness areas to mining and timbering. He attempted to eliminate moderate and successful environmental laws such as the Land and Water Conservation Fund. Watt simply refused to list species as endangered as required by the Endangered Species Act. His public demise came not from his destructive policies but in how he defended them. He claimed immunity from criticism for his decision to sell more than one billion tons of coal from federal lands in Wyoming because members of his coal advisory panel included "a black . . . a woman, two Jews, and a cripple." He was fired shortly thereafter.

Reagan's second lightening-rod appointment was corporate attorney Anne Gorsuch (later Anne Gorsuch Burford, 1942–2004) to head the

Environmental Protection Agency (EPA). She tried to dismantle the agency she was charged with leading. Gorsuch immediately cut the EPA budget by 22 percent and pressed for further reductions. Federal action affected state agencies; enforcement cases from regional EPA offices fell by 79 percent. She attempted to gut the Clean Air Act by weakening, from automobiles to furniture, pollution standards on product manufacturing. Gorsuch opposed the Clean Water Act, which eventually led Reagan to veto its reauthorization in 1987. (Congress overrode his veto and the strengthened legislation became law.) Reagan administration antipathy to the Superfund was egregious. Its administrator of the program, Rita Lavelle, was jailed for lying to Congress about corruption in her agency. (Lavelle returned to jail for fraud and lying to the Federal Bureau of Investigation while working in the private sector as an environmental consultant.) Congress was investigating Gorsuch for lying about the Superfund—they had already found her in contempt—when she resigned from public service.

The Reagan administration faced the problem of climate disruption in 1983 when two government agencies issued warnings about the issue. The National Academy of Sciences released a very cautious report that concluded "we find in the [carbon dioxide] issue reason for concern, but not panic." Three days earlier the EPA, citing nearly all the same science, also issued a report, but one with much stronger warnings. Within a few decades climate disruption could provoke "a change in habitability in many geographic regions." Overall the results could be "catastrophic." At the time the harmful consequences of climate disruption seemed far in the future. The main response to the reports was to call for further study. Throughout the 1980s climate researchers, often called to testify by Senator Al Gore of Tennessee, visited Capitol Hill where they found that Congress, in the words of one government scientist, "for the most part accepted the potential Doomsday scenarios." The issue was not yet prominent enough to trigger the public relations backlash that dominated the climate politics of the following decades.

Open contempt for the environment made Watt and Gorsuch perfect fundraising catalysts for the growing environmental movement. National organizations such as the Sierra Club and the Wilderness Society saw membership and contributions surge during Watt's tenure. In the fifteen years after Earth Day, membership in environmental organizations swelled from about five hundred thousand to 2.5 million. In the words of former Sierra Club executive director Carl Pope, President Reagan "reinvented the environmental movement by his contempt for it." The contributions and popular support helped environmentalists blunt the worst of Reagan administration policies, but in doing so the environmental agenda became largely defensive—a posture from which it has never fully recovered. As historian Richard Andrews writes, Reagan "fractured the public consensus that had been emerging in support of regulatory reform, and triggered instead a more bitter and far more partisan period of distrust and ideological trench warfare over environmental protection policy."

That fracture has had profound long-term consequences. One example come from the renewable energy industry. In 1986 Reagan removed the White House's solar panels. The panels had been manufactured in Virginia and installed by the Carter administration. Beyond the symbolism of removing the panels, Reagan cut the research and development budget for renewable energy by 85 percent. In 1986, his administration eliminated the wind investment tax credit. He opposed and then rolled back fuel economy standards. Not only did these actions result in a great deal of carbon pollution, but the market for renewable technologies—by 2016 the cheapest and cleanest producers of energy—left the United States. China now manufactures the bulk of the world's solar panels.

The conservative counterattack also fractured the environmental community. Some environmental organizations grew dependent upon outside funding from the very industries whose pollution they opposed. The Ford Foundation, for example, gave generously to environmental groups. But the money could come with strings. The Environmental Defense Fund agreed to submit proposed lawsuits to a committee, chosen by the Ford Foundation, for review. Donors, not the needs of the environment, determined whether the Environmental Defense Fund should sue.

A 1990 study of large, well-established environmental groups found that their boards of directors were well stocked with representatives from major corporate polluters such as Exxon and Monsanto. Corporate funders teamed with conservative environmental groups to create organizations such as the Corporate Conservation Council, composed of National Wildlife Federation executives and representatives from the oil, gas, and chemical industries. Sometimes the citizen-corporate alliances could even undermine the EPA, as happened when conservative environmentalists teamed up with industry to create Clean Sites Inc., which emphasized the supposed benefits of voluntary, as opposed to mandated, hazardous waste clean up. Regulation of toxic wastes, these corporate environmentalists seemed to be saying, was not needed. Grassroots environmentalists vigorously opposed such arrangements, but big money and Beltway political maneuvering compromised some environmental organizations.

Environmental law continued to evolve despite the lack of significant legislative achievement since 1980. Environmental regulation was now institutionalized as part of what political scientists Christopher McGrory Klyza and David J. Sousa call the "green state." They argue that "environmentalists' decades-old victories" are "embedded"; that is, they remain in powerful effect, "despite assaults from the right." Crucially, the green state is buoyed by "wide public support in their efforts to protect current commitments in environmental policy." As policy historian Christopher Bosso argues, "the breadth, density, and diversity of the environmental advocacy community give environmentalism itself greater resiliency and impact than are often recognized."

In place of new environmental legislation, environmental policy has been furthered by what Klyza and Sousa call "green drift." New pollution control measures that derive from existing law are continually promulgated. Public lands continue to grow. President Bill Clinton added six million acres of public lands and protected over fifty million acres of national forests by deploying administrative rules that prevent road building. Aggressive environmental advocacy organizations such as the Center for Biological Diversity have forced protections for endangered species that have altered how land is managed and how some products are made. As Clinton's Secretary of the Interior Bruce Babbitt noted, "the trajectory of environmental protection is moving ever upward over time, even as the trend line occasionally breaks downward."

If the status quo has protected environmentalism's great legislative victories, and even expanded them somewhat through green drift, it has also failed to confront profound environmental challenges. Most of those challenges are new versions of old problems. Environmentalists have responded creatively to these challenges, but the conservative backlash that has prevented major legislative victories have put the human future in increasing danger.

That danger is found in our bodies. Rachel Carson was right: what we sow in nature we reap in our health. Several hundred biomonitoring studies show that Americans house hundreds of industrial chemicals in our bodies—many of which are carcinogenic. Worries about the health effects of bodily contamination (called "body burden") are particularly acute for children. In a landmark 2015 study, The International Federation of Gynecology and Obstetrics concluded that "widespread exposure to toxic environmental chemicals threatens healthy human reproduction." The pollution is so thorough that it affects developing fetuses. The National Cancer Institute found that "to a disturbing extent babies are born 'pre-polluted.'" According to one study, the "likely low" estimate is that environmental pollutants account for 100 percent of lead poisonings, 30 percent of asthma cases, 5 percent of childhood cancers, and 10 percent of neurobehavioral disorders. The economic costs average about fifty-five billion dollars a year.

Children are born pre-polluted because America is swimming in industrial chemicals. Industry produces billions of pounds of chemicals each year. The United States uses over a billion pounds of pesticides each year—well over three pounds per person. Some forty million pounds of Agent Orange—the notorious Vietnam War herbicide—are applied to American lawns and parks annually. At least eighty-five thousand chemicals were in commercial use in 2016; fewer than 1 percent had been tested for safety.

Industrial chemicals infect every part of the globe. A total of 97 percent of America's rivers are contaminated with at least one pesticide. Deadly polychlorinated biphenyls (PCBs) are found in the snows atop Aconcagua, the highest mountain in the Andes, and in the deep-sea crustaceans that swim some ten thousand meters below the ocean's surface in the Mariana Trench. The chemicals are creating a new nature. "Synthetic chemicals have become so pervasive," observed environmental scientist Theo Colborn, "that it is no longer possible to define a normal, unaltered human physiology." The entire planet, like your body, is a toxic waste disposal site.

Industrial chemicals are so ubiquitous that it is difficult for health experts to trace their origin and health effects. In America one in three women and one in two men will die of cancer. Cancer specialist Devra Davis lamented that, "cancer has become the price of modern life." How much of that alarming truth can be traced to environmental pollution remains unknown. Even more difficult is assessing the full consequences of exposures to various combinations of chemicals.

Confounding the analysis still further is that the effects of chemical exposures can take years, even decades to appear. Damages that occur slowly over time, that are not sudden but attritional, invite less sensation and thus less interest than abrupt violence. But they are no less deadly. Literary scholar Rob Nixon theorizes incremental human and ecological poisoning as "slow violence"—a slow motion disaster, abuses that are delayed in effects and thus do not fit into our usual conception of violence as immediate and spectacular. The slow violence of chemical pollution and climate disruption are among the most profound challenges facing humanity.

Toxic pollution affects the nonwhite poor more than the wealthy. That differential is sometimes purposeful. A 1984 report prepared for the California State Waste Management Board by Cerrell Associates argued that "All socioeconomic groupings tend to resent the nearby siting of major (waste disposal) facilities, but the middle and upper socioeconomic strata possess better resources to effectuate their opposition." Thus, the report recommended that waste incineration plants should not be cited "within five miles" of "Middle and higher socioeconomic strata neighborhoods." The study concluded that the best places to cite waste incinerators were in towns with less than twenty-five thousand people whose residents are old, poor, politically conservative, and Roman Catholic.

Or toxic waste could be shipped overseas. In 1991, Lawrence Summers, chief economist of the World Bank, issued a memo in which he argued that developing countries are "underpolluted" and dirty industries should be encouraged to move to them. Summers reasoned that "the economic logic behind dumping a load of toxic waste in the lowest-wage country is impeccable and we should face up to that." The logic was that people in developing countries don't live long enough for carcinogens to fully harm them. "The concern over an agent that causes a one in a million change in the odds of prostrate (sic) cancer is obviously going to be much higher in a country where people survive to get prostrate (sic) cancer," wrote Summers. Cancers are less of a concern in "a country where under [five] mortality is [two hundred] per thousand." The logic of neoliberal capitalism overwhelmed Summers's humanity—likely in part because of the slow, rather than immediate, effects of his proposed actions.

Among the least well known but potentially most impactful chemicals are endocrine disrupters. A good example is diethylstilbestrol (DES), a "synthetic estrogen" invented in 1938 and widely prescribed as a preventative for miscarriages and premature births. Physicians discovered that the daughters of women who took DES had an increased incidence of clear-cell carcinoma, a rare vaginal cancer. Subsequent research found that the children of DES mothers suffered from increased rates of breast cancer and reproductive tract abnormalities. A key lesson from DES history is that the American approach to regulation has abandoned the idea of precaution—the notion that new chemicals should be shown to be safe before they are introduced to the public. Instead, chemicals are released upon the public and not challenged until science can prove—a key word—that they are dangerous. The perceived needs of industry largely trump the right to public health.

The problem of endocrine disruption broke onto the public consciousness with the 1996 publication of *Our Stolen Future* by Theo Colborn, Dianne Dumanoski, and John Peterson Myers. Theodora ("Theo") Colborn (1927–2014) worked in conservation before earning her doctorate at age fifty-eight. While working for the World Wildlife Fund and the Conservation Foundation, Colborn linked chemical pollutants to a variety of severe problems suffered by Great Lakes wildlife. She quickly discovered that the same chemicals were active in human metabolisms. "By drilling deep into the bowels of the earth for coal, oil and natural gas we have unwittingly and catastrophically altered the chemistry of the biosphere and the human womb," wrote Colborn.

In 2003, at age seventy-six, Colborn founded The Endocrine Disruption Exchange. Among the many upsetting findings of this work is that endocrine-mimicking chemicals affect humans at trace dosages. The dose does not make the poison—lower doses can have more profound affects for many reasons, including that they don't trigger the body's natural abilities to flush invasive substances. Trace exposures also bioaccumulate up the food chain and are passed to the next generation through the womb and breast milk. Endocrine-mimicking chemicals affect developing fetuses and can alter sexual development, undermine intelligence and behavior, and increase susceptibility to disease. The greater ecosystem effects of introduced chemicals remain unknown. Natural chemical signals organize life at all levels; disrupting those signals could profoundly affect ecosystem functioning.

Banning some pollutants has resulted in some spectacular successes. After the phaseout of leaded gasoline, elevated lead levels in children's blood declined from 88 percent in the 1970s to 1.6 percent in 2005. Not only has this reduction greatly improved childhood health, it has dramatically reduced the violent crime rate. Lead poisoning promotes apoptosis, or cell death, in the brain. It affects the prefrontal cortex—the part of the brain associated with regulation of impulses as well as attention, verbal reasoning, and mental flexibility. If those characteristics are diminished, people are more aggressive and lack impulse control: the essential traits of violent criminals. A University of Cincinnati study showed that for every five micrograms of lead in an infant's blood, their chances of being arrested later in life for a violent crime spiked by 30 percent. The effects of lead poisoning are thus simply staggering. A robust body of empirical data suggests that exposure to lead accounts for the increase and eventual decrease (after leaded fuels were banned) in violent crime in the United States. By saving America from lead poisoning, environmentalists stopped a crime wave.

While the reduction of atmospheric lead poisoning is a great achievement of environmental regulation, the lack of success in reducing biocide use counts as a stunning defeat. Part of the problem is that, following the publicity around *Silent Spring*, policy makers and the public fixated on the ecological dangers of dichlorodiphenyltrichloroethane (DDT) to the exclusion of other biocides. The government banned domestic use of DDT and other chlorinated hydrocarbons in 1972. But it ignored less persistent pesticides such as organophosphates, even though they were far more toxic. Americans traded one poison for another. Because organophosphates break down quickly, they had greater negative impacts on farmworkers than on consumers. Occupational exposure to biocides affects, minimally, some twenty thousand farmworkers each year.

Lack of biocide regulation also reflects the "regulatory capture" of the EPA. Regulatory capture occurs when a public agency such as the EPA advances commercial or private interests instead of the public good. Career EPA officials have argued that industry captured the EPA. One, Evaggelos Vallianatos, who served most of his career in the EPA's Office of Pesticides Programs, charges that "chemical and other industries have captured the EPA and turned it from an environmental protection agency into a polluter's protection agency." Vallianatos' 2014 book *Poison Spring* gives a first-hand account of the regulatory capture that political scientists had already observed. Christopher Bosso, for example, in his 1987 book *Pesticides and Politics*, wrote of the "iron triangle" of corporate interest groups, congressional subcommittees favorable to industry, and pliable civil servants that effected a "pesticides subgovernment."

The pesticide subgovernment was baked into the EPA from its beginning. Its early staff came mostly from the U.S. Department of Agriculture—an agency steeped in corporate agriculture and its vigorous use of biocides. The agency also faced the need to approve hundreds of new biocides each year, meeting its charge by relying on industry-conducted studies that attested to their safety. Eventually, audits by both the EPA and the U.S. Food and Drug Administration showed that many of the safety studies were simply fraudulent. An independent laboratory, Industrial Bio-Test laboratories (IBT), had been falsifying data and altering the results of its research for years. Hundreds, possibly thousands, of biocides deemed safe by the EPA were done so under duplicitous circumstances. Several top IBT executives were convicted of fraud. Beyond the IBT scandal, Vallianatos explained that EPA regulation suffered from an inherent conflict of interest, "in which private labs, paid by chemical companies, do [the] testing that the government relies on to protect the public." Even without outright fraud, the testing industry has a powerful monetary incentive to deliver agreeable results to the paying customer.

The EPA's reaction to the IBT scandal further demonstrates the collusion between the EPA and corporate interests. Not a single pesticide registration was cancelled due to fraudulent or nonexistent test data. Nor were any chemical industry figures who pushed for favorable results from IBT prosecuted. More contemporary accounts suggest that regulatory capture of the EPA remains a pressing issue. Ecologists used by the EPA as experts to evaluate science have published their concerns. Recent assessments of the biocide atrazine provide a good example. In the EPA's assessment of atrazine, studies that demonstrated its negative effects on amphibians were excluded from review, often for trivial reasons that had no impact on the study's conclusions. "The current regulatory system in the United States," write the scientists whose expertise on amphibians the EPA solicited then ignored, "cannot embrace precaution." It cannot do so because the EPA "primarily uses industry-supplied-and-funded data to draw its conclusions."

One objection to environmental regulations is that they are costly to the economy, specifically that they negatively impact employment. But research shows that this is not true. The benefits outweigh the costs, and the costs—including the EPA's own estimates—are consistently found to be exaggerated. In 2002 the World Resources Institute studied industries supposedly burdened by environmental regulation: pulp and paper, plastics, petroleum, and steel. It found that "additional environmental expenditure is associated with an insignificant change in employment." Furthermore, "there are strong positive employment effects in industries where environmental activities are relatively labor intensive and where demand is relatively inelastic, such as plastics and petroleum. In others . . . there is little evidence of a significant employment consequence either way." In short, research contradicts the "notion of a jobs-versus-the-environment tradeoff." Overall, economic research demonstrates that "environmental regulations end up costing far less than both industry and the EPA predict."

New research in agriculture is showing how the production of food can thrive without adopting corporate-industrial monoculture. The most promising and scientifically sound is the Natural Systems Agriculture developed at the Land Institute, a research and training center in Salina, Kansas, founded by Wes Jackson (b. 1936). A geneticist by training, Jackson is convinced that corporate industrial agriculture—with its reliance on biocides and fossil fuels to maintain the highly peculiar, unnatural monocultures that dominate the contemporary agricultural landscape—is leading humanity into an ecological disaster. (Jackson denounces the heavy use of biocides as "chemotherapy on the land.") On the Great Plains, Jackson promotes the development of a "domestic prairie," a farmland that mimics the natural functions of prairie ecosystems. The Land Institute is developing high-yield perennial grains, farmed in polycultures, that mimic the ecosystem functions of fully natural prairies. Energy comes from solar radiation. Most importantly, domestic prairies preserve and enhance soil.

Among the most salutary efforts of Jackson's project is his insistence on the connections between sustainable agriculture and sustainable communities. Sounding much like Aldo Leopold and the New Deal agricultural ecologists and bioregional theorists who are its forebears, the Land Institute defines its mission as "When people, land, and community are as one, all three members prosper; when they relate not as members but as competing interests, all three are exploited." The Land Institute seeks a revitalization of oral traditions, of communities rooted in place. In his book, *New Roots for Agriculture*, Jackson imagined Kansas farming as it might be in the year 2030. "Most communities," writes Jackson, "now emphasize the value of history, and history becomes more real when adults tell personal stories which link the past to the present." Rooting culture in place promotes love of the land. "It is possible," counsels Jackson, "to love a small acreage in Kansas as much as John Muir loved the entire Sierra Nevada."

A second exciting frontier in agriculture and social design is the urban farm. Urban farms have developed out of a vision of local production and out of necessity. Farming has emerged as a way to revitalize urban life in cities such as Detroit that have lost tens of thousands of manufacturing jobs and the workers that went with them. Urban farms can provide food, employment, and a way to help reconnect fractured communities. A 2016 study from the Johns Hopkins Center for a Livable Future found that urban agriculture could "increase social capital, community well-being and civic engagement with the food system." Local production can provide employment while reducing greenhouse gas emissions through less transportation and the carbon sequestration of the crops themselves. Building on the tradition of World War II–era victory gardens, urban agriculture can potentially supply a great deal of food. Michigan State University researchers found that Detroit could grow 70 percent of its vegetables and 40 percent of its fruit on the vacant lots covering just five thousand acres of city land.

Successful experiments in urban agriculture abound. In New York City, the Brooklyn Grange grows crops on 2.5 acres of rooftop farms. It produces more than fifty thousand pounds of organic produce each year. In Milwaukee, former professional basketball player Will Allen (b. 1949), founded Growing Power, a nonprofit farm that grows and distributes healthy food to urban residents. Allen notes that his farm is "only six blocks away from Milwaukee's largest public housing project." Rather than having to travel miles to stores that often carry substandard produce (Allen correctly describes such food deserts as "a form of redlining"), locals can acquire Growing Power food at the on-farm retail store, in schools and restaurants, at farmers' markets, and in low-cost market baskets delivered to neighborhood pickup points. Allen especially enjoys working with children. "Kids that come in here [to the Growing Power farm], they're wired and they're bouncing off the walls. But as soon as I put some soil in their hands, they just calm down." Allen understands that "There's something very spiritual about touching the soil." Innovators like Allen have updated Booker T. Washington's socially conscious agriculture for the twenty-first century.

Allen's linking of farming to children highlights another Progressive Era tradition revitalized in the environmental era: connecting children with nature. The issue preoccupied Rachel Carson. In her 1956 essay "Help Your Child to Wonder," Carson wished to meet "with the good fairy who is supposed to preside over the christening of all children." If given such an audience, she would "ask that her gift to each child in the world be a sense of wonder so indestructible that it would last through life." Reverence for the magic of nature was open to all: "The values of contact with the natural world are not reserved for the scientists. They are available to anyone . . . who will stop to think about so small a thing as the mystery of a growing seed."

Carson's nature study belief in the physical and psychological benefits of contact with nature have been robustly confirmed by modern science. A rich body of scientific evidence suggests the importance of time outdoors for the lives and education of children. Children who play outside are healthier and happier, with richer and more fulfilled psychological and cultural lives. They become more caring and grounded adults. The converse is also true: children denied contact with the outdoor world suffer from what journalist Richard Louv termed "nature deficit disorder." Rather than a medical diagnosis, nature deficit disorder refers to a society rife with maladies such as childhood obesity, depression, and attention deficit disorder that have all been substantively linked to lack of time spent in nature. Kids who do play outside are less likely to get sick, less likely to experiences severe stress, and are more creative and adaptable to life's twists and turns. Louv founded the Children & Nature Network to "connect all children, their families and communities to nature through innovative ideas, evidence-based resources and tools, broad-based collaboration and support of grassroots leadership."

Growing Power farm and the Children & Nature Network both promote local institutions to combat national (or global) environmental problems. The combination of national or global issues with local experience and activism has emerged as a central theme of contemporary environmental writing and activism. Terry Tempest Williams (b. 1955) connected the death of her mother from breast cancer to flooding that threatened the Bear River Migratory Bird Refuge and above-ground nuclear testing in her profoundly moving 1991 memoir *Refuge: An Unnatural History of Family and Place*. Birds migrating through the Great Salt Lake frame the story. Birds "were everything to me," recalled Williams; "I have always been very aware of the fragility of life." In *Refuge*, she concludes that "the losses I encountered at the Bear River Migratory Bird Refuge . . . helped me face the losses within my family."

Williams has since been arrested for protesting the federal nuclear testing facility in Nevada. ("The price of obedience has become too high," she concludes in *Refuge*.) She is a "woman wedded to wilderness." For Williams, writing helps keep us human in an age of ecological devastation. "In the act of storytelling, we do bypass rhetoric and pierce the heart," counsels Williams. "We speak from a place of honesty and receive in a spirit of empathy and compassion." The place of honesty is an actual, geographic space, and often a public one. "Open lands open minds," writes Williams, an example of what she calls the "open space of democracy."

The open lands don't need to be the grand landscapes of Utah, but can be a junkyard in Baxley, Georgia. Janisse Ray's (b. 1962) *Ecology of a Cracker Childhood* depicts the relationships her family had with the lowland Longleaf pines of south Georgia. Growing up in a loving but poor and fundamentalist family, Ray found solace in longleaf pines—and in her father's junkyard. Both offered the magic of discovery and adventure, but only the pines could offer majesty, what Ray calls the "homeland that built us." For Ray, when ecosystems are fragmented, so is human culture. "Culture springs from the actions of people in a landscape," writes Ray. When native ecosystems are lost so too are "unique folkways. . . . Our culture is tied to the longleaf pine forest that produced us, that has sheltered us, that we occupy."

Ecology of a Cracker Childhood ends with a list of endangered species and longleaf resources, as well as a list of organizations dedicated to preserving and restoring longleaf pine ecosystems. Ray has worked to restore the Pinhook Swamp, a wetland adjacent to the glorious Okefenokee Swamp. She was also instrumental in helping preserve the Moody forest, a stretch of longleaf pine bordering the Altamaha River. By restoring the deep meaning of rootedness, she hopes to revitalize southern culture.

Celebrated writers such as Williams and Ray are not the only women making these connections. Women are at the forefront of environmental justice struggles across the nation. Among the most profound are the women battling mountaintop removal, a coal mining technique widely used in Appalachia in which the tops of mountains are blasted away to expose coal seams. The coal is then collected by drag-lines, massive buckets attached to cables that gather up huge amounts of soil along with small amounts of coal. The mountaintop earth is then deposited in a neighboring valley, filling it and its streams. Mountaintop removal has destroyed over two thousand square miles of hardwood forest and has buried two thousand miles of streams. Appalachian people have protested the practice for decades. Since 2005, a movement known as "Mountain Justice" has attracted college students, activists, and Earth First! members to work with the residents of Central Appalachia to oppose mountaintop removal. Lorelei Scarboro, a West Virginian wife of a coal miner, was moved to "protect what I have left. Not only [my house and land] but the mountain behind it and the environment and the wildlife and the vegetation."

One local organization, Coal River Mountain Watch in Naoma, West Virginia, opposes mountaintop removal because it "endangers public health with airborne blasting dust, pollutes streams, increases flooding, and deprives communities of traditional use of the mountains and forests." The former director of the Coal River Mountain Watch was a true coalminer's daughter: Julia "Judy" Bonds (1952–2011). In 2001, Bonds and her family were the last residents of Marfork Hollow, a small hamlet destroyed by mountaintop removal. "There's no such thing as cheap energy," emphasized Bonds. "That's what people need to understand. We are using up all of our children's resources."

Bonds opposed mine operator Massey Energy by testifying at regulatory hearings, filing lawsuits, picketing stockholder's meetings, and working with climate activists such as NASA's James Hansen. "In Southern West Virginia we live in a war zone," thundered Bonds. "Three and one-half million pounds of explosives are being used every day to blow up the mountains. Blasting our communities, blasting our homes, poisoning us, trying to intimidate us. I don't mind being poor. I mind being blasted and poisoned." The idea that employment made environmental sacrifices a worthwhile tradeoff made no sense to Bonds: "There ARE no jobs on a dead planet." She worked to move the Marsh Fork Elementary School in Sundial, West Virginia, due to its proximity to a coal processing silo and slurry dam. "How do you tell a child that his life is a sacrifice for corporate greed?" In 2010 she helped engineer, but was too ill to attend, a "thousand hillbilly march" in Washington, District of Columbia, that occupied the offices of the Army Corps of Engineers and protested inaction on mountaintop removal by the EPA.

Over the last thirty years the efforts of socially marginalized people fighting for environmental quality have become known as "environmental justice." As Vernice D. Miller, a co-founder of West Harlem Environmental Action, writes, "By linking environmental issues to social, racial and economic justice, we have created a new and dynamic social-justice movement." Such struggles have a long history. In 1967, African-American students took to the streets of Houston to oppose a city garbage dump in their community that had claimed the lives of two children. In 1968, residents of West Harlem, in New York City, fought unsuccessfully against the siting of a sewage treatment plant in their community.

Environmental justice emerged in the national consciousness from battles over PCB disposal in North Carolina. In 1978 the Ward Transformer Company of Raleigh, North Carolina, hired drivers to dump PCB-laden liquids along the shoulders of state highways. The company assumed that once on state property, the state would be responsible for remediation. Shortly after detecting the contaminants, the state devised a plan to build a landfill for the toxins in just the kind of place Cerrell Associates recommended to the California State Waste Management Board: rural and poor. In this case, the rural poor of Warren County, North Carolina, were black. As one local put it, "The community was politically and economically unempowered; that was the reason for the siting. They took advantage of poor people and people of color." Residents of Warren County, however, were able to "effectuate their opposition." They lobbied the government but lost. Residents put their bodies on the line; over five hundred locals were arrested for protesting the landfill.

Warren County residents reached out to established civil rights organizations for help. The United Church of Christ and the Southern Christian Leadership Conference engaged in environmental justice work. Though the landfill was eventually built, the struggle garnered a lot of attention. A congressman, Walter E. Fauntroy, was among the protestors arrested. He returned to Congress and charged the Government Accountability Office (GAO) with examining the relationship between race and toxic waste disposal sites. The GAO's 1983 report found a strong correlation between minority communities and waste disposal sites.

The GAO study was supported by a second, independent study by the United Church of Christ entitled *Toxic Waste and Race*. The report documented and quantified the phenomenon of "environmental racism"—deliberately exposing nonwhite, usually poor people to environmental hazards. The study found that more than half of all blacks and Hispanics live in communities that contain at least one closed or abandoned hazardous waste site. As one Warren County local put it, "They use black people as guinea pigs. Anytime there is something that is going to kill, we'll put it in the black area to find out if it kills and how many. They don't care. They don't value a black person's life." Vernice D. Miller, who worked as a research assistant on the study, remembered "feeling that finally somebody understood . . . our community was being used as dump site."

In October 1991, several groups coalesced to convene the First National People of Color Environmental Leadership Summit. The summit produced a statement that affirmed "the sacredness of Mother Earth, ecological unity and the interdependence of all species" as well as the "environmental determination of all peoples." The summit also charged that mainstream environmental organizations had a racist blind spot with regard to environmental justice. The charge had merit. "It was a wake up call," recalled Sierra Club Director Michael Fisher. The Sierra Club responded well to the environmental justice critique. But much of the leadership of large environmental organizations remains white—a problem for the kind of inclusive, dynamic, and socially informed environmentalism needed to tackle the nation's severe ecological crisis.

The activism of First National People of Color Environmental Leadership Summit had pronounced effects on public policy after Bill Clinton (b. 1946) won the presidency in 1992. In February 1994, President Clinton issued Executive Order 12898, "Federal Actions to Address Environmental Justice in Minority Populations and Low-Income Populations." This executive order was the first presidential effort to direct federal agencies to make environmental justice part of their policy directive. It mandated federal agencies "make achieving environmental justice part of its mission by identifying and addressing, as appropriate, disproportionately high and adverse human health or environmental effects of its programs, policies, and activities on minority populations and low-income populations." Clinton's action brought attention to the issue of environmental justice and prompted a great deal of regulatory action to mandate environmental justice in governmental decision making. The George W. Bush administration subsequently weakened the order, dropping race as a factor in identifying and prioritizing populations that might be disadvantaged by federal action. In 2008, the Obama administration, led by director of the EPA Lisa Jackson, revived the order and made environmental justice a priority of the agency.

Initially, environmental justice was not linked to the issue that has dominated environmental politics since the late 1980s: climate disruption. The world seemed to get a glimpse of its climate future in 1988. Heat and drought caused severe crop losses in the American Midwest, the worst since the Dust Bowl. The Union of Soviet Socialist Republics suffered drought, as did China. Unexpected floods ravaged Africa, Brazil, Bangladesh, and India. Hurricanes struck the Caribbean, along with a cyclone in New Zealand and a typhoon in the Philippines. Colorado Senator Timothy Wirth scheduled hearings on the greenhouse effect for June 23, the anniversary of the hottest day ever recorded in Washington, District of Columbia. The hearings featured James Hansen (b. 1941), chief climate scientist at NASA's Goddard Institute for Space Studies. Hansen is a political conservative with a reputation for prudence. But rather than espousing an overabundance of caution, Hansen chided his fellow researchers by arguing that "it is time to stop waffling so much. We should say that the evidence is pretty strong that the greenhouse effect is here."

The climate crisis briefly promised to return environmental action to its bipartisan roots. In the 1988 presidential race, George H.W. Bush campaigned on the promise of being the "environmental president" and attacked the climate issue with a memorable call to action: "Those who think we're powerless to do anything about the greenhouse effect are forgetting about the White House effect!" But his administration turned its back on science. A White House policy memo, inadvertently leaked to the news media, argued that the best way to deal with global warming was "to raise the many uncertainties" that supposedly complicated the issue. The Bush administration adopted the strategy of obfuscation pioneered by the tobacco industry.

During the administrations of George H.W. Bush and his son George W. Bush, the branch of government that took the climate crisis most seriously was the Department of Defense. In a classified report that was leaked to the Knight-Ridder newspaper chain, the Department of Defense's Office of Net Assessment, an internal think-tank, speculated that the worst-case global climate change scenario "would challenge United States National Security in ways that should be considered immediately." Dryly entitled "An Abrupt Climate Change Scenario and Its Implications for U.S. National Security," the report cited "plausible" consequences of climate change that include famine in Europe and nuclear showdowns over control of the world's dwindling fresh water supply. The document suggests that climate change might result in a global catastrophe costing tens of millions of lives due to war and natural disaster. The catastrophe could include

> Eastern European countries, struggling to feed their populations with a falling supply of food, water and energy, eyeing Russia, whose population is already in decline, for access to its grains, minerals and energy supply. Or, picture Japan, suffering from flooding along its coastal cities and contamination of its fresh water supply, eyeing Russia's Sakhalin Island oil and gas reserves as an energy source. . . . Envision Pakistan, India, and China—all armed with nuclear weapons—skirmishing at their borders over refugees, access to shared rivers, and arable land.

Yet even the political framing of global climate disruption as a security concern, as opposed to an environmental or human rights issue, failed to prompt action by Republican politicians. As late as December 2002 the George W. Bush administration was still citing the "numerous uncertainties" that ostensibly remained about "global warming's cause and effect." Not surprisingly, confusion over the issue saturated the general public. A 1997 Gallup survey found that only 42 percent of the public believed that scientists mostly agreed that global warming was a real threat; the public was just as likely (44 percent) to think that scientists were divided on the issue.

Polls and focus groups from the late 1990s demonstrated that people did not connect global warming to their daily lives, were vague about its cause and effects, or simply viewed the problem apocalyptically, as an insoluble dilemma. One important study found that concern over global warming diminished significantly between 1989 (after James Hansen's congressional testimony) and 1997. At the time when science robustly confirmed the existence of anthropogenic climate disruption, the public grew less sure of its reality. Clearly, the intense media presence of climate change deniers had a profound effect. A memo from the American Petroleum Institute leaked to *The New York Times* stated that "Victory will be achieved when . . . recognition of uncertainty becomes part of the 'conventional wisdom.'" The propaganda backlash—a "brownlash" as Paul and Anne Ehrlich write—is a betrayal of science, reason, and human rights.

Both public awareness and climate policy in the United States remain years behind the rest of the developed world; climate change was barely mentioned during the 2004 presidential campaign. In early June 2005, *The New York Times* confirmed the continuing strategy of denial on the part of the Bush administration. Denial included the outright censorship of climate scientists by Republican ideological functionaries. One shocking disclosure found that the chief of staff for the White House Council of Environmental Quality, Philip A. Cooney, an oil industry lobbyist with no scientific training, edited the findings of climate research in government climate reports. *The New York Times* reported that the changes "tend[ed] to produce an air of doubt about findings that most climate experts say are robust." In many instances, the changes appeared in the final reports. Cooney resigned following the revelations, only to be hired the next day by ExxonMobil. A report from the House Oversight and Government Reform Committee found that "The evidence before the committee leads to one inescapable conclusion: The Bush administration has engaged in a systematic effort to manipulate climate change science and mislead policymakers and the public about the dangers of global warming."

Bush administration censorship of science exemplifies the transition of the Republican Party from a mainstream organization into a genuinely radical force. As the political scientists Thomas Mann and Norman Ornstein have shown, the decline of partisan restraint has rendered our democratic institutions increasingly dysfunctional: "The GOP has become an insurgent outlier in American politics," write Mann and Ornstein. "It is ideologically extreme; scornful of compromise; unmoved by conventional understanding of facts, evidence and science; and dismissive of the legitimacy of its political opposition." Key examples include Oklahoma Republican James Inhofe who described climate change as "an article of religious faith" that amounts to "the greatest hoax ever perpetrated on the American people." In February 2015, the senator brought a snowball onto the senate floor, bizarrely claiming that snow somehow disproves climate disruption.

The denial of noncontroversial climate science has become a marker of identity for ideological conservatives. Denying climate science announces political membership in conservative circles. By 2016, whether one accepts climate science or not was a more polarizing issue in America than abortion rights. Big money also enforced ideological rigidity on the climate issue. Some moderate Republican legislators entered Congress hoping to address the issue. After all, there is nothing "conservative" about wreaking havoc on the planet's life support systems. But as shown in Jane Mayer's brilliant book *Dark Money*, financial pressure can warp ideological preferences. For example, Michigan Republican Congressman Fred Upton, chairman of the Committee on Energy and Commerce, was once an environmental moderate who had said that "climate change is a serious problem that necessitates serious solutions." But faced with a well-financed conservative challenger in his congressional primary, Upton became a born-again climate change denialist. He dubbed an EPA plan to regulate carbon emissions "an unconstitutional power grab that will kill millions of jobs." He threatened to harass EPA Administrator Lisa Jackson with required testimony before his committee so often that she would need her own congressional parking space. Reasonable, science-believing legislators have no place in a Republican party addicted to oil industry funding.

Propaganda, censorship, and denial are not the only ways that conservatives have attacked climate science. Climate scientists themselves have been subject to campaigns of intimidation and harassment. Consider the plight of Michael Mann, a prominent climate scientist whose early work established the "hockey stick" graph (a visual that shows the sudden and radical increase in earth's temperature, the "blade" of a horizontal hockey stick). Mann is a moderate in politics and a fine scientist. But he has been repeatedly smeared by conservative media, especially talk radio. Mann received numerous death threats and an anthrax scare at his office, and smear agents have solicited his colleagues for any kind of damaging information about him. Well-financed pressure groups have attempted to force his removal from his academic appointments.

The consequences of this radicalism could not be more severe. Pentagon reports that assess the relationship between climate disruption and national security sound like Jeremiads from Paul Ehrlich. In a 2002 report, the Pentagon concluded that "abrupt climate change is likely to stretch (the Earth's) carrying capacity well beyond its already precarious limits." In 2015, a Pentagon report identified climate disruption as a "threat multiplier." The Department of Defense produced a 2015 report,

"National Security Implications of Climate-Related Risks and Climate Change," that forthrightly acknowledged the security implications of climate disruption. The report begins by acknowledging that

> [The Department of Defense] recognizes the reality of climate change and the significant risk it poses to U.S. interests globally. The National Security Strategy, issued in February 2015, is clear that climate change is an urgent and growing threat to our national security, contributing to increased natural disasters, refugee flows, and conflicts over basic resources such as food and water. These impacts are already occurring, and the scope, scale, and intensity of these impacts are projected to increase over time.

In 2016, a coalition of twenty-five military and national security experts warned that climate disruption poses a "significant risk to U.S. national security and international security." The costs of climate disruption are already profound, as the Arctic heatwave, Syrian civil war, bleaching of the Great Barrier Reef, spread of infectious diseases, worsening storms, prolonged droughts, wildfires, species extinctions, and unusual weather events all demonstrate. As Obama administration Science Advisor John Holdren noted, "We're not really in the business any longer of trying to avoid dangerous climate change—we're already in dangerous climate change. We're trying to avoid catastrophic climate change."

The administration of Barack Obama (b. 1961) did make some significant progress on the climate issue. The stimulus package that arrested the economic fallout of the 2008 financial crisis made large investments in renewable energy research. Prices for renewable energy sources subsequently plunged: since 2008, the price of wind power fell 41 percent, utility scale solar power fell by 64 percent, and LED lightbulbs by 94 percent. So-called alternate energies are no longer alternate, and they are the cheapest and cleanest forms of energy production.

The Obama clean power plan limited, for the first time in history, the carbon pollution that power plants—the largest contributor of greenhouse gases in America—can emit. The administration also set standards to reduce pollution from oil and gas operations, limiting, among other pollutants, the methane emissions that account for a quarter of greenhouse gases. In 2015 the administration reached an historic international climate accord in Paris. Both China and the United States agreed to reduce greenhouse gas emissions. The agreement lacks the binding power of a treaty because the Obama administration rightly understood that the Republican Senate would never ratify such a deal. Despite substantial efforts, Obama was never able to break the ideological stranglehold that climate denial has on the Republican Party.

A hopeful sign in the development of popular climate politics is the emergence of climate disruption as a social justice issue. Much activism around climate, such as Al Gore's important 2006 documentary film *An Inconvenient Truth*, focused on explaining the complex scientific issues of climate. The limitation of that necessary activism is that it presented the climate issue as an esoteric scientific matter—rather than an immediate life and death threat to regular people. Nor are those threats evenly distributed. The people most affected by climate disruption are polar and equatorial people—that is, poor, nonwhite people. And it is poor, nonwhite people in the United States most harmed by fossil fuel pollution. Moreover, only wealthy countries have the ability to mitigate some of the worst effects of climate disruption. Climate justice insists, in the spirit of the Superfund, that those who caused the pollution and benefited from fossil fuels should be the ones to pay for clean up and mitigation.

Climate justice also highlights the greatest threat to environmentally sane public policy: the overwhelming power of moneyed special interests in America's democratic political system. In 2014 two political scientists, Martin Gilens and Benjamin I. Page, tested four prominent theories meant to explain "To what extent is the broad body of U.S. citizens sovereign, semi-sovereign, or largely powerless?" To do so they examined 1,779 policy issues between 1981 and 2002 "about which it is plausible that average citizens may have real opinions and may exert some political influence." What they found was striking. "The preferences of the average American appear to have only a minuscule, near-zero, statistically non-significant impact upon public policy." Nor do organized interest groups such as environmental organizations. In contrast, "the preferences of economic elites . . . have far more independent impact upon policy change than the preferences of average citizens." In short, "the majority does *not* rule." The researchers conclude that "policymaking is dominated by powerful business organizations and a small number of affluent Americans." Given that reality, "America's claims to being a democratic society are seriously threatened." To a substantial extent, America is an oligarchy.

The lack of democracy helps explain the relative lack of legislative achievements by environmentalists since 1980. In recent years membership in environmental groups has continued to increase. Between 1997 and 2004 the Sierra Club gained over two hundred thousand members; the Audubon Society a whopping 450,000. In many ways environmentalism has proven to be the most popular and resilient progressive movement in the country. But environmentalism has not effectuated significant change in recent years because its priorities—particularly the need to abandon fossil fuels—contradict the preferences of the powerful commercial interests that dominate our politics. Despite their popularity, environmental politics are not likely to substantively change future society until America becomes a much more democratic country. This is true worldwide; many studies demonstrate that environmental quality is a strong indicator of democratic freedom (and vice versa). Democracy and environmentalism go hand in hand.

The problem of democracy is thus environmentalism's great opportunity. As Naomi Klein writes, the problem of climate disruption (and other environmental issues) "changes everything"—that is, it demands a fundamental reworking of the American social and economic structure. Humans live within a limited and increasingly fragile ecosystem. The great opportunity of the early twenty-first century is to make American society much more just, democratic, and inclusive as it is made sustainable. To do this, environmentalists must face the crisis of the present with an even greater urgency than they have faced the ecological crises of the past. Environmental success will likely hinge on the ability to form progressive coalitions such as the demand for climate justice that overtly intertwine social and environmental health.

The key to an environmentally sane future thus demands that environmentalists confront the power inequalities that define contemporary America. Our environmental problems are problems of politics and democracy. Environmentalists have a tradition of inventing new institutions and expanding democratic access to existing ones—as well as a history of failure to understand the complexities of social access to democratic institutions. Learning from that history should inform the environmentalist response to the intertwined crises of democracy and ecology. It will be the creative confrontation of this legacy to inform new institutions and strategies that will determine whether planet Earth will remain habitable for humans.

BIBLIOGRAPHY

Introduction: The Horns
in Dock Creek

Benjamin Franklin is by now his own academic industry. Edmund Morgan's superb *Benjamin Franklin* (Yale, 2002) is an excellent beginning to any study of Franklin. For Franklin as scientist, see Joyce E. Chaplin, *The First Scientific American* (Basic Books, 2006). For the Dock, see A. Michael McMahon, "'Small Matters': Benjamin Franklin, Philadelphia and the Progress of Cities," *Pennsylvania Magazine of History and Biography* 66:2 (April 1992). Philadelphia eventually gave up and turned the Dock into an actual sewer. See Charles S. Olton, "Philadelphia's First Environmental Crisis," *The Pennsylvania Magazine of History and Biography* 98:1 (January 1974). In 1744 Franklin published "An Account of the Newly Invented Pennsylvanian Fire-Places." Franklin's thoughts on population can be found by reading his *Observations Concerning the Increase of Mankind, Peopling of Countries, &c.* (Boston, 1755). For Franklin's interaction with Joseph Priestley, see Steven Johnson, *The Invention of Air* (Riverhead Books, 2009).

Francis Bacon and Enlightenment philosophy also command their own libraries. Bacon's utopian novel *The New Atlantis* (1627) and his philosophical work *The New Organon*

(1620) readily demonstrate his ideology that human advancement depends upon the control of nature. Readers interested in environmental criticism of this complicated legacy can begin with three classics of the genre: William Leiss, *The Domination of Nature* (McGill-Queen's University Press, 1994 [1972]); Donald Worster, *Nature's Economy: A History of Ecological Ideas* (Cambridge University Press, 1977); and Carolyn Merchant, *The Death of Nature: Women, Ecology and the Scientific Revolution* (HarperCollins, 1980). For colonial Americans' understanding nature as commodities, see William Cronon's classic environmental history of New England, *Changes in the Land* (Hill and Wang, 1983), from which many of my quotes of colonial Americans reveling in abundance are taken. Timothy Silver's *A New Face on the Countryside: Indians, Colonists and Slaves in South Atlantic Forests, 1500-1800* (Cambridge University Press, 1990) does for the South what Cronon did for New England. Mark Kurlansky's *Cod: Biography of a Fish that Changed the World* (Walker Books, 1997) ably details the "[one thousand]-year fishing spree" that helped enable colonization of the New World. J. Hector St. John Crevecoeur's *Letters from an American Farmer*, originally published with the cumbersome subtitle *Describing Certain Provincial Situations, Manners, and Customs Not Generally Known; and Conveying Some Idea of the Late and Present Interior Circumstances of the British Colonies in North America*, was originally published by Davies & Davis in 1782. For a cultural history of notions of abundance, see Jackson Lears, *Fables of Abundance: A Cultural History of Advertising in America* (Basic Books, 1994). Alexis de Tocqueville's classic work is *Democracy in America*, originally published by Saunders and Otley in London, 1835–1840. Benjamin Rush's letter to Jefferson in support of sugar maple protection may be found in Benjamin Rush, *Essays, Literary, Moral and Philosophical* (Bradford, 1806).

Even in my introduction I have benefited and drawn from other books that tackle the longer history of North American environmentalism. Benjamin Kline's *First Along the River: A Brief History of the U.S. Environmental Movement*, third edition (Rowman & Littlefield, 2007) is the closest analog to the book you hold in your hands. Philip Shabecoff's *A Fierce Green Fire: The American Environmental Movement* (Hill and Wang, 1993) was easily the best history of environmentalism when it was published and remains most valuable. Richard N.L. Andrews has written a truly comprehensive yet readable history of environmental policy from which I have greatly benefited, including his discussion of the Constitution. See Andrews, *Managing the Environment, Managing Ourselves: A History of American Environmental Policy* (Yale University Press, 2006). Finally, Bill McKibben's anthology of American nature writing, *American Earth: Environmental Writing Since Thoreau* (The Library of America, 2008) is both a great scholarly source and a delight.

The Science and Nature of Empathy

Not enough scholarly attention has been given to early American naturalists; an important exception is Richard W. Judd, "A 'wonderfull order and balance': Natural History and the Beginnings of Forest Conservation in America, 1730-1830," *Environmental History* 11 (January 2006), 8–36. Two key texts that investigate the history of early American naturalists are Raymond Phineas Stearns, *Science in the British Colonies of America* (University of Illinois Press, 1970), and Wayne Handley, *Natural History in America: From Mark Catesby to Rachel Carson* (Quadrangle, 1977). Philip J. Pauly's *Biologists and the Promise of American Life: From Meriwether Lewis to Alfred Kinsey* (Princeton University Press, 2000) is a superb evaluation of the social impacts of biological research. Primary documents include "American Forest Trees," *North American Review* 44 (April 1837): 361; Benjamin Waterhouse, *The Botanist* (Joseph T. Buckingham, 1811); Alexander Wilson and Charles Lucian Bonaparte, *American Ornithology: or, the Natural History of the Birds of the United States* (Philadelphia: Porter and Coates, n.d.); Benjamin Smith Barton, "On the Animals of North America" (1793); "Forest Trees," *The Naturalist* 1 (November 1831); and George Barrell Emerson, *A Report on the Trees and Shrubs Growing Naturally in the Forests of Massachusetts* (Dutton and Wentworth, 1846). For Nicholas Collin, see Whitfield J. Bell Jr., "Nicholas Collin's Appeal to American Scientists," *The William and Mary Quarterly* 13:4 (October 1956). On John James Audubon, see Richard Rhodes, *John James Audubon: The Making of an American* (Vintage, 2004), and Peter B. Logan, *Audubon: America's Greatest Naturalist and His Voyage of Discovery to Labrador* (Ashbryn Press, 2016).

Thoreau is one of the few American figures who has attracted scholarly consideration that rivals that of Benjamin Franklin. To begin, see Robert D. Richardson Jr., *Henry Thoreau: A Life of the Mind* (University of California Press, 1986), and Lawrence Buell, *The Ecological Imagination: Thoreau, Nature Writing, and the Formation of American Culture* (Belknap Press, 1995). Insightful essays that helped shape my own outlook on Thoreau are Rebecca Solnit, "The Thoreau Problem," *Orion* (May/June 2007); Kent Curtis, "The Virtue of Thoreau: Biography, Geography, and History in Walden Woods," *Environmental History* 15:1 (January 2010); and James Finney, "'Justice in the Land': Ecological Protest in Henry David Thoreau's Antislavery Essays," *The Concord Saunterer: A Journal of Thoreau Studies* (2013). Accessible slave narratives that include an ecological critique of slavery are Charles Ball, *Slavery in the United States* (John S. Taylor, 1837); Frederick Douglass's second autobiography, *My Bondage and My Freedom* (Miller, Orton & Mulligan 1855) and *Narrative of the Life and Adventures of Henry Bibb* (Author, 1849); and Solomon Northup's *12 Years a Slave* (Derby, Orton, and Mulligan, 1853). For ecology in Douglass's autobiography, see Buell and Cristin Ellis, "Amoral Abolitionism: Frederick Douglass and the Environmental Case Against Slavery," *American Literature* 86:2 (2014). Discussion of the Lowell mills comes from Chad Montrie's most valuable *A People's History of Environmentalism in the United States* (Continuum, 2011).

For Catlin, see John Hausdoerffer, *Catlin's Lament: Indians, Manifest Destiny, and the Ethics of Nature* (University Press of Kansas, 2009). The scholarly renewal of interest and my own introduction to Humboldt comes from two sources: Aaron Sachs, *The Humboldt Current: Nineteenth Century Exploration and the Roots of American Environmentalism* (Viking, 2006), and Andrea Wulf, *The Invention of Nature: Alexander von Humboldt's New World* (Knopf, 2015). George Perkins Marsh's great book is *Man and Nature; or, Physical Geography as Modified by Human Action* (Belknap Press of Harvard University, [1864] 1965). The standard biography of George Perkins Marsh is David Lowenthall, *George Perkins Marsh: Prophet of Conservation* (Weyerhaeuser, 2003). For the history of conservation in New York, see David Stradling, *The Nature of New York: An Environmental History of the Empire State* (Cornell University Press, 2010). A compelling blend of ecological and economic history can be found with John Bellamy Foster, *The Vulnerable Planet: A Short Economic History of the Environment* (Monthly Review Press, 1999). For more on the Peshtigo fire, see Scott Knickelbine, *The Great Peshtigo Fire: Stories and Science from America's Deadliest Firestorm* (Wisconsin Historical Society Press, 2012).

For the story of public lands in America, see Randall K. Wilson, *America's Public Lands: From Yellowstone to Smokey Bear and Beyond* (Rowman & Littlefield, 2014). The relationship between ideas of nature, native peoples, and national parks has attracted much scholarly attention. For the story of parks in the lower forty-eight states, see Philip Burnham, *Indian County, God's Country: Native Americans and the National Parks* (Island Press, 2000), and Mark D. Spence, *Dispossessing the Wilderness: Indian Removal and the Making of the National Parks* (Oxford University Press, 1999). My discussion of urban planners and public space comes from Aaron Sachs, *Arcadian America: The Death and Life of an Environmental Tradition* (Yale, 2013).

Pehr Kahn's work is long-windedly entitled *Travels into North America: Containing Its Natural History, and a Circumstantial Account of Its Plantations and Agriculture in General; with the Civil, Ecclesiastical and Commercial State of the Country, the Manners of the Inhabitants, and Several Curious and Import-ant Remarks on Various Subjects* (T. Lowndes, 1772). Agriculture in the early republic has been most insightfully explored by Steven Stoll, *Larding the Lean Earth: Soil and Society in Nineteenth Century America* (Hill and Wang, 2002). See also Harry J. Carman, "Jesse Buel, Early Nineteenth-Century Agricultural Reformer," *Agricultural History* 17:1 (January 1943). Edmund Ruffin, *An Essay on Calcareous Manures* (J.W. Randolph, 1832). Edmund Ruffin's writings were collected and edited by Jack Temple Kirby; see *Nature's Management: Writings on Landscape and Reform, 1822–1859* (University of Georgia Press, 2000).

The environmental history of the Civil War (and war in general) is a rapidly emerging subfield. A great popular overview comes from *The New York Times*'s "Disunion" blog, Ted Widmer's "The Civil War's Environmental Impact," http://opinionator.blogs.nytimes.com/author/ted-widmer/. Widmer also provides a short bibliography. For more on the Civil War begin with Megan Kate Nelson, *Ruin Nation: Destruction and the American Civil War* (University of Georgia Press, 2012); Lisa M. Brady, *War Upon the Land: Military Strategy and the Transformation of Southern Landscapes during the American Civil War* (University of Georgia Press, 2012); Kathryn Shively Meier, *Nature's Civil War: Common Soldiers and the Environment in 1862 Virginia* (University of North Carolina Press, 2015); and Brian Allen Drake, ed. *The Blue, the Gray, and the Green: Toward an Environmental History of the Civil War* (University of Georgia Press, 2015). The best examination of extinction and its impact on environmental thought is Mark V. Barrow Jr., *Nature's Ghosts: Confronting Extinction from the Age of Jefferson to the Age of Ecology* (University of Chicago Press, 2009).

Progressive Publics and the Social Natural Order

For more on Mary Ellen Wilson, see Eric A. Shelman and Stephen Lazoritz, *Out of the Darkness: The Story of Mary Ellen Wilson* (Dolphin Moon Publishing, 1999). On and the connection between animal and child welfare, see Susan J. Pearson, *The Rights of the Defenseless: Protecting Animals and Children in Gilded Age America* (University of Chicago Press, 2011). Early interpretations of conservation emphasized that it was an elite movement. This interpretation has been greatly modified by more recent scholarship. One pioneering study that emphasized the "bottom up" nature of conservation is Richard Judd's important book, *Common Lands, Common People: The Origins of Conservation in Northern New England* (Harvard University Press, 1997). The world of *Garden and Forest* magazine has been beautifully recreated by Shen

Hou in *The City Natural: Garden and Forest Magazine and the Rise of American Environmentalism* (University of Pittsburgh Press, 2013). Daniel J. Philippon explores the work of Mabel Osgood Wright in his excellent *Conserving Words: How American Nature Writers Shaped the Environmental Movement* (University of Georgia Press, 2005). Mira Lloyd Dock's career is ably explored by Susan Rimby in *Mira Lloyd Dock and the Progressive Era Conservation Movement* (Penn State University Press, 2012).

Urban conservation is still understudied, but several books have established a great understanding of this vital topic. See David Stradling, *Smokestacks and Progressives: Environmentalists, Engineers, and Air Quality in America, 1881-1951* (Harvard University Press, 1998). F. Elizabeth Crowell, "Painter's Row: The Company House," in Paul U. Kellogg, *The Pittsburgh District, The Civic Frontage* (Russell Sage Foundation Publications, 1914). John Opie writes of "negative infrastructure" in his fine environmental history, *Nature's Nation: An Environmental History of the United States* (Harcourt Brace College Publishers, 1998). For the Russell Sage Foundation investigation of Pittsburgh, see Maurine W. Greenwald and Margo Anderson, *Pittsburgh Surveyed: Social Science and Social Reform in the Early Twentieth Century* (University of Pittsburgh Press, 1996). For women's municipal housekeeping, see Suellen Hoy, *Chasing Dirt: The American Pursuit of Cleanliness* (Oxford University Press, 1995). For the work of the Ladies Health Protective Association, see Edith Parker Thompson, "What Women Have Done for the Public Health," *The Forum* (September 1897). For Ellen Swallow Richards, see Robert Clarke, *Ellen Swallow: The Woman Who Founded Ecology* (Follett Publishing Company, 1973); Pamela C. Swallow, *The Remarkable Life and Career of Ellen Swallow Richards: Pioneer in Science and Technology* (Wiley, 2014); and Robert Musil, *Rachel Carson and Her Sisters: Extraordinary Women Who Have Shaped America's Environment* (Rutgers University Press, 2014).

A great overview of Progressive Era public health environmentalism can be found with Robert Gottlieb, *Forcing the Spring: The Transformation of the American Environmental Movement* (Island Press, 1993). Chicago's urban reform is explored by Hoy, *Chasing Dirt*; Chad Montrie, *A Peoples History of Environmentalism in the United States* (Bloomsbury Academic, 2011); and Sylvia Hood Washington, *Packing Them In: An Archaeology of Environmental Racism in Chicago, 1865–1954* (Lexington Books, 2004). Jane Addams, *Twenty Years at Hull-House with Autobiographical Notes* (MacMillan Company, 1912). On Alice Hamilton, see her *Exploring the Dangerous Trades: The Autobiography of Alice Hamilton, M.D.* (Atlantic Monthly Press, 1943); and Barbara Sicherman, *Alice Hamilton. A Life in Letters* (Harvard University Press, 1984). On urban horses, see Clay McShane and Joel A. Tarr, *The Horse in the City: Living Machines in the Nineteenth Century* (Johns Hopkins University Press, 2007).

For more general studies of urban pollution, see Joel Tarr, *The Search for the Ultimate Sink: Urban Pollution in Historical Perspective* (University of Akron Press, 1996), and two from Martin Melosi: *Pollution and Reform in American Cities, 1870-1930* (University of Texas Press, 1980) and *The Sanitary City: Urban Infrastructure in America from Colonial Times to the Present* (Johns Hopkins University Press, 2000). For smoke see Stradling, *Smokestacks and Progressives*, and Frank Uekoetter, *The Age of Smoke: Environmental Policy in Germany and the United States, 1880-1970* (University of Pittsburgh Press, 2009). Some of my information on Cincinnati comes from "The History of Air Pollution Control in Cincinnati, Ohio," http://www.southwestohioair.org/uploads/Department%20History.pdf.

Teddy Roosevelt and Progressive Era conservation are intensely studied—arguably more so than recent environmentalism—but as with all fascinating subjects, new information and interpretations keep emerging. For Roosevelt's conservation activism, see Douglas Brinkley's magisterial study, *The Wilderness Warrior: Theodore Roosevelt and the Crusade for America* (HarperCollins, 2009). A great collection of primary documents from the era is David Stradling, *Conservation in the Progressive Era: Classic Texts* (University of Washington Press, 2004). Gifford Pinchot published *The Fight for Conservation* (Doubleday, Page, and Company) in 1910. The classic study of conservation is Samuel Hays, *Conservation and the Gospel of Efficiency* (Harvard University Press, 1959). For hunters as conservationists, see John F. Rieger, *American Sportsmen and the Origins of Conservation* (Oregon State University Press, 1975). A newer, different interpretation focusing on how hunting regulations could be imperial is Louis Warren, *The Hunter's Game: Poachers and Conservationists in Twentieth Century America* (Yale University Press, 1997). The standard source on Gifford Pinchot is Char Miller's great biography, *Gifford Pinchot and the Making of Modern Environmentalism* (Island Press, 2001).

Organized womanhood is explored by Anne Firor Scott, *Natural Allies: Women's Associations in American History* (University of Illinois Press, 1991). On women, birds, and hats, see Nancy C. Unger, "Gendered Approaches to Environmental Justice: An Historical Sampling," in Sylvia Hood Washington, Heather Goodall, and Paul C. Rosier, eds., *Echoes from the Poisoned Well: Global Memories of Environmental Injustice* (Lexington Books, 2006). For more on gender and amazing women conservationists, see Unger, *Beyond Nature's Housekeepers: American Women in Environmental History* (Oxford University Press, 2012). See also Jennifer Price's great book, *Flight Maps: Adventures with Nature in Modern America* (Basic Books, 1999). *Harper's Bazar* wrote about bird fashion in its December 4, 1897, issue. Marion Crocker's words are recorded in "Mrs. Marion Crocker on the Conservation Imperative," *Proceedings of the Fourth Conservation Congress* (National Conservation Congress, 1912). Lydia Adams-Williams argued that "Conservation Is Woman's Work," in *Forestry and Irrigation*, 14 (June 1908). On Florence Merriam Bailey, see Madelyn Holmes, *American Women Conservationists* (McFarland & Company, 2004); Mark V. Barrow, *A Passion for Birds: American Ornithology after Audubon* (Princeton University Press, 1998); and Thomas R. Dunlap, *In the Field, Among the Feathered: A History of Birders & Their Guides* (Oxford University Press, 2011). For the all-important Antiquities Act, see David Harmon, Francis P. McManamon, and Dwight T. Pitcaithley, eds., *The Antiquities Act: A Century of American Archaeology, Historic Preservation, and Nature Conservation* (University of Arizona Press, 2006).

On nature study, see Kevin C. Armitage, *The Nature Study Movement: The Forgotten Popularizer of America's Conservation Ethic* (University Press of Kansas, 2009), and Sally Gregory Kohlstedt, *Teaching Children Science: Hands-On Nature Study in North America, 1890–1930* (University of Chicago Press, 2010). Margaret W. Morley, "Nature Study and its Influence," *Outlook* 68 (July 27, 1901). Anna Botsford Comstock, *Handbook of Nature Study* (Comstock Publishers, 1911). For Booker T. Washington, see *Up from Slavery: An Autobiography* (Doubleday, 1901), and especially his second book, *Working with the Hands: Being a Sequel to "Up from Slavery"* (Doubleday and Page, 1904), which fully articulates Washington's nature study pedagogy. On Liberty Hyde Bailey, see Armitage, *The Nature Study Movement*; "'The Science-Spirit in a Democracy': Liberty Hyde Bailey, Nature Study, and the Democratic Impulse of Progressive Conservation," in Michael Egan and Jeff Crane, eds., *Natural Protest: Essays on the History of American Environmentalism* (Routledge, 2008); and A.D. Rogers, *Liberty Hyde Bailey: A Story of American Plant Sciences* (Princeton University Press, 1949). On the country life commission, see Scott J. Peters and Paul A. Morgan, "The Country Life Commission: Reconsidering a Milestone in American Agricultural History," *Agricultural History* 78:3 (Summer 2004); and David B. Danbom, "Rural Education Reform and the Country Life Movement, 1900-1920," *Agricultural History* 53:2 (April 1979).

A Green New Deal

My opening quotes from Franklin D. Roosevelt (FDR) come from two of his key speeches: The January 24, 1935, "A Message to Congress on the Use of Our National Resources," and the February 26, 1937, "Letter to all State Governors on a Uniform Soil Conservation Law." In the last fifteen years many talented environmental historians have appraised the environmental legacy of the New Deal. A good overview is D. Woolner and H. Henderson, eds., *FDR and the Environment* (Palgrave Macmillan, 2005). The authoritative source that appraises FDR and the environment is Douglas Brinkley, *Rightful Heritage: Franklin D. Roosevelt and the Land of America* (HarperCollins Publishers, 2016). The most compelling single-volume overview of the green deal is Sarah T. Phillips, *This Land This Nation: Conservation, Rural America and the New Deal* (Cambridge University Press, 2007). More specific volumes include Neil M. Maher's invaluable study of the Civilian Conservation Corps, *Nature's New Deal: The Civilian Conservation Corps and the Roots of the American Environmental Movement* (Oxford University Press, 2008), and Joseph M. Speakman's *At Work in Penn's Woods: The Civilian Conservation Corps in Pennsylvania* (Pennsylvania State University Press, 2006). The quote from Lewis Mumford comes from "Regions—To Live In," *Survey Graphic* (May 1925). The issue includes an essay from Benton MacKaye. For Kudzu, see Bill Finch, "The True Story of Kudzu, the Vine That Never Truly Ate the South," *Smithsonian* (September 2015).

Benton MacKaye is finally receiving the scholarly attention he deserves. For MacKaye, see Paul Sutter, *Driven Wild: How the Fight Against Automobiles Launched the Modern Wilderness Movement* (University of Washington Press, 2002); and Ben A. Minteer, *The Landscape of Reform* (Cambridge, MA: MIT Press, 2009). The first full-length biography of MacKaye is Larry Anderson, *Benton MacKaye: Conservationist, Planner, and Creator of the Appalachian Trail* (Johns Hopkins University Press, 2002). The Appalachian Trail itself finally has its historian with Sarah Mittlefehldt's fine *Tangled Roots: The Appalachian Trail and American Environmental Politics* (University of Washington Press, 2013). MacKaye's "An Appalachian Trail: A Project in Regional Planning," can be found in the *Journal of the American Institute of Architects* 9 (1921). Hugh Hammond Bennett is ripe for further scholarly attention. Wellington Brink's *Big Hugh: The Father of Soil Conservation* (MacMillan Company, 1951) is a hagiographic appreciation of Bennett. For Bennett as science salesman, see Kevin C. Armitage, "The Soil Doctor: Hugh Hammond Bennett, Soil Conservation and the Search for a Democratic Science," in *New Natures: Joining Environmental History with Science and Technology Studies* (University of Pittsburgh Press, 2013).

Donald Worster's Bancroft Prize–winning *Dust Bowl: The Southern Plains in the 1930s*, twenty-fifth anniversary edition (Oxford University Press, 2004), remains the best book on the dirty 1930s. A valuable book on soils that combines science with history is David R. Montgomery, *Dirt: The Erosion of Civilizations* (University of California Press, 2008). For the current state of dry land farming in Kansas, see http://www.kansascity.com/news

/state/kansas/article28640722.html. See also https://coyotegulch.wordpress .com/category/colorado-water/pipeline-projects/pipeline-from-the-missouri -river/. The go-to source on the underappreciated George Washington Carver is Mark D. Hersey, *My Work is that of Conservation: An Environmental Biography of George Washington Carver* (University of Georgia Press, 2011). Harold Ickes's biographer is Jeanne Nienaber Clarke, *Roosevelt's Warrior: Harold L. Ickes and the New Deal* (Johns Hopkins University Press, 1996). The roots of land use planning its impact on rural people can be studied with Sara M. Gregg, *Managing the Mountains: Land Use Planning, the New Deal, and the Creation of a Federal Landscape in Appalachia* (Yale University Press, 2010). For William J. Trent and desegregation of campgrounds, see Terence Young, "'A Contradiction in Democratic Government': W. J. Trent, Jr., and the Struggle to Desegregate National Park Campgrounds," *Environmental History* 14:4 (October 2009). Du Bois's essay "Of Beauty and Death" can be found in his book *Darkwater: Voices from Within the Veil* (Harcourt, Brace, and Howe, 1920).

Arthur Kallet and F.J. Schlink, *100,000,000 Guinea Pigs: Dangers in Everyday Foods, Drugs and Cosmetics* (Vanguard Press, 1933). For the elixir sulfanilamide debacle, see Daniel Carpenter, *Reputation and Power: Organizational Image and Pharmaceutical Regulation at the FDA* (Princeton University Press, 1910), and Jef Akst, "The Elixir Tragedy, 1937," *The Scientist* (June 1, 2013). Leopold commands a large laboratory. His most famous book is *A Sand County Almanac and Sketches Here and There* (Oxford University Press, 1949). The go-to biography is Curt Meine, *Aldo Leopold: His Life and Work* (University of Wisconsin Press, 1988). Susan Flader's *Thinking Like a Mountain: Aldo Leopold and the Evolution of an Ecological Attitude Toward Deer, Wolves and Forests* (University of Missouri Press, 1974) remains a valuable examination of Leopold's thinking. For vegetation surveys and the deer irruption on the Kaibab Plateau, see Dan Binkley, Margaret M. Moore, William H. Romme, and Peter M. Brown, "Was Aldo Leopold Right about the Kaibab Deer Herd?" *Ecosystems* 9:2 (March 2006). For Van Jones, see "Working Together for a New Green Deal," *The Nation* (October 29, 2008), and his book *The Green Collar Economy: How One Solution Can Fix Our Two Biggest Problems* (HarperOne, 2008).

A Wilderness Society

Any appreciation of Muir should begin with Donald Worster's brilliant biography *A Passion for Nature: The Life of John Muir* (Oxford University Press, 2008). Still relevant—indeed necessary—is a book I first read while backpacking through the wilds of Alaska: Stephen Fox's *John Muir and His Legacy:*

The American Conservation Movement (Little, Brown, 1981). While Worster penned the go-to source, several other excellent biographies have examined Muir. Two valuable texts are Steven J. Holmes, *The Young John Muir: An Environmental Biography* (University of Wisconsin Press, 1999), and Frederick Turner, *Rediscovering America: John Muir in His Time and Ours* (Sierra Club Books, 1985). Muir's writings are vast. A good beginning can be found in Edwin Way Teale, ed., *The Wilderness World of John Muir* (Houghton Mifflin, 1954). For larger doses of Muir's words, begin with the following, all by John Muir, *The Mountains of California* (The Century Company, 1894), *The Yosemite* (The Century Company, 1912), *The Story of My Boyhood and Youth* (Houghton Mifflin, 1913), and *A Thousand-Mile Walk to the Gulf* (Houghton Mifflin, 1916).

The classic intellectual history of wilderness is Roderick Nash's *Wilderness and the American Mind*, fourth edition (Yale, 2001). Michael Lewis's *American Wilderness: A New History* (Oxford, 2007) couples well with Nash's work, as it contains many provocative and insightful essays. Online sources also informed this history and are very useful for classroom teaching. J. Baird Callicott's "The Puritan Origins of the American Wilderness Movement" can be found at http://nationalhumanitiescenter.org/tserve/nattrans/ntwilderness/essays/puritan.htm. I found the quote from Jonathan Edwards in Clarence Faust and Thomas Johnson, eds., *Jonathan Edwards: Representative Selections* (American Book Company, 1935).

For the Hudson Valley School of landscape painters, begin with Barbara Babcock Millhouse, *American Wilderness: The Story of the Hudson River School of Painting* (Black Dome Press Corp, 2007); Linda Ferber, *Kindred Spirits: Asher B. Durand and the American Landscape* (D. Giles Ltd, 2007); and John K. Howat et al., *American Paradise: The World of the Hudson River School*, exhibition catalog (Metropolitan Museum of Art, 1987). The battle over Hetch Hetchy has occupied the talents of many fine historians; readers interested in further details should see Worster, *A Passion for Nature*, and Robert W. Righter, *The Battle Over Hetch Hetchy: America's Most Controversial Dam and the Birth of Modern Environmentalism* (Oxford University Press, 2005). For contemporary biodiversity and the reduction of the Yosemite protected area, see Rachel E. Golden Kroner, Roopa Krithivasan, and Michael B. Mascia, "Effects of Protected Area Downsizing on Habitat Fragmentation in Yosemite National Park (USA), 1864–2014," *Ecology and Society* 21:3 (2016).

On the gender politics of the controversy, see Adam Rome, "'Political Hermaphrodites,' Gender and Environmental Reform in Progressive America," *Environmental History* 11:3 (July 2006). The full-scale study of Enos Mills is Alexander Drummond, *Enos Mills: Citizen of Nature* (University Press of Colorado, 1995). Enos Mills and Rocky Mountain National Park are great examples of the tensions between protecting nature and tourist development that have defined so much of the history of public lands in America. An excellent examination of that history is Jerry Frank, *Making Rocky Mountain National Park: The Environmental History of an American Treasure* (University Press of Kansas, 2013). Wallace Stegner was a prolific writer. His musings on public lands are scattered, but a good place to start, and the source of his quote, is Wallace Stegner, *Marking the Sparrow's Fall: The Making of the American West* (Henry Holt and Company, 1948). For contemporary attitudes about parks, see Michelle Haefele, John Loomis, and Linda J. Bilmes, "Total Economic Valuation of the National Parks Service Lands and Programs: Results of a Survey of the American Public," *HKS Working Paper No. 16-024*, http://papers .ssrn.com/sol3/papers.cfm?abstract_id=2821124.

In recent years the story of wilderness areas and their creation has occupied a number of excellent scholars. Begin with Sutter, *Driven Wild*. For women and the fight against billboards, see Catherine Gudis, *Buyways: Billboards, Automobiles and the American Cultural Landscape* (Routledge, 2004). For Rosalie Edge, see Dyana Furmansky, *Rosalie Edge, Hawk of Mercy: The Activist Who Saved Nature from the Conservationists* (University of Georgia Press, 2009). Bob Marshall needs more scholarship. For now, see Sutter, *Driven Wild*, as well as James M. Glover, *A Wilderness Original: The Life of Bob Marshall* (The Mountaineers, 1986). See also Glover's article, "Romance, Recreation, and Wilderness: Influences on the Life and Work of Bob Marshall," *Environmental History Review* 14:4 (Winter 1990). The go-to source on Marjorie Stoneman Douglas is Jack E. Davis's magnificent biography, *An Everglades Providence: Marjorie Stoneman Douglas and the American Environmental Century* (University of Georgia Press, 2009). For a more general treatment of wetlands in American history, see Ann Vileisis, *Discovering the Unknown Landscape: A History of America's Wetlands* (Island Press, 1999). Howard Zahniser had long been neglected in the literature on American environmentalism. That gap has now been filled by Mark Harvey's *Wilderness Forever: Howard Zahniser and the Path to the Wilderness Act* (University of Washington Press, 2005). Harvey has also collected many of Zahniser's wilderness writings in *The Wilderness Writings of Howard Zahniser* (University of Washington Press, 2014). Thanks to Harvey, Zahniser is finally getting his due as both an activist and a writer.

Alaska commands its own section in the literature of wilderness. I have relied heavily on a chapter on Alaska from James Morton Turner's *The Promise of Wilderness: American Environmental Politics Since 1964* (University of Washington Press, 2012). Also valuable is Douglas Brinkley, *The Quiet World: Saving Alaska's Wilderness Kingdom, 1879-1960* (Harper, 2011). Theodore

Catton, *Inhabited Wilderness: Indians, Eskimos and National Parks in Alaska* (University of New Mexico Press, 1997), is the most insightful examination of the interaction of native peoples with national parks. See also E. Barrett Ristroph and Anwar Hussain, "Wilderness: Good for Alaska: Legal and Economic Perspectives on Alaska's Wilderness," *Washington Journal of Environmental Law and Policy* 4:2 (2015).

Damming the Arid West

The American encounter with desert southwest is detailed by Patricia Nelson Limerick in *Desert Passages: Encounters with the American Deserts* (University of New Mexico Press, 1985). Powell has had the good fortune to be the recipient of excellent biographies from two of the west's most passionate and thoughtful historians. First was Wallace Stegner in *Beyond the Hundredth Meridian: John Wesley Powell and the Second Opening of the West* (University of Nebraska Press, 1954) and more recently, Donald Worster, *A River Running West: A Life of John Wesley Powell* (Oxford University Press, 2001).

Western water development commands a large and complex literature. My review is based on the following classics of the genre: Mark Reisner, *Cadillac Desert: The American West and its Disappearing Water* (Penguin, 1986); Donald Worster, *Rivers of Empire: Water, Aridity and the Growth of the American West* (Oxford University Press, 1985); Norris Hundley Jr., *The Great Thirst: Californians and Water, 1770s-1990s* (University of California Press, 1992); and two books by Donald Pisani: *Water, Land and Law in the West: The Limits of Public Policy, 1850-1920* (University Press of Kansas, 1996) and *Water and the American Government: The Reclamation Bureau, National Water Policy, and the West, 1902-1935* (University of California Press, 2002). My appreciation of Mary Hunter Austin comes from her book *Land of Little Rain* (Houghton Mifflin, 1903) and two academic sources: Madelyn Holmes's chapter on Austin in her *American Women Conservationists: Twelve Profiles* (McFarland & Company, 2004) and Benay Blend, "Mary Austin and the Western Conservation Movement: 1900-1927," *Journal of the Southwest* 30:1 (Spring 1988). The full history of the Colorado River Compact can be found in Norris Hundley's *Water and the West: The Colorado River Compact and the Politics of Water in the American West* (University of California Press, 2009). Herbert Hoover's conservationism is most deeply explored by Kendrick A. Clements in *Hoover, Conservation, and Consumerism: Engineering the Good Life* (University Press of Kansas, 2000).

For Minerva Hamilton Hoyt, see Connor Sorenson, "'Apostle of the Cacti': The Society Matron as Environmental Activist," *Southern California Quarterly* 58:3 (Fall 1976). A helpful overview of dams can be found with

David P. Billington, Donald C. Jackson, and Martin V. Melosi, *The History of Large Federal Dams: Planning, Design, and Construction in the Era of Big Dams* (U.S. Department of the Interior: Bureau of Reclamation, 2005). The story of Echo Park Dam is masterfully told in Mark Harvey's *A Symbol of Wilderness: Echo Park and the American Conservation Movement* (University of New Mexico Press, 1994). More academic study needs to be done on anti-environmental backlash. For now, see E. Louise Peffer, *The Closing of the Public Domain: Disposal and Reservation Policies 1900-1950* (Stanford University Press, 1951), and Jacqueline Vaughn Switzer, *Green Backlash: The History and Politics of Environmental Opposition in the U.S.* (Lynne Reinner Publishers, 1997).

David Brower, who died in 2000, is beginning to receive the scholarly interest he deserves. Brower wrote an autobiography, *For Earth's Sake: The Life and Times of David Brower* (Gibbs Smith, 1990). The classic portrait that reveals Brower's brilliance, irascibility, and maddening impetuousness is John McPhee, *Encounters with the Archdruid* (Farrar, Straus & Giroux, 1971). The most up-to-date biography is Tom Turner, *David Brower: The Making of the Environmental Movement* (University of California Press, 2015). For the political history of the debate over Grand Canyon dams, see Byron E. Pearson, *Still the Wild River Runs: Congress, the Sierra Club, and the Fight to Save Grand Canyon* (University of Arizona Press, 2002). Barry Goldwater is a major political figure and is beginning to receive a lot of scholarly attention. For Goldwater and the rise of conservatism, see Rick Perlstein, *Before the Storm: Barry Goldwater and the Unmaking of the American Consensus* (Nation Books, 2009). For Goldwater as an environmentalist, see Brian Allen Drake, *Loving Nature Fearing the State: Environmentalism and Antigovernment Politics Before Reagan* (University of Washington Press, 2013).

Earth First! and Edward Abbey are beginning to demand quite a library. On Abbey see Drake and James M. Cahalan, *Edward Abbey: A Life* (University of Arizona Press, 2001). On Earth First! and the "Redwood Summer" campaign, see David Harris, *The Last Stand: The War Between Wall Street and Main Street over California's Ancient Redwoods* (Times Books, 1995). On Earth First! See Susan Zakin, *Coyotes and Town Dogs: Earth First! and the Environmental Movement* (University of Arizona Press, 1993). See also Christopher Manes, *Green Rage: Radical Environmentalism and the Unmaking of Civilization* (Back Bay Books, 1991). A great source of early Earth First! writings is John Davis, ed., *The Earth First! Reader: Ten Years of Radical Environmentalism* (Gibbs Smith, 1991). Dave Foreman's autobiography is *Confessions of an Eco-Warrior* (Crown Publishing Group, 1991). See also Howie Wolke, *Wilderness on the Rocks* (A Ned Ludd Book, 1991). Paul B. Sears, *Deserts on the March* (University of Oklahoma Press, 1935).

The Atomic Body Politic

To read McCormick's writing on the bomb, see Anne O'Hare McCormick, "The Promethean Role of the United States," *The New York Times* (August 8, 1945), p. 22. For conservation on the World War II homefront, see Mike Davis, "Home-Front Ecology: What Our Grandparents Can Teach Us about Saving the World," *Sierra* (July/August 2007). Historian Timothy Snyder links World War II with resource anxiety in *Black Earth: The Holocaust as History and Warning* (Tim Duggan Books, 2015). On the United Nations Scientific Conference on the Conservation and Utilization of Resources and the International Technical Conference on the Protection of Nature, see Thomas Jundt, "Dueling Visions for the Postwar World: The UN and UNESCO 1949 Conferences on Resources and Nature, and the Origins of Environmentalism," *The Journal of American History* 101:1 (June 2014). Maria Telkes wrote on "The Uses of Solar Energy" for the *Bulletin of the Atomic Scientists* 7:7/8 (August 1, 1951). Fairfield Osborn's great book is *Our Plundered Planet* (Little, Brown and Company, 1948); Vogt's is *The Road to Survival* (William Sloane Associates, 1948).

Malthus must be one of the most influential but least read writers of the modern era. Thomas Malthus, *An Essay on the Principle of Population, as it affects the future improvement of society with remarks on the speculations of Mr. Godwin, M. Condorcet, and other Writers* (Anonymously published, 1798). On Thomas Malthus, see Robert Mayhew, *Malthus: The Life and Legacies of an Untimely Prophet* (Harvard University Press, 2014). A good examination of the legacy of Malthusian thinking is Björn-Ola Linnér, *The Return of Malthus: Environmentalism and Postwar Population–Resource Crises* (White Horse Press, 2003).

For American Malthusianism, see Thomas Robertson's most valuable study, *The Malthusian Moment: Global Population Growth and the Birth of American Environmentalism* (Rutgers University Press, 2012). For a background on Pearl and American eugenics, see Robertson, *The Malthusian Moment*, as well as Daniel Kevles, *In the Name of Eugenics: Genetics and the Uses of Human Heredity* (Alfred A. Knopf, 1985). Barry Commoner is beginning to gather the attention of historians. A great first book on his environmental activism is Michael Egan, *Barry Commoner and the Science of Survival: The Remaking of American Environmentalism* (Massachusetts Institute of Technology, 2007).

For a history of nuclear enthusiasm, see Charles Seife, *Sun in a Bottle: The Strange History of Fusion and the Science of Wishful Thinking* (Viking, 2008). One example of Panglossian technological enthusiasm can be found with

A.M. Weinberg, "Nuclear Energy and the Agro-industrial Complex," *Nature* 222 (1969). Paul Ehrlich seems to write books more quickly than most people read them. Begin with *The Population Bomb* (Ballantine Books, 1968). The most important follow up is *The Population Explosion* (Touchstone Books, 1990). The Ehrlichs have continued writing on population and resource issues for decades, and have reflected on *The Population Bomb* and its legacy. See Paul R. Ehrlich and Anne H. Ehrlich, "The Population Bomb Revisited," *Electronic Journal of Sustainable Development* 1:3 (2009). Ehrlich's pioneering work on coevolution is Paul R. Ehrlich and Peter H. Raven, "Butterflies and Plants: A Study in Coevolution," *Evolution* 18:4 (December 1964). Historians writing about Ehrlich include Robertson and Paul Sabin, who has penned a rich portrait of Ehrlich in *The Bet: Paul Ehrlich, Julian Simon and Our Gamble Over Earth's Future* (Yale University Press, 2013).

Stephanie Mill's valedictory address can be found in McKibben, *American Earth*. Her website is http://www.smillswriter.com.

Few historians have examined Dennis and Donella Meadows and *The Limits to Growth*. To begin, see D.H. Meadows, D.L. Meadows, J. Randers, and W.W. Behrens III, *The Limits to Growth: A Report for the Club of Rome's Project on the Predicament of Mankind* (Universe Books, 1972). Christian Parenti's essay, "'The Limits to Growth': A Book That Launched a Movement," appeared in the December 24/31, 2012, issue of *The Nation*. The best historical source on the book comes from Donald Worster, *Shrinking the Earth: The Rise and Decline of American Abundance* (Oxford University Press, 2016). John W. Gofman and Arthur Tamplin wrote *"Population Control" Through Nuclear Pollution* (Nelson-Hall Co, 1970).

John Kenneth Galbraith's essay "How Much Should a Country Consume?" can be found in Henry Jarrett, *Perspectives on Conservation* (Johns Hopkins University Press, 1958). For more on Norman Borlaug, see Leon Hesser, *The Man Who Fed the World: Nobel Peace Prize Laureate Norman Borlaug and His Battle to End World Hunger* (Durban House, 2006). Borlaug's Nobel acceptance speech can be found online at http://www.nobelprize.org/nobel_prizes/peace/laureates/1970/borlaug-acceptance.html. For the Oil Crisis of 1973, see Karen R. Merrill, *The Oil Crisis of 1973-1974: A Brief History with Documents* (Bedford/St. Martin's, 2007), and Meg Jacobs, *Panic at the Pump: The Energy Crisis and the Transformation of American Politics in the 1970s* (Hill and Wang, 2016).

The global history of oil can be examined with Brian Black's *Crude Reality: Petroleum in World History* (Rowman & Littlefield, 2012). James Akins, "The Oil Crisis: This Time the Wolf is at the Door," *Foreign Affairs* 51 (April 1973). Jimmy Carter's "malaise" speech is analyzed by Kevin Mattson in *"What the*

Heck Are You Up To, Mr. President?": Jimmy Carter, America's "Malaise," and the Speech that Should Have Changed the Country (Bloomsbury, 2009).

On the battle over the ozone layer, see Lydia Dotto and Harold Schiff, *The Ozone War* (Doubleday, 1978), and Michael Hoffmann, *Ozone Depletion And Climate Change: Constructing A Global Response* (State University of New York Press, 2005). On nuclear weapons, see William A. Schwartz and Charles Derber, *The Nuclear Seduction: Why the Arms Race Doesn't Matter - And What Does* (University of California Press, 1990). The famous "TTAPS" paper on nuclear winter is P. Turco, O.B. Toon, T.P. Ackerman, J.B. Pollack, and Carl Sagan, "Nuclear Winter: Global Consequences of Multiple Nuclear Explosions," *Science* 222:4630 (December 23, 1983). Paul Ehrlich et al., "Long-Term Biological Consequences of Nuclear War," *Science* 222:4630 (December 23, 1983.) Paul R. Ehrlich, Carl Sagan, Donald Kennedy, and Walter Orr Roberts, *The Cold and the Dark: The World After Nuclear* War (W.W. Norton, 1985). A more up-to-date appreciation of the nuclear autumn is O.B. Toon, R.P. Turco, A. Robock, C. Bardeen, L. Oman, and G.L. Stenchikov, "Atmospheric Effects and Societal Consequences of Regional Scale Nuclear Conflicts and Acts of Individual Nuclear Terrorism," *Atmospheric Chemistry and Physics* 7:8 (2007). Herman Daly's first important volume is *Toward a Steady-State Economy* (W.H. Freeman, 1973). For a brief history of ecological economics, see M. Common and S. Stagl, *Ecological Economics: An Introduction* (Cambridge University Press, 2005).

Abundance in the Age of Ecology

For a more recent environmental and social critique of the suburb, see James Howard Kunstler, *The Geography of Nowhere: The Rise and Decline of America's Man-Made Landscape* (Simon & Schuster, 1993). Histories of modern environmentalism include Hal K. Rothman, *Saving the Planet: The American Response to the Environment in the Twentieth Century* (Ivan R. Dee, 2000) and his *The Greening of a Nation? Environmentalism in the United States since 1945* (Harcourt Brace, 1998). Two classics of the genre are Samuel P. Hays, *Beauty, Health and Permanence: Environmental Politics in the United States, 1955-1985* (Cambridge University Press, 1987), and Kirkpatrick Sale, *The Green Revolution: The American Environmental Movement 1962–1992* (Hill and Wang, 1993). A most valuable sociological study is Robert J. Brulle, *Agency, Democracy and Nature: The U.S. Environmental Movement from a Critical Theory Perspective* (MIT Press, 2000). A fine collection of documents is Steven Stoll, *U.S. Environmentalism Since 1945* (Bedford/St. Martin's, 2007).

William Leach's *Land of Desire: Merchants, Power, and the Rise of a New American Culture* (Pantheon Books, 1993) is a great study of American commercialism. Victor Liebow's fascinating ruminations are in "Price Competition in 1955," *Journal of Retailing* (Spring 1955). For Brooks Stevens, see Glenn Adamson, *Industrial Strength Design: How Brooks Stevens Shaped Your World* (MIT Press, 2003). For the story of the Chesapeake and Ohio Canal and Douglas's hike, see Harvey, *Wilderness Forever*. Rachel Carson has attracted a great deal of scholarly attention. A good short biography is Mark Hamilton Lytle, *The Gentle Subversive: Rachel Carson, Silent Spring, and the Rise of the Environmental Movement* (Oxford University Press, 2007); the definitive scholarly work on her life is Linda Lear, *Rachel Carson: Witness for Nature* (Houghton Mifflin Harcourt, 2009). Lear also maintains a helpful website: http://www.rachelcarson.org. For reaction to *Silent Spring*, see Maril Hazlett, "'Woman vs. Man vs. Bugs': Gender and Popular Ecology in Early Reactions to Silent Spring," *Environmental History* 9:4 (October 2004). For fish kills in the Mississippi River, see Pete Daniel, *Toxic Drift: Pesticides and Health in the Post-World War II South* (Louisiana State University Press, 2005).

The environmental hazards of post–World War II suburbanization and its relationship to the environmental movement are explored by Adam Rome in his prize-winning *The Bulldozer in the Countryside: Suburban Sprawl and the Rise of American Environmentalism* (Cambridge University Press, 2001). Stewart Udall's career is summarized by the American National Biography online: http://www.anb.org/articles/07/07-00863.html. For Lady Bird Johnson, see Lewis L. Gould, *Lady Bird Johnson: Our Environmental First Lady* (University Press of Kansas, 1999). Ralph Nader's muckraking classic is *Unsafe at Any Speed: The Designed-In Dangers of the American Automobile* (Grossman Publishers, 1965). Jane Jacob's landmark book is *The Death and Life of Great American Cities* (Random House, 1961). For the Donora, Pennsylvania, smog and the regulations it spawned, see Lynne Page Snyder, "'The Death-Dealing Smog Over Donora, Pennsylvania': Industrial Air Pollution, Public Health Policy, and the Politics of Expertise, 1948-1949," *Environmental History Review* 18:1 (Spring 1994).

For labor union environmentalists, see Scott Dewey, "Working for the Environment: Organized Labor and the Origins of Environmentalism in the United States, 1948-1970," *Environmental History* 3:1 (January 1998), and Chad Montrie, *Making a Living: Work and Environment in the United States* (University of North Carolina Press, 2008). Cesar Chavez is one of the most important labor organizers of the post–World War II era. For his environmentalism, see Cesar Chavez, "Address by Cesar Chavez," Pacific Lutheran University, Tacoma, Washington, March 1989. Reprinted in Stoll, *U.S. Environmentalism Since 1945*. Ruth Harmer, "Poisons, Profits and Politics," *The*

Nation (August 25, 1969). Dolores Huerta, "Amor por el terruño—Our Love for the Land," http://sierraclub.org/amor-por-el-terru-o-our-love-land. The most detailed account of the farmworker struggle against pesticides is told by Adam Tompkins, *Ghostworkers and Greens: The Cooperative Campaigns of Farmworkers and Environmentalists for Pesticide Reform* (Cornell University Press, 2016). For the history of lead poisoning, see David Rosner and Gerald Markowitz, *Lead Wars: The Politics of Science and the Fate of America's Children* (University of California Press, 2014). For Ivory Perry, see George Lipsitz, *A Life in the Struggle: Ivory Perry and the Culture of Opposition* (Temple University Press, 1988).

King spoke of polluted air and water in "Conscience for Change" in *The Lost Massy Lectures* (House of Anansi Press, 2007). For Cleveland and Carl Stokes, see David Stradling and Richard Stradling, *Where the River Burned: Carl Stokes and the Struggle to Save Cleveland* (Cornell University Press, 2015). Robert Heilbroner, "Ecological Armageddon," *The New York Review of Books* (April 23, 1970). *Audubon* magazine's joy in everyone being a conservationist is from May 1970.

Earth Day was an amazing event and is finally attracting the historical attention it demands. See Adam Rome, *The Genius of Earth Day: How a 1970 Tech-In Unexpectedly Made the First Green Generation* (Hill and Wang, 2013). A collection of primary documents, including the play "Black Survival: A Collage of Skits" and Arturo Sandoval's speech, is Environmental Action, ed., *Earth Day—The Beginning: A Guide for Survival Compiled by the National Staff of Environmental Action* (Bantam, 1970). For Richard Nixon, see Brooks Flippen, *Nixon and the Environment* (University of New Mexico Press, 2000). For successes of the Clean Air Act, see U.S. Environmental Protection Agency, *The Benefits and Cost of the Clean Air Act, 1970 to 1990* (October 1997), http://www.epa.gov/oar/sect812/1970-1990/chptr1_7.pdf. Andrew Kirk, *Counterculture Green: The Whole Earth Catalogue and American Environmentalism* (University Press of Kansas, 2007). Amory Lovins, "Energy Strategy: The Road Not Taken?" *Foreign Affairs* (October 1976). Lovins followed up that idea with *Soft Energy Paths: Towards a Durable Peace* (HarperCollins, 1976).

On Love Canal, see Elizabeth D. Blum, *Love Canal Revisited: Race, Class, and Gender in Environmental Activism* (University Press of Kansas, 2008), and Richard Newman, *Love Canal: A Toxic History from Colonial Times to the Present* (Oxford University Press, 2016). Gibbs's memoir is *Love Canal: My Story* (State University of New York Press, 1982). She is also the author of *Love Canal and the Birth of the Environmental Health Movement* (Island Press, 2010). Greenpeace is the lucky recipient of a great book from Frank Zelko, *Make it a Green Peace* (Oxford University Press, 2013).

Science Denial in the Age of Global Disruption

On smog in Los Angeles, see Chip Jacobs and William J. Kelley, *Smogtown: The Lung-Burning History of Pollution in Los Angeles* (Overlook Press, 2008). President Johnson's special message to Congress can be read online. See "Special Message to the Congress on Conservation and Restoration of Natural Beauty," http://www.presidency.ucsb.edu/ws/?pid=27285.

For the 1968 science on the collapse of Antarctic ice sheets, see J.H. Mercer, "Antarctic Ice and Sangamon Sea Level," *International Association of Scientific Hydrology, Commission of Snow and Ice, General Assembly of Bern, Publ. No. 79.* For a history of this specific research, see William Thomas, "Research Agendas in Climate Studies: The Case of West Antarctic Ice Sheet Research," *Climatic Change* 122 (2014). A terrific history of scientific research on climate change is Spencer Weart, *The Discovery of Global Warming* (Harvard University Press, 2008). Weart maintains a great website, full of rich information: http://history.aip.org/climate/index.htm. For the deep history of climate change denial by the oil industry, see the rich collection of primary documents published on the website Smoke and Fumes (https://www.smokeandfumes.org/smoke) produced by the Center for International Environmental Law. The Environmental Protection Agency's 1983 report is Stephen Seidel and Dale Keyes, *Can We Delay a Greenhouse Warming?* (Environmental Protection Agency, 1983.) The already-classic history of institutionalized climate change denial is Naomi Oreskes and Erik Conway, *Merchants of Doubt: How a Handful of Scientists Obscured the Truth on Issues from Tobacco Smoke to Global Warming* (Bloomsbury Press, 2010).

A stark critique of recent environmentalism is Mark Dowie, *Losing Ground: American Environmentalism at the Close of the Twentieth Century* (MIT Press, 1995). See also Jeffrey St. Clair, *Ben Brown So Long It Looked Green to Me: The Politics of Nature* (Common Courage Press, 2004). For the corporate boards of environmental organizations, see Jim Donahue "Environmental Board Games," *Multinational Monitor* 11:3 (March 1990). For the rise of corporate conservative politics in America, see Thomas Byrne Edsall, *The New Politics of Inequality* (W.W. Norton, 1985); Jacob Hacker and Paul Pierson, *The Paradox of American Democracy: Elites, Special Interests, and the Betrayal of the Public Trust* (Routledge, 2001); and Daniel T. Rodgers, *The Age of Fracture* (Harvard University Press, 2011). On green drift, see Christopher McGrory Klyza and David J. Sousa, *American Environmental Policy: Beyond Gridlock* (MIT Press, 2013). Christopher J. Bosso, *Environment, Inc.: From Grassroots to Beltway* (University Press of Kansas, 2005).

For body burden, see P.J. Landrigan, et al., "Environmental Pollutants and Disease in American Children: Estimates of Morbidity, Mortality, and Costs for Lead Poisoning, Asthma, Cancer, and Developmental Disabilities," *Environmental Health Perspectives* 110:7 (July 2002). The International Federation of Gynecology and Obstetrics report is Gian Carlo Di Renzo, et al., "International Federation of Gynecology and Obstetrics Opinion on Reproductive Health Impacts of Exposure to Toxic Environmental Chemicals," *International Journal of Gynecology and Obstetrics* 131:3 (October 2015). Curt DellaValle, "The Pollution in People: Cancer Causing Chemicals in Americans' Bodies," Environmental Working Group, http://static.ewg.org/reports/2016 /cancer_main/the-pollution-in-people/EWG_Cancer_BioMonitoring _Report_C02pages.pdf?_ga=1.138201975.650986466.1473623583 (2016). A great book on body burden is McKay Jenkins, *What's Gotten Into Us?*: *Staying Healthy in a Toxic World* (Random House, 2011), reprinted as *ContamiNation: My Quest to Survive in a Toxic World* (Avery, 2016). For pesticide use, see Michael C.R. Alavanja, "Pesticides Use and Exposure Extensive Worldwide," *Reviews in Environmental Health* 24:4 (Oct.–Dec. 2009). On slow violence, see Rob Nixon, *Slow Violence and the Environmentalism of the Poor* (Harvard University Press, 2011). On endocrine disruptors, see Mary Sue Marty, Edward W. Carney, and Justin Craig Rowlands, "Endocrine Disruption: Historical Perspectives and Its Impact on the Future of Toxicology Testing," *Toxicological Sciences* 120:1 (2010). For diethylstilbestrol, see Nancy Langston's great book, *Toxic Bodies: Hormone Disruptors and the Legacy of DES* (Yale University Press, 2010). The environmental classic on endocrine disruptors is Dianne Dumanoski, John Peterson Myers, and Theo Colborn, *Our Stolen Future*: *Are We Threatening Our Fertility, Intelligence and Survival?—A Scientific Detective Story* (Penguin Books, 1996).

On lead and crime, see Rick Nevin, "How Lead Exposure Relates to Temporal Changes in IQ, Violent Crime, and Unwed Pregnancy," *Environmental Research* 83:1 (May 2000), and "Understanding International Crime Trends: The Legacy of Preschool Lead Exposure," *Environmental Research* 104 (2007). See also Jessica Wolpaw Reyes, "Environmental Policy as Social Policy? The Impact of Childhood Lead Exposure on Crime," NBER Working Paper No. 13097 (May 2007). For a popular overview of this research, see Kevin Drum, "America's Real Criminal Element: Lead," *Mother Jones* (January/February 2013). For a history of toxicology and pesticide regulation, see Frederick Rowe Davis, *Banned: A History of Pesticides and the Science of Toxicology* (Yale University Press, 2014). On regulatory capture of the Environmental Protection Agnecy, see E.G. Vallianatos with McKay Jenkins, *Poison Spring: The Secret history of Pollution and the EPA* (Bloomsbury, 2014). Michelle D. Boone, et al., "Pesticide Regulation Amid the Influence of Industry," *Bioscience* 64:10 (2014). See also David Heath, "How Politics Derailed EPA Science on Arsenic, Endangering Public Health," Center for Public Integrity, https://www.publicintegrity.org/2014/06/28/15000/how-politics-derailed-epa-science-arsenic-endangering-public-health. On Industrial Bio-Test Laboratories see Keith Schneider, "IBT-Guilty," *Amicus Journal* (Winter 1983). World Resources Institute reports on the costs of regulations are Richard D. Morgenstern, William A. Pizer, and Jhih-Shyang Shih, "Jobs versus the Environment: An Industry-level Perspective," and Ruth Greenspan Bell, "For EPA Regulations, Cost Predictions are Overstated." See also Eban Goodstein, *The Trade-off Myth: Fact and Fiction About Jobs and the Environment* (Island Press, 1999).

Wes Jackson and the Land Institute are just beginning to receive historical attention. The best treatment so far comes from Minteer, *The Landscape of Reform*. See also Judy Soule and Jon Piper, *Farming in Nature's Image* (Island Press, 1991). Jeffrey Filipiak wrote a dissertation on Jackson and Wendell Berry, "Learning from the Land: Wendell Berry and Wes Jackson on Knowledge and Nature" (University of Michigan, 2004). For Jackson's writings, begin with *New Roots for Agriculture* (University of Nebraska Press, 1980) and *Becoming Native to This Place* (Counterpoint, 1996). The most useful Johns Hopkins study on urban agriculture is Raychel Santo, Anne Palmer, and Brent Kim, "Vacant Lots to Vibrant Plots, " http://www.jhsph.edu/research/centers-and-institutes/johns-hopkins-center-for-a-livable-future/_pdf/research/clf_reports/urban-ag-literature-review.pdf. Will Allen writes about his work in urban farms in *The Good Food Revolution: Growing Healthy Food, People and Communities* (Penguin Random House, 2013). For a profile of Allen, see Elizabeth Royte, "Street Farmer," *The New York Times Magazine* (July 1, 2009). Richard Louv, *Last Child in the Woods* (Workman Publishing, 2005). The Children & Nature Network is online at http://www.childrenandnature.org.

Terry Tempest Williams, *Refuge: An Unnatural History of Family and Place* (Vintage Books, 1991), and *The Open Space of Democracy* (Wipf & Stock, 2004). Janisse Ray, *Ecology of a Cracker Childhood* (Milkweed Editions, 1999). Mountaintop removal and its activists have attracted a good deal of scholarship. See Chad Montrie, *To Save the Land and People: A History of Opposition to Surface Coal Mining in Appalachia* (University of North Carolina Press, 2003), and Shannon Elizabeth Bell, *Our Roots Run Deep as Ironweed: Appalachian Women and the Fight for Environmental Justice* (University of Illinois Press, 2013). Vernice D. Miller, "The Quest for Environmental Justice," in Richard Hofricher, ed. *Toxic Struggles: The Theory and Practice of Environmental Justice* (New Society Publishers, 1993). For a history of environmental justice, see

Eileen Maura McGurty, "From NIMBY to Civil Rights: The Origins of the Environmental Justice Movement," *Environmental History* 2:3 (July 1997).

For the George H.W. Bush policy memo, see *The New York Times*, April 19, 1990. The Office of Net Assessment report is now readily available online: Peter Schwartz and Doug Randall, "An Abrupt Climate Change Scenario and Its Implications for United States National Security" (October 2003). For a review of climate denial, see Kevin C. Armitage, "State of Denial: The United States and the Politics of Global Warming," *Globalizations* 2:3 (December 2005). More detailed examinations of the campaign to deny the realities of climate disruption can be found in Oreskes and Conway, *Merchants of Doubt*, and also Ross Gelbspan, *Boiling Point: How Politicians, Big Oil and Coal, Journalists and Activists Are Fueling the Climate Crisis—And What We Can Do to Avert Disaster* (Basic Books, 2004), and James Hoggan, *Climate Cover-Up: The Crusade to Deny Global Warming* (Greystone Books, 2009). The Union of Concerned Scientists produced a good report of Bush administration censorship of climate science, *Scientific Integrity in Policy Making* (2004). "Brownlash" was coined by Paul R. and Anne H. Ehrlich in *Betrayal of Science and Reason: How Anti-Environmental Rhetoric Threatens Our Future* (Island Press, 1996). Philip A. Cooney's editing of climate science, complete with examples of rewritten scholarship, are seen in Andrew C. Revkin, "Bush Aide Softened Greenhouse Gas Links to Global Warming," *The New York Times* (June 8, 2005). For the extremism of the Republican party, see Thomas E. Mann and Norman J. Ornstein, *It's Even Worse Than It Was: How the American Constitutional System Collided With the New Politics of Extremism* (Basic Books, 2016). Jane Mayer, *Dark Money: The Hidden History of the Billionaires Behind the Rise of the Radical Right* (Doubleday, 2016). Michael Mann tells his story in *The Hockey Stick and the Climate Wars: Dispatches From the Front Lines* (Columbia University Press, 2012). The political scientists testing American democracy are Martin Gilens and Benjamin I. Page, "Testing Theories of American Politics: Elites, Interest Groups, and Average Citizens," *Perspectives on Politics* 12:3 (September 2014). Naomi Klein, *This Changes Everything: Capitalism vs. The Climate* (Simon & Schuster, 2014).

INDEX

ABOUT THE AUTHOR

KEVIN C. ARMITAGE has worked as a bouncer, bartender, bus driver, commercial fisherman, and field ecologist. He currently teaches inter-disciplinary studies, environmental studies and history at Miami University of Ohio. He is the author of *The Nature Study Movement: The Forgotten Popularizer of America's Conservation Ethic.*